Les langages de l'interprétation personnalisée

L'animation dans les musées

The Languages of Live Interpretation

Animation in Museums

Sous la direction de   Edited by
Jean-Marc Blais

Collection Mercure   Mercury Series
Directorat   Directorate
Dossier n° 9   Paper 9

Publié par le   **Published by the**
Musée canadien des civilisations   **Canadian Museum of Civilization**

© Musée canadien des civilisations 1997

DONNÉES DE CATALOGAGE AVANT PUBLICATION (CANADA)

Vedette principale au titre :

Les langages de l'interprétation personnalisée = The languages of live interpretation

(Collection Mercure = Mercury series)
(Directorat Dossier / Musée canadien des civilisations = Directorate paper / Canadian Museum of Civilization; no. 9)
Symposium tenu au Musée canadien des civilisations en mai 1994 — Préf.
Comprend des articles en français et en anglais.
ISBN 0-660-50757-9

1. Art du spectacle dans les musées — Congrès.
2. Musées — Aspect éducatif — Congrès.
3. Muséologie — Congrès.
I. Blais, Jean-Marc.
II. Musée canadien des civilisations.
III. Titre: The languages of live interpretation.
IV. Coll.
V. Coll.: Bureau du directeur, dossier (Musée canadien des civilisations); no. 9.

AM7.L36 1997   069'.16   C97-980073-0F

© Canadian Museum of Civilization 1997

CANADIAN CATALOGUING IN PUBLICATION DATA

Main entry under title :

Les langages de l'interprétation personnalisée = The languages of live interpretation

(Collection Mercure = Mercury series)
(Directorat Dossier / Musée canadien des civilisations = Directorate paper / Canadian Museum of Civilization; no. 9)
Symposium held at the Canadian Museum of Civilization in May 1994 — Pref.
Includes articles in English and French.
ISBN 0-660-50757-9

1. Performing arts in museums — Congresses.
2. Museums — Educational aspects — Congresses.
3. Museum techniques — Congresses.
I. Blais, Jean-Marc.
II. Canadian Museum of Civilization.
III. Title: The languages of live interpretation.
IV. Series
V. Series: Bureau du directeur, dossier (Canadian Museum of Civilization); no. 9.

AM7.L36 1997   069'.16   C97-980073-0E

BUT DE LA COLLECTION

La collection Mercure vise à diffuser rapidement le résultat de travaux dans les disciplines qui relèvent des sphères d'activités du Musée canadien des civilisations. Considérée comme un apport important dans la communauté scientifique, la collection Mercure présente plus de trois cents publications spécialisées portant sur l'héritage canadien préhistorique et historique.

Comme la collection s'adresse à un public spécialisé, elle est constituée essentiellement de monographies publiées dans la langue des auteurs.

Vous pouvez vous procurer la liste des titres parus dans la collection Mercure en appelant au 1 800 555-5621, ou en écrivant au :   Service des commandes postales
            Musée canadien des civilisations
            100, rue Laurier
            C.P. 3100, succursale B
            Hull (Québec)
            J8X 4H2

Télécopieur : 1 819 776-8300

OBJECT OF THE MERCURY SERIES

The Mercury Series is designed to permit the rapid dissemination of information pertaining to the disciplines in which the Canadian Museum of Civilization is active. Considered an important reference by the scientific community, the Mercury Series comprises over three hundred specialized publications on Canada's history and prehistory.

Because of its specialized audience, the series consists largely of monographs published in the language of the author.

Titles in the Mercury Series can be obtained by calling in your order to 1-800-555-5621, or by writing to:

            Mail Order Services
            Canadian Museum of Civilization
            100 Laurier Street
            P.O. Box 3100, Station B
            Hull, Quebec
            J8X 4H2

Fax: 1-819-776-8300

Chef de la production : Deborah Brownrigg
Graphiste : Roger Langlois Design
Révision : Communications Choquette
Photographe : Steven Darby

Photos de la couverture :
1. David Parry en spectacle au MCC.
2. Une animatrice du MCC.
3. Comédiens de Dramamuse au MCC.
4. Un comédien de Dramamuse au MCC.

Photos : Sauf indication contraire, les photographies proviennent du Musée canadien des civilisations.

Senior Production Officer: Deborah Brownrigg
Graphic design: Roger Langlois Design
Editing: Jennifer Rae-Brown
Photographer: Steven Darby

Front cover photos:
1. David Parry performing at CMC.
2. A CMC animator.
3. Actors from CMC's Dramamuse.
4. An actor from CMC's Dramamuse.

Photos: Photographs belong to the Canadian Museum of Civilization unless otherwise stated.

 IMPRIMÉ AU CANADA

Canada

 PRINTED IN CANADA

❖ Résumé

Les langages de l'interprétation personnalisée sont multiples et tirent leurs origines de nombreuses sources. Cet ouvrage renferme les articles de collaborateurs provenant de trois continents et œuvrant dans le domaine. David Parry fut en charge de la troupe permanente de théâtre du Musée canadien des civilisations depuis l'ouverture du Musée en 1989 jusqu'à son décès soudain en juin 1995 et fut l'instigateur du symposium de 1994 sur *Les langages de l'interprétation personnalisée*. C'est à sa mémoire que nous publions ce collectif.

❖ Abstract

The languages of live interpretation are many, and they derive from various sources. This book contains articles from three continents by people working in the field. David Parry was in charge of the resident theatre company at the Canadian Museum of Civilization from the time the Museum opened in 1989 until his untimely death in June 1995. He instigated the symposium on "The Languages of Live Interpretation" held in 1994. This book is published in his memory.

À ta mémoire, David!
In your honour, David!

❖ Remerciements

Je tiens à exprimer mes plus sincères remerciements à :

Monique Carnell, pour son aide et ses précieux conseils; Ron McRae, pour son appui face au projet; Marie-Josée Therrien, pour les réponses à mes nombreuses questions; Caroline Parry, pour son enthousiasme et son engagement personnel.

❖ Acknowledgements

I would like to express my sincere thanks to:

Monique Carnell, for her help and invaluable advice; Ron McRae, for supporting the project; Marie-Josée Therrien, for answering numerous questions; Caroline Parry, for her enthusiasm and personal contribution.

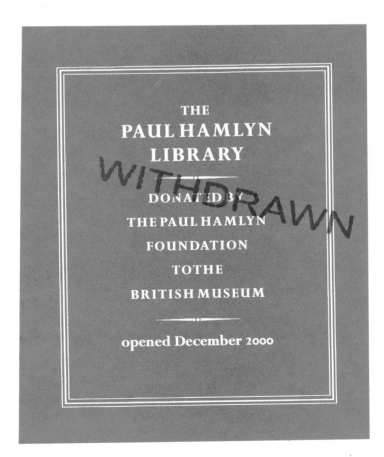

❖ Table des matières
Table of Contents

❖ Dédicace

Sylvie Morel
Directrice générale, Expositions et programmes
Musée canadien des civilisations
Hull (Québec)

C'est avec grand plaisir que chacun de nous, au Musée canadien des civilisations, dédie cet ouvrage à la mémoire de son instigateur, David Parry, un collègue talentueux et très spécial, un ami rare et un membre respecté du personnel du Musée dont nous avons été séparés par la mort soudaine.

Le 20 juin 1995, David aurait célébré son septième anniversaire au Musée. Je me souviens clairement de son arrivée parmi nous en 1988. Nous étions dans un état de panique absorbés par la construction et l'ouverture de ce magnifique et grand musée. Les gens demandaient : «Qui est cet homme qui chante à pleins poumons et qu'est-ce qu'on fait avec un "comédien" dans un musée?» Au cours des mois qui suivirent, David formait une troupe de théâtre et comptait parmi le groupe réuni à l'ouverture du Musée, en 1989, pour donner vie à l'histoire et faire en sorte, au dire même de David, «qu'une visite au Musée ne soit jamais ordinaire». Nous n'avions alors plus de doute quant à l'utilité de ce comédien à l'intérieur du Musée. Pendant les sept années qui ont suivi, David a joué un rôle de premier plan dans la renommée internationale du Musée avec son utilisation novatrice du théâtre. En effet, les programmes du Musée ne tardèrent pas à servir de modèle à d'autres musées et établissements du patrimoine du monde entier. Ses réalisations dans ce domaine sont bien connues.

La contribution de David au Musée va au-delà du théâtre. En joignant le Musée, David voulait plus que simplement s'ajouter à son effectif, mais devenir une force motrice, l'âme, de l'établissement. Travailleur inlassable et engagé, il était aussi entièrement dévoué à l'amélioration des nombreux projets et programmes dont il assurait la direction. Il était un véritable partisan de l'esprit d'équipe et du respect et soutien du rôle et des talents d'autrui. Plus important, David était toujours positif et optimiste. Malgré les obstacles ou l'impossibilité de l'échéance, il pouvait nous faire croire qu'il était encore possible d'atteindre nos objectifs. Nous nous souviendrons de lui pour son grand talent, ses qualités de chef, sa passion, son enthousiasme et son énergie débordante et, avant tout, pour sa grande chaleur et sa bonté.

Le colloque «Les langages de l'interprétation personnalisée» qui a eu lieu au Musée canadien des civilisations en mai 1994 avait été organisé par David Parry et ses collègues. Nous sommes ravis que cette publication serve de témoignage durable de la réunion des talents les plus novateurs dans le domaine de l'interprétation muséale et d'hommage à David Parry, un de ses pionniers célèbres.

Sylvie Morel

❖ Dedication

Sylvie Morel
Director General
Exhibitions and Programmes
Canadian Museum of Civilization
Hull, Quebec

All of us at the Canadian Museum of Civilization take great pleasure in dedicating this volume to the memory of the person who instigated it — David Parry — a very special and talented colleague, whose sudden death took from us a much valued friend and a respected member of the Museum staff.

On June 20, 1995, David would have celebrated his seventh anniversary at the Museum. I remember vividly when he joined us in 1988: we were in a state of panic in the throes of trying to build and open this great new Museum. I heard numerous people asking, "Who is that guy singing at the top of his voice and what's an "actor" doing in a museum anyway?"! Over the next year, David built up a company of several actors and when we opened the Museum in 1989, he was among the group assembled, in full costume, bringing history to life and, to use David's own words, "making sure a visit to the Museum was never ordinary." At that point it was clear to us all what this actor was doing here. Over the next seven years, David brought the Museum international acclaim for its innovative use of theatre and the Museum's programme soon became a model for other museums and heritage institutions around the world. His achievements in this area are well known.

But David brought much more than theatre to this institution. For him, joining the Museum meant not simply becoming part of a workforce but rather, becoming a driving force — a beating heart — within it. In addition to being a tireless and committed worker, he was wholly dedicated to improving the many projects and programmes under his direction; he was a true believer in teamwork and in respecting and supporting each person's role and talents. More importantly, David was always positive and upbeat; he made us believe that no matter how huge the impediments or tight the deadlines, we could still achieve our goals. We will remember him for his great talent and leadership, his passion, his enthusiasm and incredible energy, but most of all for his warmth and his kind heart.

"The Languages of Live Interpretation" symposium held at the Canadian Museum of Civilization in May 1994 was organized by David Parry and his colleagues. We are delighted that this publication will serve as a lasting account of the coming together of the most innovative minds in the field of museum interpretation, as well as a tribute to David Parry, one of its renowned pioneers.

Sylvie Morel

❖ Préface

Caroline Parry

Le symposium international de 1994 du Musée canadien des civilisations (MCC) sur «Les langages de l'interprétation personnalisée» a été tout un accomplissement pour David, mon défunt mari. Cette rencontre a non seulement été une occasion d'évaluer comment les établissements publics utilisent - et pourraient utiliser - cette ressource que sont les interprètes et les comédiens - une première dans le monde muséal -, mais elle représente également un jalon significatif dans la vie professionnelle aux multiples facettes de David. Dans cet ouvrage, les lecteurs en apprendront beaucoup au sujet du symposium et de Dramamuse, la compagnie de théâtre du MCC. Je voudrais vous raconter ici comment David en est venu à être le directeur du programme et à réaliser le projet - de la conception à la tenue - du symposium.

Quand j'ai rencontré David pour la première fois, en 1968, il conduisait une *Land Rover* en Inde. Après avoir enseigné quelques années la chimie et travaillé comme administrateur de théâtre, il s'est engagé comme professeur bénévole à l'école expérimentale de Kerala, où j'étais déjà. À 25 ans, son répertoire était déjà très varié - Bob Dylan, vieilles balades en passant par le western. Il était aussi fasciné - c'est bien de lui - par la culture locale. Au festival du temple du village, nous restions debout toute la nuit pour assister au kath~kali, un spectacle qui allie au théâtre proprement dit la danse, la musique, le mime et le chant. Il a étudié par la suite le théâtre sanskrit au deuxième cycle.

Après une année passée ensemble à l'école et notre mariage, nous sommes revenus en Europe en auto, puis nous sommes venus en visite aux États-Unis, mon pays d'origine. Nous nous sommes ensuite installés à Hull, en Angleterre (pays d'origine de David), et il a complété avec grande distinction un baccalauréat spécialisé en art dramatique et en anglais (1972). David est alors venu au Canada pour faire sa maîtrise (1974) et son doctorat (1983) en théâtre médiéval. Il a mis un temps fou à terminer son doctorat parce que, durant cette même période, il faisait sa marque en tant que conteur et chanteur folklorique, au plan international, et il donnait des représentations ou agissait comme directeur artistique de dizaines de pièces. Celles-ci étaient grosses ou petites, créées pour la salle ou pour le plein air, médiévales (de l'Europe et de l'Inde) ou modernes. Nous avons partagé l'emploi d'administrateur de la Poculi Ludique Societas de Toronto pendant quelques années. Nous avons partagé, pendant tant d'années, un intérêt philosophique et artistique pour la manière de communiquer des humains dans les arts en général, mais sur les planches en particulier.

Le temps que David obtienne ses diplômes et il était devenu un directeur artistique, un professeur et un conférencier d'expérience. Mais il était aussi dans la quarantaine. Les portes des universités se fermaient - plus d'emploi -, et il était trop qualifié pour occuper des postes de débutant. Alors il a continué à faire toutes sortes de choses! Nous avons passé deux magnifiques années à l'étranger avec nos enfants alors que David était professeur invité, d'abord à Cambridge et ensuite à l'Hebrew University de Jérusalem. Mais à notre retour au Canada, il n'a trouvé aucun poste à son niveau. Alors il a investi une année supplémentaire comme professeur invité, cette fois au Trinity College de Hartford (Connecticut), aux États-Unis. Il est résulté de cette affectation un important congrès et une pièce musulmane chiite. Il a fait la navette - et s'est fait du mauvais sang à propos de son avenir.

Au printemps 1988, une nouvelle carrière semblait s'ouvrir à lui, qui pourrait combiner ses nombreux talents et intérêts. Le Musée canadien des civilisations était sur le point d'ouvrir et cherchait quelqu'un pour diriger une compagnie de théâtre de musée novatrice qui travaillerait sur place. Le directeur du Musée, George MacDonald, avait rêvé qu'une telle compagnie de théâtre puisse créer des pièces qui jetteraient des ponts entre les visiteurs et les expositions. Ce concept de compagnie de théâtre ayant l'appui d'un musée a emballé David. Il a tout de suite aimé à la folie le nouvel édifice de Douglas Cardinal. Et il a pris l'emploi à l'essai. Encore une fois, il a fait la navette entre notre maison de Toronto et son travail. Ça été une période fatigante, difficile, spécialement pour la famille (nos deux enfants étaient alors adolescents). Encore qu'il était clair qu'un grand voyageur expert du théâtre médiéval pouvait en fait contribuer pour beaucoup à ce nouveau concept d'interprétation des artefacts par l'entremise de comédiens. Deux ans plus tard, en 1990, nous sommes déménagés à Ottawa.

L'enthousiasme tous azimuts et les intérêts éclectiques de David l'ont bien servi durant les sept années presque complètes qu'il a passées au MCC. Les pièces qu'il a créées avec la petite compagnie constituaient des centres d'attraction fascinants et variés pour les visiteurs qui y ont répondu de façon très positive. Ces pièces comprenaient un conte sur la vieille légende amérindienne de Corbeau qui dérobe la lumière, un spectacle sans aucune parole qui passe en revue différentes versions culturelles du Déluge, une pièce trilingue qui invite à faire un «voyage autour du monde» à bord de l'autobus du Musée des enfants et une pièce intimiste au sujet des relations entre les Français et les Anglais après 1765. David a aidé la compagnie à donner vie à des personnages aussi différents qu'un castor qui décrivait l'histoire par le biais d'une série de bâtonnets (et qui invitait le public à commencer sa propre collection) et une femme de bûcheron, dans les années 1820, qui attendait tout l'hiver que son mari revienne du chantier - leur seul gagne-pain. La compréhension profonde qu'avait David du théâtre médiéval - à distance rapprochée, à petit auditoire et d'une manière efficace quoique didactique - lui a facilité la tâche alors qu'il devait diriger les courtes pièces qui allaient devenir la marque de commerce de la compagnie de théâtre.

Au printemps 1992, David a contribué à notre bulletin d'information familial épisodique et ses mots traduisent les défis à relever, la satisfaction et la frustration -souvent pêle-mêle! Il a écrit :

> [Nous] essayons de comprendre ce que nous faisons dans du «théâtre de musée», et pourquoi, ce qu'en sont les principes de base - spécialement les principes philosophiques - et comment les mener à bien. Ce qui est le plus fantastique, c'est de voir à quel point la technique requise s'apparente à celle du théâtre du Moyen Âge et du début de la Renaissance. Non, pas seulement parce que c'est moi qui fais l'ouvrage, mais parce que, à l'origine, les deux sont des formes d'enseignement livrées à l'occasion d'une relation très intimiste et directe avec le public. Du bon théâtre populaire, aussi... quand la paperasserie et les chinoiseries administratives ne me dépriment pas complètement; c'est très emballant, cette forme de théâtre vraiment nouvelle et populaire. Comme du théâtre de rue à l'intérieur.

Dans ces mêmes années mouvementées où il devait composer avec son travail d'artiste et la bureaucratie, David est devenu parfaitement bilingue et il a trouvé le tour de travailler à divers rôles de création à l'extérieur du Musée. En plus de publier plusieurs articles au sujet de son nouveau rôle et de la compagnie de théâtre Dramamuse, il a aussi été le directeur artistique de deux spectacles importants pour la Gilbert and Sullivan Society. De plus, il a enregistré deux disques de musique traditionnelle et de contes, ces derniers s'inspirant de l'œuvre de Robert Service. Il a continué de donner des spectacles solos ou avec le groupe Friends of Fiddlers Green, qui chante en celtique et avec lequel David a joué plus de vingt ans et avec Ian Robb, son concitoyen anglais expatrié et chanteur de talent. Au moment de son infarctus, David était en train de préparer un troisième enregistrement et il parlait de monter un spectacle solo sur la vie et les poèmes (il avait écrit la musique de beaucoup d'entre eux) de Robert Service. Les «Friends» ont aujourd'hui fait paraître une cassette posthume (intitulée 'E Liked It All) où David chante avec le groupe, en direct, dans divers festivals. Les profits de la vente de cette cassette sont versés, à titre d'appui, pour la tenue de deux festivals folkloriques en Ontario où David se produisait.

Il ne fait aucun doute que la vie même de David a façonné sa capacité de diriger les autres. Il avait un instinct sûr pour ce qui fait le bon théâtre et pour faire passer une chanson, un poème ou une histoire avec juste l'effet qu'il faut. De plus, il pouvait enseigner ce qu'il savait aux autres - avec énormément d'enthousiasme et de générosité. Dans un récent hommage à David Parry au festival des chants de la mer du Mystic Seaport Museum du Connecticut, beaucoup ont salué la capacité de David de concentrer son attention sur une tâche ou sur la personne en face de lui. Ses différentes et nombreuses réalisations témoignent du soin qu'il apportait à son travail.

David a vu l'énorme potentiel du théâtre de musée et il a partagé sa vision de bien des manières, spécialement au symposium dont les actes sont rapportés ici. Je suis reconnaissante au Musée non seulement d'avoir suivi son plan original de publication de ces actes, mais je suis aussi reconnaissante aux femmes et aux hommes avec qui il a travaillé de 1988 à 1995 - les comédiennes et les comédiens, les auteures et les auteurs, le personnel technique et de production, les gestionnaires - d'avoir mis en œuvre, avec tant de compétence, sa vision du théâtre.

❖ Foreword

Caroline Parry

The Canadian Museum of Civilization's 1994 international symposium on "The Languages of Live Interpretation" was a major achievement for David Parry, my late husband. This gathering to consider how public institutions use — and could use — live actors and interpreters was not only a first of its kind throughout the museum world, it was also a significant milestone in David's multifaceted professional life. In this volume readers will learn a great deal about the symposium and about Dramamuse, the Museum's resident theatre group; in this foreword I would like to explain how David Parry came to be the person who directed the programme and also put the symposium — from conception to final reception — together.

When I first met David, in 1968, he was driving a Land Rover around India, after a few years of post-grammar school work in chemistry and as a theatre administrator. Soon he became a volunteer teacher at the experimental school in Kerala where I was ensconced. At age 25, his interests were already eclectic — for example, his singing repertoire included Bob Dylan songs, cowboy ditties and old ballads. David was also fascinated — characteristically — with the local culture, and in season we would stay up all night to see Kathakali dance drama performances at our village temple festival. Eventually he would follow up this interest by studying Sanskrit drama at the graduate level!

After our marriage and a year together at the school, we travelled back to Europe over-land, and then visited the United States, my original home. We settled in Hull, England (David's country of origin), where he earned a First Class Honours degree in drama and English (1972). He then went on to pursue both an M.A. (1974) and a Ph.D. (1983) in medieval theatre here in Canada. The latter took far too long to complete, but along the way David directed and acted in dozens of plays, huge and tiny, indoors and out, medi-eval European (and Indian) and modern, as well as establishing himself as a fine singer and storyteller on the international folk circuit. For a few years we shared the administrator's job at the University of Toronto's *Poculi Ludique Societas*; for many, many years we shared an artistic and philosophical interest in how humans communicate through the arts in general, and on the stage in particular.

By the time David had completed his degrees, he was an experienced director, teacher and lecturer, but he was also over 40. The university world was shrinking in terms of employment, and he found he was overqualified for entry-level jobs — so his work life continued to be varied! We had two wonderful years abroad with our children while

David taught as a visiting professor, first at Cambridge University in England and then at the Hebrew University in Jerusalem, but on our return there were no suitable openings for him in Canada. And so David put in one more year as a visiting academic, this time in the United States, at Trinity College in Hartford, Connecticut. That appointment culminated in a massive conference about and production of a Shiite Muslim drama. He commuted — and fretted about his future.

In the spring of 1988, a new career path seemed to beckon, one that might combine many of David's talents and interests. The Canadian Museum of Civilization was about to open and was looking for someone to head up an innovative, museum-based company of actors. Dr. George MacDonald, the Museum's Director, had dreamed that such a company could create plays that would serve as an engaging bridge between exhibits and museum-goers. David was excited by this concept of a theatre company supported by a museum, he fell totally in love with the new Douglas Cardinal building, and he took the job on a trial basis. Once again, he commuted between our home in Toronto and his work. It was a difficult, exhausting period, especially in terms of family life (our two children were teenagers at that time). Still, it became clear that a world-traveller and expert in medieval drama actually had a great deal to contribute to the ground-breaking concept of using actors to interpret artifacts. Two years later, in 1990, we moved to Ottawa.

David's eclectic interests and wide-ranging enthusiasms served him well during his almost seven years at the Museum. The plays he created with his small company were diverse and fascinating focal points for the museum public and evoked very positive responses. These plays included a storytelling monologue based on the ancient Native tale of Raven stealing the light, a totally non-verbal performance drawing on common cultural myths about the great flood, a trilingual dramatic attempt to take a bus trip from the Children's Museum "around the world," and an intimate drama about French-English neighbourly relations after 1765. David helped the company bring to life such varied characters as a beaver who collected historic sticks (and encouraged the audience to start their own significant collections), and a young, cabin-bound mother of the 1820s who paced through winter days until her husband returned from the logging that was their only livelihood. David's deep understanding of how medieval drama worked — at close range, with small audiences, and in a didactic yet effective manner — facilitated his job as director of the short plays that came to be the hallmark of the Museum's resident theatre company.

In the spring of 1992, David contributed to our sporadic family newsletter, and his own words spell out the challenges, frustrations and satisfactions that he felt — often simultaneously! He wrote:

> [We are] trying to really figure out what we are doing in "museum theatre," and why. What the basic principles are — philosophical principles especially — and how to achieve them. One of the most fascinating parts of that is how much of the technique required relates to the theatre of the Middle Ages and early Renaissance. No, not just because it's me doing the job, but because at root both are teaching forms, with a very direct and intimate relationship with their audiences. Good popular theatre, too . . . When the government paperwork and bureaucratic red tape don't utterly depress me, it's very exciting — a truly new and truly popular theatre form. Like street theatre indoors.

In these same hectic years as an artist working in a bureaucracy, David became fluently bilingual and found time to work outside the Museum in various creative roles, as well! He not only published several articles about his new role and Dramamuse, but also directed two major performances for the local Gilbert and Sullivan society. In addition, he recorded two albums of traditional music and storytelling, the latter based on the works of Robert Service. He continued to perform solo or with the Friends of Fiddlers Green, the ceilidh band he played with for over 20 years, and with Ian Robb, a fellow English expatriate and a fine singer. At the time of his unexpected heart attack, David was actively planning a third recording and talking about a solo show based on Robert Service's life and poems (many of which David has set to music). "The Friends" have now released a posthumous tape recording (called "'E Liked It All") of David singing live with the band at various festivals. The proceeds of the sales of this tape are being used to support two different Ontario folk events at which he was a frequent performer.

There is no doubt that David's own life as a performer shaped his ability to direct others. He had a keen instinct for what makes good theatre and how to convey a song, poem or story with just the right effect. Plus, he was able to teach others what he knew — with a great deal of generosity and enthusiasm. In a recent tribute to David at the Sea Music Festival at the Mystic Seaport museum in Connecticut, many people praised David's ability to focus intently on whatever task or person was in front of him. His many different achievements do indeed testify to his careful, caring attentiveness.

David saw that the possibilities for museum theatre were enormous, and he shared his vision in many ways, especially at the symposium documented here. I am grateful not only that the Museum has followed through with its original plan to support David in the publication of these proceedings, but also that the men and women he worked with between 1988 and 1995 — actors, writers, technical and production staff, administrators — have so ably continued to put that inspired vision into practice.

Le théâtre au Musée devrait amener son public à re-
mettre en question tout ce qu'il croyait connaître sur
la condition humaine, faire en sorte qu'il se
sente à l'aise de le faire, et lui laisser l'impression
qu'il a appris quelque chose de vraiment nouveau
tout en s'étant souverainement amusé.

David Parry

Theatre in the Museum should make its audiences
question everything they thought they knew about
the human condition, allow them to feel comfortable
in doing so, and leave them feeling they've learned
something quite new and have been royally
entertained in the process.

David Parry

❖ Introduction

Symposium «Les langages de l'interprétation personnalisée»

David Parry

Du 7 au 10 mai 1994, le Musée canadien des civilisations (MCC) a accueilli un symposium international, «Les langages de l'interprétation personnalisée», organisé par la Division des programmes publics. Cette rencontre a attiré plus de 100 participants, parmi lesquels trois compagnies de théâtre de musées du Canada, des États-Unis et de l'Angleterre. Durant quatre jours, des délégués d'Europe, d'Australie et d'Amérique du Nord ont étudié des questions relatives à la manière dont les musées et les établissements de patrimoine utilisent les techniques et la «langue» du théâtre pour communiquer avec les visiteurs - par le biais de diverses formes d'interprétation personnalisée - et ainsi aider à faire face à une société de plus en plus multilingue.

Le symposium a commencé par deux jours d'interprétation personnalisée, de manière à offrir des exemples de travail vivants et à soulever en chacun un tas de questions d'ordre pratique pour discuter dans la seconde moitié de la rencontre. Après un court mot de bienvenue de M. MacDonald et des organisateurs de même qu'un survol des activités à venir, la matinée du samedi a été consacrée à la visite du Musée canadien des civilisations en compagnie des guides, des animateurs et de certains de nos personnages historiques. Nous avons également assisté à plusieurs pièces jouées par la compagnie de théâtre du MCC (*Measure for mesure*, *Deux sœurs / Two Sisters*, *Ma collection / My Collection* et *Elle souffle! / There She Blows!*). Après le dîner, les délégués se sont rendus en autobus au Musée national des sciences et de la technologie (MNST) pour assister à d'autres pièces présentées par le MNST (*Micro*, une pièce de théâtre de marionnettes - au sujet de l'exploration spatiale - jouée dans les deux langues officielles) et par la Platform 4 Theatre Company du musée ferroviaire national du Royaume-Uni (*Le tunnel sous la Manche* et *Running the Risk*).

Après avoir assisté à ces trois spectacles au MNST, les délégués ont été conduits, toujours en autobus, au Musée canadien de la nature, où ils ont vu cette fois une pièce montée par le Musée à propos du monarque (*Gaga pour les monarques / Mad about Monarchs*), deux pièces présentées par la Boston Museum of Science Company, soit *The Ballad of Chico Mendes* et *The Bog Man's Daughter* et, dernière représentation de l'aprèsmidi, la pièce *Science is Fun* de l'Evergreen Coop de Calgary. Pour terminer la journée, Joseph Dandurand, stagiaire autochtone au Musée qui a travaillé huit mois avec les

Programmes d'interprétation, a organisé un spectacle de cabaret informel au Stone Angel Institute, où des musiciens, des poètes et des conteurs autochtones se sont produits. Il y est venu pas mal de monde et les délégués qui y ont assisté (ceux qui tenaient encore debout après leur journée!) en ont été enchantés.

Tôt le dimanche matin, les autobus ont quitté le MCC en direction de l'Upper Canada Village à Morrisburg (Ontario) et de Pointe-à-Callière à Montréal. Le but était de discuter et de connaître l'expérience en interprétation personnalisée du personnel en interprétation de ces deux établissements. Ça a été deux visites très profitables, bien que la journée ait encore une fois été longue. Notre tentative de combiner l'expérience dans deux sites du patrimoine aux antipodes linguistiques - l'un où l'anglais était prépondérant et l'autre où c'était le français qui l'était - était peut-être un peu trop ambitieuse.

La visite de l'Upper Canada Village a été très productive et source de réflexion. Des interprètes en costume d'époque ont fait faire un tour complet du site aux délégués, et des personnages ont fait plusieurs interventions théâtrales «à la première personne». Après les visites guidées, Paul Deault, directeur du site, a présidé une table ronde sur les approches de l'interprétation à la première personne au village. Deux des interprètes du site qui ont le plus d'expérience y ont participé.

La visite à Pointe-à-Callière a été plus courte, mais a alimenté notre réflexion dans le sens qu'on utilise ici certaines techniques nouvelles d'art dramatique dans les visites guidées. L'expérience de ces techniques par les délégués a servi de matériel de discussion en atelier, plus tard au cours du symposium. La visite s'est terminée par un souper à Montréal, puis ça a été le retour au MCC tard le soir.

Le lundi et le mardi, il y a eu des présentations plus formelles. De nombreux spectacles, donnés par la compagnie de théâtre du MCC et les trois troupes de théâtre de musées - en visite - dans les salles d'expositions et dans le salon Marius-Barbeau, se sont encore intercalés entre ces séances. *Tsonoqua*, lecture-spectacle offerte par Joseph Dandurand, a été l'une de ces prestations. Il s'agit d'une version de travail d'une pièce de théâtre d'interpréation écrite par l'auteur comme projet principal dans le cadre du Programme de formation en muséologie pour les Autochtones. Plus de quarante personnes ont présenté un total de neuf séances plénières et dix-neuf ateliers.

À la fin des séances du lundi, les délégués ont été accueillis dans les édifices du Parlement, qu'ils ont visités avec les guides. La soirée s'est terminée sur des spectacles spécialement organisés pour le symposium par la Commission de la capitale nationale, *À vous de juger / You be the Jury*.

Le partage de différentes approches et perspectives, tout au long du symposium, a été très stimulant et l'alignement de perspectives venant de partout dans le monde a été particulièrement utile. En fait, cette rencontre a favorisé la réflexion, a été source d'énergie et, malgré un horaire qui a quelquefois laissé les délégués à bout de souffle, ils en ont redemandé à la fin. Il y a un besoin évident, dans le domaine, de ce genre de rencontre qui réunit les théoriciens et les praticiens du domaine de l'interprétation personnalisée, et le MCC semble l'endroit idéal pour tenir ce genre d'activité. Des discussions ont commencé à l'effet de tenir ce type de rencontre tous les deux ans.

Enfin, bien que le symposium se soit tenu au MCC, son développement est dû à la collaboration entre plusieurs établissements. Il n'aurait pas pu se tenir sans l'expérience, le travail acharné et les ressources humaines qu'ont fournis Parcs Canada et la CCN, qui nous ont aidés à planifier et à organiser la rencontre et à faire qu'elle se déroule bien. Nous tenons à remercier aussi d'autres établissements qui ont accueilli nos délégués et les compagnies de théâtre invitées, spécialement le Musée national des sciences et de la technologie, le Musée canadien de la nature, l'Upper Canada Village et Pointe-à-Callière.

❖ Le symposium en images
Photographs of the symposium

❖ Introduction

"The Languages of Live Interpretation" Symposium

David Parry

From May 7-10, 1994, the Canadian Museum of Civilization (CMC) hosted an international symposium, "The Languages of Live Interpretation," which was organized by the Interpretive Programmes section of the Public Programmes Division. The symposium attracted over a hundred participants, including three visiting museum theatre companies from Canada, the United States and England. Over the course of four days, delegates from Europe, Australia and North America explored a wide spectrum of issues relating to the ways in which museums and heritage institutions use theatrical techniques and "languages" to communicate with visitors through various forms of live interpretation, and to assist in meeting the communication challenges we all face in our increasingly multilingual society.

The symposium began with two days of live presentations in order to set everyone up with lots of lively working examples and practical issues for the second half of the gathering. After a brief welcome by Dr. MacDonald, the Museum's Director, and the organizers, and an orientation to the event, Saturday morning was spent at the Museum of Civilization with the guides, the animators and some of our interactive historical characters, and in viewing several plays by the CMC's theatre company (*Measure for mesure, Two Sisters/Deux soeurs, My Collection/Ma collection* and *There She Blows!/Elle souffle!*). Delegates lunched and were then taken by bus to the National Museum of Science and Technology (NMST) to see plays presented by the NMST (*Micro*, a puppet play about space exploration, performed in both official languages) and by the Platform 4 Theatre Company from the National Railway Museum in the U.K. (*Le Tunnel sous La Manche* and *Running the Risk*).

Following these three presentations at NMST, delegates were taken by bus to the Canadian Museum of Nature, to watch their presentation of a piece on the Monarch butterfly (*Mad About Monarchs*), the Boston Museum of Science Company's presentation of *The Ballad of Chico Mendes* and *The Bog Man's Daughter,* and the Evergreen Co-op from Calgary's piece entitled *Science is Fun.* To conclude the day's activities, Joseph Dandurand, one of CMC's Aboriginal Programme trainees who worked with Interpretive Programmes for eight months in 1994, had arranged an informal cabaret by Native storytellers, poets and musicians at the Stone Angel Institute as an evening social event. This was well attended and much enjoyed by those delegates who were still on their feet after the long day of performances!

Early on Sunday morning, buses left the CMC to take delegates to Upper Canada Village in Morrisburg, Ontario and the Pointe-à-Callière archaeological museum in Montreal. At each institution, delegates had the opportunity to meet interpretive staff and discuss their respective live interpretation programmes. These were both successful visits, though once again it was a rather long day, and our attempt to combine the language experiences of a primarily anglophone and a primarily francophone heritage site on a single day was perhaps a little too ambitious.

The visit to Upper Canada Village, where delegates were given an extended tour of the site by costumed interpreters and experienced a number of theatrical interventions by "first-person" characters, was extremely productive and thought-provoking. The tours were followed by a panel session (led by site manager Paul Deault and including two of the most experienced site interpreters) on approaches to first-person interpretation at Upper Canada Village.

The visit to Pointe-à-Callière was shorter, but gave further worthwhile food for thought on the use of some new dramatic techniques during guided tours. Experiencing these techniques provided delegates with a good background for a workshop given later in the symposium. The day's tour concluded with supper in Montreal before the return to the CMC.

Two days of more formal presentations, papers and workshops followed at the CMC on Monday and Tuesday. These plenary and workshop sessions were again interspersed with numerous live performances by the CMC's own interpretive theatre company and by the three visiting museum theatre groups in the exhibition halls and the Salon Marius Barbeau. These performances included the staged reading of *Tsonoqua*, a working version of the interpretive theatre piece written by Joseph Dandurand as his major project for the Aboriginal Training Programme. In all, 9 plenary presentations and 19 workshops were given by more than 40 presenters.

At the end of the Monday sessions, delegates enjoyed a reception hosted by CMC in the Parliament Buildings, and guided tours of the buildings given by their interpretive staff. The evening concluded with special performances of the National Capital Commission's own interactive summer theatre presentations, *You Be the Jury/À vous de juger.*

The sharing of different approaches and perspectives throughout the symposium was very stimulating, and the juxtaposition of wide-ranging international perspectives was particularly useful. Indeed, the whole gathering was extremely thought-provoking and energizing, and although the schedule sometimes left delegates gasping for breath, it also left them asking for more! There is a clear need in the field for the kind of forum that brings theorists and practitioners in the field of live interpretation together in this way, and the CMC seems an ideal place for it to happen. Discussions have already started regarding the possibility of making this a biennial event.

Finally, while the symposium was officially a CMC event, its development was the result of collaboration among a number of institutions, and it would not have been possible without the experience, hard work and physical resources extended by Parks Canada and the National Capital Commission, who helped us plan, organize and conduct the gathering, and by other institutions, especially the National Museum of Science and Technology, the Canadian Museum of Nature, Upper Canada Village and the Pointe-à-Callière Museum of Archeology and History of Montreal, who hosted our delegate visits and our visiting performance groups.

Les langages

PART ONE

The Languages

❖ Les langages de l'interprétation personnalisée

David Parry

(adapté et révisé par Caroline Parry, d'après des notes accompagnant le manuscrit de David)

[Note de Caroline Parry : David a donné une version de cet exposé dans son discours-programme du symposium, qui n'a malheureusement pas été enregistré. Le brouillon qu'il a laissé n'est pas complet non plus. Certaines de ses notes sur le texte lui-même constituent désormais d'énigmatiques références et la seconde moitié de son manuscrit est un mélange de grandes lignes, de notes, de citations de même que de phrases complètes et incomplètes. J'ai essayé de décrypter son griffonnage, de compléter ses références et de peaufiner le brouillon de manière que ce texte soit le plus près possible de sa pensée, de son style et de ses mots. Ce que je n'ai pu faire, cependant, parce qu'il a laissé trop peu d'indices, c'est de structurer le tout en discours achevé, avec une introduction et une conclusion. Je le regrette, mais c'est encore heureux qu'il reste autant de la pensée stimulante de David.

Pour rendre les choses encore plus compliquées pour les lecteurs qui ont assisté au symposium, rappelons que David a oublié son discours et les diapositives qui l'accompagnaient dans le taxi qui l'amenait au Musée ce jour-là. Alors je n'ai aucune certitude que ce que je livre ici soit la même chose que ce qu'il a dit ce jour-là. Néanmoins, il s'agit d'un texte à propos et d'une source de réflexion, et David aurait certainement voulu que nous en reproduisions ce que nous pouvons - et que nous continuions la discussion!]

[*Notes au sujet de la procédure de présentation du texte : Quand j'ai inséré mes mots dans les paragraphes écrits par David ou quand j'ai écrit de nouveaux paragraphes, j'ai mis les mots en italique. Les questions qui ont trait à sa pensée, les notes à propos de ses notes ou mes commentaires sont aussi en italique et entre crochets - comme ici.*]

«Venez, alors, commençons par les Muses, qui ont ravi par leurs chants le grand esprit de Zeus, leur père qui habite l'Olympe, puisqu'elles révèlent de leurs voix harmonieuses ce qui a été, ce qui est et ce qui sera.»

Cette citation provient de la *Théogonie,* un ouvrage d'Hésiode, éminent contemporain d'Homère. Cette œuvre a été créée en Grèce vers le VIIIe siècle avant Jésus-Christ. Hésiode y raconte la création du monde, de l'univers, y fait la généalogie des dieux, des monstres de la terre et, le plus important pour nous, des Muses. Des écrivains qui sont venus plus tard en dénombrent neuf. Les Muses présidaient : Clio à l'Histoire, Therpsichore à la Danse, Uranie à l'Astronomie, Melpomène à la Tragédie et ainsi de suite - quoique les écrivains n'ont jamais vraiment été d'accord sur laquelle des Muses faisait quoi. *Mais*, à l'évidence, *les Muses étaient* source d'inspiration pour les poètes, les dramaturges, les chanteurs *et les autres créateurs.*

Hésiode nous a aussi raconté, ailleurs, que la mère des Muses s'appelait Mnémosyne (Mémoire). Et si vous vous demandez où je veux en venir avec mon introduction pompeuse à caractère classique, eh bien! simplement à ça : Muses et Mémoire. Notre mot «musée» provient du grec *mouseîon* qui, en plus de faire référence à un lieu consacré aux Muses - celles du Chant, de la Danse, de la Tragédie... -, renvoie à la mémoire. Mnémosyne a, *de toute évidence*, été le référent des musées au cours des siècles précédents, mais ce n'est que depuis relativement peu que les musées ont renoué sérieusement avec les Muses dans leurs salles d'expositions. *Bien entendu*, quand je dis «musée», je parle de tous ces établissements, centres, sites, parcs *et autres* avec lesquels nous avons en commun *le rôle et les préoccupations.*

Au sujet de ce que nous avons en commun, j'espère que ce discours-programme mènera à encore plus d'«envolées créatives» que ce qui a déjà commencé. Après tout, nous partageons beaucoup des buts de cette rencontre, et peut-être pourrons-nous encore plus mettre en commun nos compétences de manière à pouvoir construire sur nos expériences communes.

Pour en revenir à la mémoire, dans le temps d'avant l'invention de l'écriture, toute la connaissance reposait sur la mémoire pour sa continuité. Il en va de même aujourd'hui pour ceux qui ne peuvent pas lire la musique; ils la retiennent. *Ce que les gens «savaient» se transmettait verbalement de toutes sortes de manières, par exemple,* dans des proverbes, des dictons sur la température ou sur la navigation, des formulettes enfantines, *etc.* Les Muses de l'Histoire, de la Danse, de la Tragédie étaient en partie les hôtes de la mémoire. Et il semble évident que la mémoire soit devenue, en partie, tributaire des Muses. Au contraire de la nôtre, la culture d'Hésiode était orale. Je vais revenir plus loin sur Hésiode et les Muses.

Mais avant, je veux mettre l'accent sur le fait que nous, les interprètes, *travaillons* essentiellement dans la tradition orale. *J'ai lu un livre magnifique de Walter J. Ong, dernièrement,* **Orality and Literacy**[1]. *Il décrit comment marche la tradition orale, que «la pensée profonde s'imbrique dans les systèmes de la mémoire.»* Plus loin, il appelle à «penser à des choses inoubliables.» Je crois que l'un de nos défis, en tant qu'interprètes, consiste à créer ces *pensées inoubliables en offrant à notre public des* images inoubliables sans *s'encombrer* du langage. [Emphase de David sur «*s'encombrer*» : pour cela, le rythme *est* très important *de même que la* rime *et le* son *en général.* Toutes sortes de choses non verbales *sont* utiles *aussi, comme les* costumes et les accessoires.]

Même alors, beaucoup, sinon la plus grande partie, de ce que nous apprenons au sujet de notre art, l'information que nous communiquons quand nous jouons, nous vient directement ou indirectement des livres, ou à tout le moins sous forme écrite. Dans les musées, comme dans le monde en général, nous sommes toujours, de manière frappante et malgré la vidéo, liés à l'écrit. Comme Walter Ong mentionne :

> Le mot continue d'arriver à vous par l'écrit, peu importe ce que vous faites. De plus, dissocier les mots de l'écrit fait peur, psychologiquement, parce que le sens du contrôle des lettrés sur la langue est intimement lié à sa transformation visuelle. Sans les dictionnaires, les règles de grammaire, la ponctuation ou tout autre matériel qui leur permet de chercher les mots, comment les lettrés pourraient-ils vivre?

Cela peut être démoralisant de se rappeler que l'intellect ne contient pas de dictionnaire. À part les cultures de relativement haute technologie, la plupart des usagers de la langue se sont toujours assez bien arrangés sans quelque transformation visuelle de l'oral que ce soit. Comprenez-moi bien, je ne critique pas l'écriture. Comme l'a dit M. Ong, «l'oralité a besoin de produire et elle est destinée à produire de l'écrit.» Sans cela, la conscience humaine ne peut voir s'épanouir son potentiel. Ce que j'aimerais suggérer c'est qu'en tant qu'interprètes de musées, nous avons besoin de cerner certains aspects de l'héritage que nous ont laissé les Muses, en particulier la puissance - la puissance pure, concrète, physique, magique des mots que nous devons imbriquer, avec l'aide des Muses, à tous les autres langages que nous connaissons.

Mais ce besoin comporte cependant un paradoxe. Nous sommes tellement tributaires de l'écrit que c'est souvent difficile, particulièrement pour les interprètes qui aiment communiquer des choses de manière dynamique, *comme parler au public, d'exploiter aussi la pleine puissance des langages non verbaux.*

Ici David a écrit, sur la page, «Discours à Mystic - Robert R». La référence au nom n'est pas claire, mais nous savons que David a joué en juin 1991 et 1993 au festival Sea Music du Mystic Seaport, le musée d'histoire vivante du Connecticut. La diapositive qu'il se proposait de montrer pourrait bien être celle du Charles P. Morgan, le dernier bateau de chasse à la baleine en bois du XIXᵉ siècle, magnifiquement conservé dans le port. David aurait entonné - c'est bien de lui - une chanson de bord, peut-être la puissante Bully in the Alley, *de manière à faire sentir à son auditoire la puissance de ce navire - et de ce lieu magique qu'il aimait - et, grâce au langage de la musique, le rythme du chantier [l'accent porte sur les syllabes soulignées] ajoutant son sens à celui des mots.*

> *So 'elp me, bob, I'm <u>bully</u> in the alley,*
> <u>*Way*</u>*, ay, <u>bully</u> in the alley;*
> *'elp me, bob, I'm <u>bully</u> in the alley,*
> <u>*Bully*</u> *down in Shinbone <u>Al</u>!*

Musée Mystic Seaport, Mystic (Connecticut)

Les chansons de bord sont bien entendu des chansons de travail chantées principalement par les marins dans le but de coordonner les grosses corvées telles que hisser et baisser les voiles ou manœuvrer le cabestan de l'ancre.[2] Ces mots n'ont en fait pas beaucoup de «sens», mais le rythme représentait une manière de donner des «instructions» aux travailleurs - une autre sorte de langage.

Il est intéressant de constater qu'en montrant l'image du bateau en même temps qu'il entonnait la chanson de bord, David effectuait une sorte de «transformation visuelle [d'un] son» - ajoutant littéralement une image au son, bien que sans écrire les mots sur papier - il venait à peine d'affirmer que «les usagers de la langue pouvaient très bien faire sans.» Cela vient peut-être simplement renforcer le paradoxe mentionné précédemment. Peut-être aussi que l'apparente contradiction vient du fait que David n'a jamais totalement résolu la question qu'il voulait soulever dans cet article - il est clair qu'il n'a jamais écrit ni esquissé de conclusion dans ses notes.

Ce symposium a vraiment débuté par une simple question au sujet d'un problème complexe : «Comment pouvons-nous, au sein de cet établissement, utiliser plus efficacement le théâtre d'interprétation de manière à résoudre les problèmes que pose le bilinguisme?» Cette simple question s'est rapidement compliquée. *Mais avant de se pencher plus avant sur la complexité de cette question, permettez-moi faire le bilan de la situation.* Le MCC est un établissement officiellement bilingue. C'est-à-dire que, par son mandat, l'organisation doit fonctionner dans les deux langues et que nous devons communiquer ce que nous désirons communiquer aux visiteurs dans la langue de leur choix. La langue de leur choix, c'est-à-dire le français ou l'anglais. À dire vrai, alors que nous pourrions ne *parler* que l'anglais ou le français - à l'occasion, on peut entendre un membre du personnel qui travaille auprès du public parler espagnol, allemand, russe ou autre -, nous *utilisons* bien des langages pour communiquer ce qu'est notre musée à nos visiteurs et ce que notre musée a le désir de partager avec eux. En tant que musée, notre premier langage est celui des «objets». Voici certains des langages que nous utilisons :

- visuel (forme / fonctionnel)
- visuel (contextuel)
- visuel (esthétique)
- tactile (habituellement des reproductions, mais parfois l'objet authentique)

Nous devons peut-être joindre ce langage des «objets» - le visuel, le tactile, l'oral non verbal, les langages de l'odorat et du goût (beaucoup plus sur les sites historiques que dans les musées) - à notre communication verbale.

Comme vous savez, nous nous efforçons de maintenir un équilibre réel des deux langues officielles en tout temps dans la programmation de théâtre d'interprétation au MCC. Tous les jeux de rôles, toutes les représentations à la première personne sont conçus pour être joués dans les deux langues, et les comédiens passent continuellement d'une langue à l'autre lorsqu'ils jouent, selon qu'ils s'adressent à tels ou tels visiteurs à tel moment.

Le Bus!

Certaines pièces telles que *Elle souffle! / There She Blows!* viennent en deux versions et sont jouées dans chaque langue officielle correspondante. D'autres, comme *Le vase brisé* ne sont, pour diverses raisons, jouées que dans une langue, mais dans un tel cas, nous offrons une contrepartie équivalente dans l'autre langue. Et puis il y en a d'autres, comme *Measure for mesure*, dont le scénario est bilingue et dans lesquelles les deux langues se côtoient. L'une d'entre elles, *Déluge*, se passe de mots et n'a recours qu'à des sons ou à des jeux de voix; elle possède sa propre langue. Et une autre, *Le Bus!* mélange le bilinguisme et les sons.

À mesure que nous développions notre programme, il nous est apparu *de plus en plus clair* que les visiteurs perçoivent le choix de la langue de chaque texte comme une prise de position politique et il est souvent remis en question pour cette raison.

Extrait d'une conférence donnée à Chicago, en 1992, dont le but était de provoquer.

Parry: As far as language is concerned, the bilingual mandate of the theatre programme, like that of the museum, means the programme has to provide comprehensive and balanced access for visitors to all its presentations in both official languages. In fact, we thought that because of this mandate the next part of our presentation should be given in both the official languages of Canada. So, for the next few minutes, Sara will speak in French and I will give my part of the presentation in English.

Snow: Merci, David. D'abord, il faut que j'explique le contexte et la perspective des pièces. La plupart des auteurs de pièces du musée sont des Canadiens anglais. À cause de ça, il existe un point de vue anglophone dans les pièces. Cette perspective pose un problème pour les visiteurs francophones.

Parry: As Sara has just stated, we must first describe the context in which these performances take place and the perspective of the plays' creators. Because the majority of playwrights and curators for the exhibitions are French Canadians, there is a strong theatrical bias towards a French-Canadian perspective on English history. This direction often poses problems for English-Canadian visitors to the museum.

Snow: (*To David in English*) David ....

Parry: Sara, we'd better move on.

Snow: (*To David, unwillingly, in English*) Okay, okay. (*In French*) Par exemple, la majorité des comédiens sont anglophones - alors quand ils jouent les rôles français, ils ont un accent anglais. Quand ils jouent les rôles français, ces mauvais accents posent un grand problème pour les visiteurs francophones.

Parry: Most of the actors are francophone. Therefore, when they speak English they have a strong and disturbing French accent, and this presents a problem when they are performing histori-cally English-speaking characters for anglophone visitors.

Snow: (*Protesting, in English*) But David ....

Aud. 1: (*Jumping up from the audience in anger*) O.K. Ça suffit! Arrête! Is bad enough you have anglophone avec cet accent terrible qui parle en français. Est-ce que vous voulez me dire qu'il n'y a pas un francophone au musée qui était disponible pour venir ici à Chicago pour faire cette présentation! Mais, c'est toujours comme ça - c'est les Anglais qui ont tous les privilèges. C'est mes impôts aussi qui paie pour vos voyages et ....

Aud. 2: (*Looking at Aud. 1 in disgust*) Oh, can it! I'm so sick of hearing you francophones whining about this stuff. So no francophone is speaking. So what? And what's the big deal about her accent? I don't really speak French anyway, but I'm sure her accent is fine. Obviously you understand what they were saying anyway, so what's the big problem ...?

Convenor: Excuse me. Perhaps it would be best if you continued your discussion outside so that we can get on with the papers — we do have a very tight time schedule.

(*Aud. 1 stomps out. Aud. 2 mutters and subsides*).

Source : David Parry et Sara Snow, «A Question of Identity: Interpretive Theatre and the Politics of Language at the Canadian Museum of Civilization», conférence donnée au congrès de la Speech Communication Association, Chicago, 1992, pp. 5-6.

Il y a environ un an et demi, j'ai donné une conférence lors d'un congrès à Chicago avec une collègue, Sara Snow, au sujet du programme d'interprétation didactique et des politiques sur la langue au MCC. Nous avons été étonnés de constater l'intérêt que suscitait là-bas la question du bilinguisme. Nous nous sommes rendus compte que Chicago comptait en gros 30 % d'hispanophones et, juste avant l'ouverture du congrès, la question de la langue a provoqué un tumulte. En effet, la question était de savoir si les bulletins de vote, aux élections présidentielles, allaient être en anglais seulement ou s'ils seraient bilingues, anglais-espagnol. Nombre des participants qui travaillaient dans le domaine des arts d'interprétation au sein d'établissements culturels cherchaient des solutions aux défis linguistiques et culturels que nous posions.

Alors en quoi consistent, précisément, ces défis?

Tout d'abord, la langue, en tant que symbole et véhicule de l'identité culturelle, a été, et demeure, une très grande question. [*David, dans ses notes, mentionne le sexe et la couleur comme deux autres défis, mais il n'y a pas de texte qui vienne étayer ce qu'il avait l'intention d'en dire. Il soulève cependant ces questions dans d'autres articles.*] La langue ne peut pas être autre chose qu'un élément clé dans la programmation d'un musée national d'histoire humaine et c'est, pour reprendre les mots de notre directeur, «un symbole du rôle que joue le gouvernement fédéral dans la culture.»[3] *Nous savons que* le langage verbal a un rapport avec la culture de bien des façons. *Nous savons aussi que* les musées sont des lieux où les gens découvrent et réaffirment leur identité.

Comédien de Dramamuse, MCC
Dramamuse actor, CMC

La réflexion que nous avons portée sur ces questions à l'occasion de la conférence de Chicago m'a amené à penser à diverses choses. L'une était de relever le défi que posait l'usage des langues comme telles (bilinguisme et multilinguisme) et d'essayer de développer des moyens de communiquer par-delà les silences de la langue (*par* le langage visuel que sont le mime, le costume, la danse et les marionnettes de même que la musique et d'autres moyens); nous avons vraiment commencé à définir d'autres langages - des langages qui vont avec, mais qui parfois remplacent et quelquefois contredisent carrément, les langues que nous parlons.[4]

Nous pouvons, en tant qu'interprètes, être d'accord ou pas avec ce que nous disons *dans* plusieurs de *ces* autres langages : le langage corporel, les yeux - contact ou pas -, la langue, le timbre vocal et autres. À mesure que notre programme s'est développé, nous avons trouvé des moyens, et les avons intégrés à notre travail, pour que le programme d'interprétation et celui de l'animation s'apportent mutuellement quelque chose. C'est devenu évident pour moi que *nous devons avoir recours à toutes les formes de langage et prêter attention, particulièrement, aux formes non verbales, et invoquer les Muses pour nous aider à tous les niveaux.*

Il y a le langage des objets - pas seulement de l'information au sujet de l'objet et son utilisation, mais la sensation qu'il dégage, son odeur, son poids, sa texture, son goût même. Par exemple, l'expérience *que j'ai faite, alors que je visitais Louisbourg*, du pain cuit dans les fours, et toute l'information que j'ai eu à ce sujet, *a été très intéressante. Et puis il y a le* langage corporel, *et la voix, naturellement, et l'attitude* - vous devez aimer les gens et leur montrer que vous les aimez, que vous *voulez* leur parler, que vous désirez partager avec eux votre enthousiasme pour le musée et ce qu'il représente.

M. Sullivan *soulève un autre point au sujet de ce que nous communiquons quand nous mettons quelque chose en exposition. Il nous rappelle que la décision même d'exposer A plutôt que B relève toujours d'un jugement de valeur. Nous passons un «message» au public* simplement en mettant, ou en ne mettant pas, des objets ou des images dans les expositions.[5]

Et puis Julian Spalding, dans le discours-programme qu'il a prononcé au congrès annuel de l'AMC en 1993, faisait mention d'un autre facteur qui fait que nous communiquons - seulement QUI communique? Ce texte a paru sous forme d'article, intitulé «Interpréter? Non, communiquer». Sous cet aspect, M. Spalding nous inspire énormément, et il confirme ma propre réponse à la question : «Qui sont les interprètes?». Il explique que dans les musées et les galeries d'art de Glasgow, tous les membres du personnel qui s'adressent au public sont des communicateurs. Il affirme que les assistants de notre musée [autrefois tout le monde, des nettoyeurs ou des officiers de sécurité à ceux qui aident à la boutique] sont, à certains égards, les membres de notre personnel les plus importants. Ce sont eux que le public voit... Ils sont notre principal contact humain avec le public - et vital pour la bonne marche du musée. M. Spalding ajoute qu'on devrait juger un musée sur sa capacité de bien communiquer.[6]

Mais revenons aux Muses avec lesquelles nous avons commencé... Ces Muses trouvent voix et expression dans notre capacité, en tant qu'interprète, non seulement de bien utiliser le langage verbal, mais aussi d'avoir recours aux nombreux langages non verbaux dont nous avons discuté. La communication humaine est si complexe!

De plus, nous devons nous rappeler que la notion même de théâtre est fugace. L'interprétation personnalisée - dans un musée, sur un site historique, dans un centre des sciences ou dans un parc du patrimoine (nous venons tous de l'un ou l'autre de ces établissements) - est, de toute évidence, éphémère, qu'il s'agisse de théâtre proprement dit, de jeux de rôles historiques ou de démonstrations (costumées ou autres).

Il y a du pour et du contre *à cela*. C'est extrêmement efficace dans l'immédiat, mais on ne peut pas vraiment le prendre avec soi. On ne peut non plus l'ouvrir comme un livre et le lire. On ne peut également en faire jouer la cassette vidéo et s'attendre à en retirer la même impression. Quelquefois, cela donne quelque chose de concret, de tangible que l'on peut apporter avec soi - un clou forgé dans une boutique (reconstituée) de forgeron du XIXe siècle, une calligraphie que l'on a soi-même réalisée avec les conseils des interprètes, une brochure manuscrite qui décrit ce que l'on a vu et fait. Mais c'est du sur-le-champ et, par définition, éphémère. C'est fait et ça passe.

Nous verrons *Déluge* dans sa version conçue pour l'intérieur[7], et une autre version qui pousse plus loin certains des choix de langages qui commençaient à être connus au moment de la production de la pièce. Et il m'est apparu évident, à mesure que nous explorions des façons de faire passer le contenu, l'essence des divers «messages», que *la pièce pourrait avoir plus de succès si nous n'utilisions pas de «langue vraiment connue», mais bien plutôt des sons combinés avec le langage non verbal dont nous venions d'entrevoir les immenses possibilités.*

Que devrait être, alors, notre réponse à ces questions de langues? Nous avons en commun, dans nos établissements respectifs, le développement et l'animation par l'interprétation personnalisée. Et que nous ayons ou non, actuellement, ce sentiment de faire face à un problème de langues, je crois qu'il faut dire que cela s'en vient, à mesure que l'internationalisme gagne du terrain. D'un côté, nous nous dirigeons vers l'utilisation d'une langue des affaires internationale, l'anglais. De l'autre, nous allons vers l'expression violente du besoin de préserver son identité culturelle, sa culture, par le biais de la langue.

[*Il faut faire ici un détour du côté de la manière dont le MCC a utilisé ou reconnu les langues des Premiers Peuples du Canada. En fait, la question y fait l'objet, depuis longtemps, de préoccupations et de débats constants, sans parler de la bataille financière qu'elle soulève. Cependant, David n'a que peu de notes à ce sujet.*][8] Au Canada, nous avons connu jusqu'à assez récemment, une politique qui semblait avoir pour but d'éradiquer les langues autochtones en en défendant l'usage dans les écoles *publiques. Heureusement, nous prenons nos distances de cette position d'oppression aussi bien en termes de règlements édictés par le gouvernement qu'en tant que société.* [*David donne, à ce sujet, l'exemple*] *du populaire groupe de chanteurs montagnais Kashtin, qui montre l'intérêt naissant des Canadiens pour leurs autres cultures et que* la musique traverse les frontières. [*Il donne aussi l'exemple*] de Coyote's Cabaret, *le spectacle qui a eu lieu le samedi soir dans le cadre du symposium.*

De façon plus générale, et comme nous nous efforçons de communiquer du mieux possible avec nos visiteurs, je pense que nous avons besoin de répondre aux défis que posent les questions de langues inhérentes à l'interprétation personnalisée en invoquant les Muses. Dans un sens, je pense que les interprètes de toutes sortes, dans un musée ou sur un site du patrimoine, ont hérité de la cape (ou d'un petit morceau de cette cape, peut-être la bordure) des conteurs d'histoires, des bardes, de ceux qui racontent des légendes, des poètes, des comédiens, des gardiens de la loi et de la culture orale. Nous comprenons notre passé et nous nous identifions à lui *par l'action de nos interprètes.* [*Ici David a inscrit «Taziyeh» et avait visiblement l'intention de parler de ce qu'il avait appris avec d'autres du Trinity College, au Connecticut, à un congrès et à une pièce musulmane chiite de premier ordre, en 1988.*][9]

[*Bien que David n'ait pas écrit de conclusion, il a imprimé à nouveau la citation avec laquelle il a commencé son allocution et l'a placée à la fin de son travail. Ainsi nous finissons avec cette citation - laissant bien des aspects de sa discussion sous forme de questions. C'est non seulement le plus que nous pouvons faire avec le matériel qu'il a laissé, mais c'est aussi ce qui est le plus approprié, parce que dans son allocution de bienvenue au symposium, il espérait que les travaux de ces quatre jours permettraient de soulever bien d'autres questions plutôt que de trouver des solutions définitives.]*

«Venez, alors, commençons par les Muses, qui ont ravi par leurs chants le grand esprit de Zeus, leur père qui habite l'Olympe, puisqu'elles révèlent de leurs voix harmonieuses ce qui a été, ce qui est et ce qui sera.»

Notes

1. Walter J. ONG. *Orality and Literacy*, Londres et New York, Methuen, 1982. [*Toutes les citations proviennent des cinquante premières pages du livre, fortement soulignées par David.*]

2. Cette chanson de bord est décrite comme «chanson de bord de drisse que chantaient les Noirs des Antilles» dans le livre de Stan Hugill *Shanties from the Seven Seas*, Londres, Routledge et Kegan Paul, 1961, p. 522. [*David a chanté une version différente de celle de M. Hugill, qu'il a apprise de John Townley qui dit qu'il s'agit d'une chanson de bord de cabestan d'après la guerre civile et que «Shinbone Alley» était la rue principale du quartier du port à Saint George, aux Bermudes. On peut entendre David chanter* Bully in the Alley *sur la cassette posthume intitulée* 'E Liked It All *(on peut se la procurer par la Boutique du Musée).*]

3. George F. MACDONALD et Stephen ALSFORD. *Un musée pour le village global*, Hull, Musée canadien des civilisations, 1989.

4. [*David fait ici référence à l'ouvrage de Jay INGRAM,* Talk Talk Talk, *Toronto, Penguin Books, 1992, qui contiendrait des exemples d'appui et de contradiction. Je n'ai pas pu localiser ces exemples.*]

5. Référence à SULLIVAN. «The Museum and Moral Artifact», dans *Moral Education Forum*, n° X, 1985, [*peut-être entre les pages 2 et 18, que David cite dans un article écrit avec Stephen Alsford*].

6. Dans *Muse*, vol. XI, n° 3, automne (novembre) 1993, p. 10-14.

7. [*David a senti que cette pièce conçue pour être jouée à l'intérieur était très différente de celle conçue originalement pour être jouée à l'entrée (à l'extérieur) du MCC.*]

8. [*Voir le document «Live Interpretation at CMC» de David Parry et Louise Boucher, 1988, p. 33-35, pour une étude plus poussée.*]

9. [*Cela a constitué le point culminant de l'année 1987-1988 où David a été professeur invité, après qu'il ait eu enseigné un an à l'Hebrew University de Jérusalem. Les deux expériences ont accru son intérêt pour les divergences de points de vue culturels sur la signification et l'usage du théâtre, sans parler de la langue et du défi qu'elle a représenté pour lui durant ces années.*]

❖ The Languages of Live Interpretation

David Parry

Adapted and edited by Caroline Parry from notes attached to David Parry's incomplete manuscript.

Editor's note: David gave a version of this speech as the keynote address of the symposium, which, unfortunately, was not tape-recorded. Nor is the existing draft he left complete: some of his notes on the text itself are now cryptic references, and the entire second half of his manuscript is a handwritten mix of outline, notes, quotes and both full and incomplete sentences. I have attempted to decipher his scrawl, supplement his references and add to the unfinished draft in such a way as to make this text as true to his thinking, style and words as possible. What I have not been able to do, however, because he left too few clues, is structure the whole as if it were a complete speech, with a beginning thesis and tidy conclusion. I regret this, but am glad we do still have as many of David's stimulating thoughts from that time as we do.

To make matters even more confusing, readers who also attended the symposium may remember that David left his speech and the accompanying slides in the taxi he took to the Museum. So we have no real guarantee that what David wrote (and we have given here) corresponds completely to what he actually said! Nonetheless, it is germane and thought-provoking, and surely David would have wanted us to reproduce what we could — and to continue the discussion! CP

[Notes on editorial procedure: Where I have inserted my words in any pre-existing paragraphs of David's or where I have created new paragraphs of text, my words are in italics — as is this paragraph. Questions about David's meaning, notes about his notes, or my textual comments are in italics and within square brackets.]

Come, then, let us begin from the Muses, who by their singing delight the great mind of Zeus, their father, who lives in Olympos, as they tell of what is, and what is to be, and what was before now, with harmonious voices.

That was Homer's great contemporary, Hesiod, speaking in a work called the *Theogony*, created in Greece sometime in the eighth century B.C., in which he tells of the earliest ages of the world, the universe, the gods, the monsters of the earth and — most importantly for us — the Muses. Later writers reckoned there were nine of them — Clio, the Muse of History, Terpsichore, the Muse of Dance, Urania, the Muse of Astronomy, Melpomene, the Muse of Tragedy, and so on — although writers could never quite agree on exactly which Muse did precisely what. *But* clearly *the Muses were the* inspirers of poets, playwrights, singers *and other creators.*

Hesiod also tells us, elsewhere, that the mother of the Muses was Mnemosyne — Memory. And if you're wondering what all this high-falutin' classical introduction of my subject is all about, well, it's just that: The Muses, and Memory. A museum — and our word "museum" — derives from the Greek "mouseion," which meant not only a home for the Muses (such as those of song, dance, dramas and so on) but also the place of memory. Museums through the last few centuries have *obviously* retained their sense of connection with Mnemosyne, but it's only relatively recently that they have begun to welcome the Muses back into their exhibition halls in any substantial way. *Of course,* when I speak of "museum," I am speaking of all those institutions, centres, sites, parks *and so on* that share our *role and concerns here.*

While I am talking about sharing, let me add that I hope this keynote will prompt even more "creative swiping" *than has already begun to happen. After all,* we share many of the same aims at this conference*, and perhaps we can share a lot more of what we have already achieved with each other, so that we can build on our joint experiences.*

But to return to memory. In the days before the invention of writing, all knowledge was dependent on memory for its preservation, as music is today, for those who can't read it. *What people "knew" was passed on through all sorts of oral forms or processes — such as* proverbs, weather or navigation rhymes, children's rhymes, *et cetera.* The Muses of History, Song,

Dance and Drama were in part patronesses of memory. And it seems clear that memory became, in part, dependent on the Muses. Hesiod lived in an oral culture, unlike ourselves. I'll return to him, and to the Muses, shortly.

But first I want to emphasize that we live interpreters *are working,* essentially, in the oral tradition. *I have been reading a fascinating book by Walter J. Ong, called* Orality and Literacy, *lately.*[1] *He discusses how the oral tradition works, and he says that "serious thought is intertwined with memory systems." Further, he exhorts us to* "Think memorable thoughts." I believe one of the challenges for us as live interpreters is to create these *memorable thoughts by giving our audience* memorable images, without language as such **getting in the way**. [*David's emphasis: For this,* rhythm *is* very important *and* rhyme *and* sound *in general.* All sorts of *ancillary,* non-verbal things *are* useful, *too* — costumes, props *and so forth.*]

Even so, much, if not most, of what we learn about the content of our art, the informational substance of what we communicate through live interpretation, comes to us directly or indirectly from books, or at any rate the written word. In museums, as in our world at large, we are still — despite video — still strikingly tied to the written word. As Walter Ong puts it:

> The words keep coming to you in writing no matter what you
> do. Moreover, to dissociate words from writing is psychologically
> threatening, for literates' sense of control over language is closely tied
> to the visual transformation of language: without dictionaries, written
> grammar rules, punctuation, and all the rest of the apparatus that
> makes words in something you can look up, how can literates live?

It can be demoralizing to remind yourself that there's no dictionary in the mind. Outside of relatively high-technology cultures most users of language have always got along pretty well without any visual transformations whatsoever of oral sound. Don't get me wrong, I'm not putting down writing: as Ong says, "orality needs to produce and is destined to produce writing." Without it human consciousness cannot achieve its fullest potentials. What I would like to suggest here is rather that as museum interpreters, we need to embrace particular aspects of our inheritance from the Muses, and in particular the power — the sheer concrete, physical, magical potency and power of words, and to knit them with the help of the Muses, to all those other languages to which we have access.

There is a paradox embodied in this need, however. We are so tied to the written word that it's often difficult, particularly as interpreters who actively **like** to communicate things, *like to talk to our audiences, to tap the full power of our non-verbal languages, as well.*

Mystic Seaport museum, Mystic, Connecticut

Here David wrote on the page, "Mystic talk — Robert R." The name reference is unclear, but we do know David had been a performer in June 1991 and 1993 at the Sea Music Festival at Mystic Seaport, the living history museum in Connecticut. The slide he was planning to use may well have been one of the Charles P. Morgan, *the last surviving wooden whaling ship from the nineteenth century, beautifully preserved and sited at the Seaport. David would, characteristically, have broken into a shanty at this point, perhaps the powerful "Bully in the Alley," to give his audience a deeper feel of the power of that ship and the magical place he loved, through the language of music, the rhythm of the shanty [heavy emphasis on underlined syllables below] adding its own meaning to the actual words.*

> *So 'elp me, bob, I'm <u>bully</u> in the alley,*
> *<u>Way,</u> ay, <u>bully</u> in the alley;*
> *'elp me, bob, I'm <u>bully</u> in the alley,*
> *<u>Bully</u> down in Shinbone <u>Al</u>!*

Shanties of course are work songs sung mostly by sailors to help coordinate heavy chores such as hauling sails up and down or winding up the capstan to weigh anchor.[2] The actual words may not make much "sense," but the rhythms were a way of conveying "instructions" to the workers involved — another sort of language.

It's interesting that by his very juxtaposition of the ship image and the shanty, David was himself giving a kind of "visual transformation [to] oral sound" — literally adding a visual image to the sound, albeit not putting words on paper, which he had just claimed most "users of language have always got along pretty well without." Perhaps this is merely further reinforcement of the paradox above. Or perhaps the apparent contradiction is due to David never fully resolving the issues he wanted to present in this paper — certainly it is clear that David neither wrote nor indicated a conclusion in his notes.

This symposium really began life as a simply stated question about a complex problem: "How can we in this institution use interpretive theatre more effectively to meet the challenges posed by bilingualism?" The simply stated question rapidly grew more complex. *But before getting into the complexities, let me review the basic situation.* The CMC is an officially bilingual institution. That is to say, our mandate is to function bilingually as an organization, and to communicate whatever we wish to communicate to each and every visitor in the language of their choice. That is to say, the language of their choice just so long as it's French or English. The truth is that while we may only *speak* English and French, with perhaps an occasional member of the floor or programme staff offering some Spanish, German, Russian or whatever, we *use* many languages in our museum to communicate to our visitors just what our museum is, and what it wants to share with them. As a museum, we start with a language of "things." Some of the languages we use:

- Visual (form/functional)
- Visual (contextual)
- Visual (aesthetic)
- Tactile (usually reproductions, but sometimes the real thing)

We need perhaps to connect this language of "things" — the visual, the tactile, the non-verbal aural, the languages of smell and taste (much more on historic sites than museums) with our verbal communication.

As you know, the interpretive theatre programme at the CMC is one in which we strive to maintain an effective balance of programming in the two official languages at all times. All of the first-person, role-playing presentations are designed to function in both

languages, and the actors are constantly switching from one to the other as they perform, depending on what visitors they are addressing at any given moment.

As for the plays, some, like *There She Blows!/Elle souffle!,* are performed in two versions, one in each of the official languages. Others, like *Le vase brisé,* are for various reasons performed only in one language, though in such a case we will almost certainly have a balancing play of some kind in the other language. Yet others, like *Measure for mesure,* are bilingual scripts, in which the two languages are used in the same play alongside each other. One, *The Deluge,* which you will see in the Grand Hall, dispenses with language entirely and employs pure vocal and other sound — essentially creating its own language. And yet another, *Le Bus!,* mixes the bilingual and the non-lingual formats.

Le Bus!

The creation of this piece (*Le Bus!*) took as its starting point the idea of interpreting in a completely open-ended way the statement made by a certain part of the Children's Museum space and the interactive objects it contained (all from different parts of the world): a full-size bus from Pakistan; a British telephone booth; a rickshaw; a fruit and vegetable stand; a puppet theatre; and so on. The piece simply plays with the various ideas and possibilities generated by *these* objects in *this* space.

When visitors to the Children's Museum lift up the telephone in the booth, for example, they may get a "personal telephone call" in any one of a number of languages. *Le Bus!* picks this idea up, and plays with its language implications. Of the three characters in the play, the Driver speaks only French, the Mechanic only English, the Traveller is a mute, and communicates only visually. With the audience's assistance, they eventually succeed in communicating in a somewhat bizarre, but perfectly effective manner.

The bus itself as a part of the Museum is clearly a static object representing the possibilities of travel. *Le Bus!* plays on this by taking it as a dramatic premise that the bus is broken. The Mechanic tries to fix it, but cannot. The play then attempts to get the audience to decide how the Traveller can fulfil his travel aspirations in these circumstances.

The fruit and vegetable stand is loaded with plastic fruit and vegetables. When the Driver and Mechanic in their theatrical reality offer the Traveller apples from the stand to eat, and are about to "eat" some themselves, the Traveller responds to the non-theatrical reality, looks at the audience, then back at the apples, and then begins to juggle them. And so on. The attempt is all the time to provoke questions about the objects, their "reality," and the host of different possible meanings inherent in them as part of the museum experience.

Again in *Le Bus!*, as with the examples of *Frame by Frame* or *There She Blows!* described above, one of the potentially most exciting and fertile new territories for theatre museum to explore would seem to be the different kinds of dialectic it can create with the physical actuality of an exhibition — or even of the museum as a whole — as encountered by the public.

Source: Jeanne Cannizzo and David Parry, "Museum Theatre in the 1990s: Trail-blazer or Camp-follower?" in *Museums and the Appropriation of Culture* (London: The Athlone Press, 1994), pp. 60-61.

Comédienne de Dramamuse, MCC

Dramamuse actor, CMC

As we have developed our programme, it has become *more and more* clear that the choice of language for each text is increasingly seen by visitors as a political statement and often specifically questioned by them as such.

About a year and a half ago, I gave a paper at a conference in Chicago with a colleague, Dr. Sara Snow, about the interpretive theatre programme and the politics of language here at the CMC. We were amazed at the level of interest and the power of the response in Chicago to the bilingual question, till we discovered that Chicago has a roughly 30 per cent Hispanic population and that just before the conference opened the city had experienced a furore over whether or not ballot-papers for the presidential elections were going to be in an English-only, or a bilingual English-Spanish format. A number of people in our audience who worked in the performance or interpretive arts in cultural institutions were looking for solutions to the particular kinds of linguistic and cultural challenges we had articulated.

So what were these challenges, precisely?

Well, firstly, that language as a primary symbol of and vehicle for cultural identity was, and is, an extremely big issue here. *[In David's notes he lists gender and colour as two other challenges, but there are no further notes to develop what he might have intended to cover — or at least touch on — concerning these. He does discuss these issues in his other papers, however.]*

Language cannot be other than a key element in the programming of a national museum of human history which is, in our director's words, "a symbol of the federal government's role in cultural affairs."[3] In very many ways, *we know that* verbal language is connected to culture. *We also know that* museums are places where people discover or reaffirm their cultural identity.

The thinking we had done about these issues for the Chicago paper set me to thinking in several different directions at the same time. One was that in confronting the challenges of language as such (bilingualism and multilingualism), and in trying to develop ways of communicating across language gaps (*using* the visual languages of mime, costume, music, dance, puppets and so on), we were really beginning to describe other kinds of languages — all the languages that go along with and support, occasionally replace, sometimes even contradict, the languages we speak.[4]

On a simple level, we *can*, as live interpreters, either support or contradict what we are saying *through* many of *these* other languages: *our* body language, eye — contact, or not — language, vocal tone and so on.

And as our programme here developed, and we began to integrate and find techniques for the mutual support of interpretive theatre and the animation programme, it became very apparent to me that *we have to use all forms of language, paying particular attention to the non-verbal ones, and invoking the Muses to help on every possible level.*

There is the language of objects — not just information about the object and its use, but its feel, its smell, its weight, its texture, its taste, even — for instance the bread baked in the Louisbourg ovens, and the information about it *that I gained as a visitor there, which was very* interesting. *And there is* body language *and of course* voice, *plus attitudinal language* — you have to like people and show them you like them, **want** to talk to them, want to share your enthusiasm for the museum and what it represents, with them.

A further consideration about just what we *communicate* when we exhibit something *comes from* Sullivan, *who reminds us that the very act of choosing to exhibit "A" rather than "B" is* always a value judgement. We give "messages" *to our audience* simply by our inclusion or non-inclusion of objects and images in exhibitions.[5]

And yet another factor in what we communicate — just WHO does the communicating — comes from Julian Spalding, *whose keynote address to the 1993 CMA annual conference is now an article entitled "Interpretation? No, Communication." Spalding is tremendously* inspirational in this regard, *and he confirms my own answer to the question* "Who are live interpreters?" *by explaining that in the Glasgow museums and art galleries,* **all** staff who come into contact with the public *are communicators. He says, "Our Museum Assistants [formerly everyone from cleaners and guards to shop assistants] are, in some ways, our most important members of staff. They are the*

Le Déluge / The Deluge

staff the public sees . . . They are our main human contact with our public — and vital to the effectiveness of the museum." Spalding does not hesitate to affirm that "A museum should be judged on how well it communicates."[6]

But now back to the Muses we began with . . . Those Muses find voice and expression not only through our ability, as live interpreters, to use verbal language well, but also through the many non-verbal languages we have been discussing. Human communication is so complex!

In addition, we need to remember that theatre itself is evanescent. Live interpretation — in a museum, on a historical site, in a science centre or a heritage park — any one of these institutions from which we variously come — is clearly ephemeral, whether it be theatre proper, historical role-playing, or a demonstration (costumed or otherwise). *This is* both a plus and a minus, *because it is* extraordinarily effective in the present tense, but you can't really take it away with you. You can't open it like a book and read it. You can't turn on a video of it and expect it to have the same effect.

Sometimes live interpretation *does* provide you *with* a tangible, material piece of something to take away with you — a nail forged in a re-created nineteenth-century blacksmith shop, a piece of calligraphy that you have done yourself, coached by an interpreter, a written pamphlet or booklet about what you have seen and experienced. But it is live and therefore by definition ephemeral. It is done and it passes.

Our theatre programme at the Canadian Museum of Civilization may reasonably be said to have as many different, and equally justifiable roles as there are different agendas in the visitors who constitute its audiences. As Stephen Weil points out, "Museum-goers may legitimately be seeking frivolous diversions, consolation, social status, an opportunity for reverence, companionship, solitude, or innumerable other groups or individual goals. Museum-going is neither a tidy or a predictable activity" (Stephen Weil, *Rethinking the Museum and Other Meditations* (Washington, D.C.: Smithsonian Institution Press, 1990) p. 63). But in its approach to the intertwined challenges of language and identity, the CMC theatre programme has certainly taken Sola's suggestions to heart, and striven to generate in all its audiences more understanding, appreciation and tolerance for "the other."

In approaching these challenges it has also, we believe, striven to move beyond the roles for which Sola argues, to embrace two further roles articulated by Weil: stimulation and empowerment (Ibid., pp. 53-56). Our presentations consciously and constantly make the attempt to provoke visitors into a fresh interaction with the museum through surprise and a kind of subversive activity — challenging their assumptions about what a museum is, challenging their responses to it, challenging their interpretations of history and culture, with the ultimate goal of enlisting each individual as a collaborator who might, in Weil's words, "in turn develop his own sense of heritage, causality, connectedness and taste — his own links to both an individual and a communal past" (Ibid., p. 55).

In the course of developing such an approach in a theatre programme appropriate to the CMC, it has become increasingly clear that language, the political *bête noire* and probably the most divisive issue in recent Canadian history, is also potentially one of the most useful, provocative, stimulating, entertaining and recreative theatrical tools at our disposal. If we grasp it with both hands, and use it with insight, subtlety and good humour it may assist us in empowering museum visitors to see their own identities afresh and transform the Brechtian "historical field" into what they themselves would truly have it be.

Source: David Parry and Sara Snow, "A Question of Identity: Interpretive Theatre and the Politics of Language at the Canadian Museum of Civilization," paper presented at the annual conference of the Speech Communication Association, Chicago, 1992, pp. 24-25.

You will see *The Deluge* in a version designed for indoor performance,[7] and one that pursues further some of the emerging language choices which came to the fore in producing that play. For it became increasingly apparent to me as we explored the ways in which it could communicate its essence, its content, its various "messages," that *this play could be most successful if we used no "real known spoken language" at all in our script, but relied on pure sound combined with the non-verbal languages we were coming to realize had such power.*

What *then* should our response be *to all these language issues? We have in common the use of and development of live interpretation in our various institutions. And* whether we feel we *currently* face a direct language challenge or not, I think it's fair to say that we all will, increasingly, as globalism accelerates. On the one hand, *we are* moving towards an international business language — English? On the other, towards fiercely expressed needs to preserve and retain cultures and cultural identity through language.

[An obvious tangent at this point would be some consideration of how the CMC has used or recognized the languages of Canada's First Nations. Indeed, this has been a long-term concern and subject of continuing debate, not to mention financial struggle, at the CMC. However, David gives only minimal notes on this topic, which are incorporated here.[8]] We have been faced until quite recently in Canada with a policy which seemed bent *on* eradicating Native languages by forbidding their use in *government* schools. *Happily we are moving away from this oppressive stance as a society as well as in terms of government regulations. [David noted the two examples of]* The popular Montagnais band/singing group Kashtin *is a fine example of burgeoning Canadian interest in our other cultures, of* music crossing boundaries, *as was the entertainment provided for this conference on Saturday night,* at Coyote's Cabaret.

In the larger picture, I believe we need to respond to the challenges of the language questions inherent in live interpretation by remembering to invoke the Muses as we strive to communicate as fully as possible with our visitors. In some senses I believe that interpreters of all kinds in a museum or a heritage site are the inheritors of the mantle (or a little piece, maybe the hem of the mantle) of the storytellers, the bards, the singers of tales, the poets, the actors, the keepers of the law and of oral culture. We understand our past and identify ourselves with it *in the hands of our interpreters. [Here David noted* Taziyeh *and obviously expected to expand on what he and others at Trinity College, Connecticut learned at a 1988 conference and performance of a major Shiite Muslim drama.[9]]*

[Although David wrote no concluding paragraphs, he did print the quotation that he began with again at the end of his draft. And so it is that quotation we finish with — leaving many aspects of David's discussion as open-ended questions. It is not only the most we can do with the materials he left, but it is also appropriate, for in his welcoming remarks at the beginning of the symposium David hoped that the proceedings of these four days together would indeed generate far more open-ended questions than find final solutions.]

> Come, then, let us begin from the Muses, who by their singing delight the great mind of Zeus, their father, who lives in Olympos, as they tell of what is, and what is to be, and what was before now, with harmonious voices.

Notes

1. Walter J. Ong, *Orality and Literacy* (London and New York: Methuen, 1982). *[All quotes appear to be from the first 50 pages of the book, which David underlined heavily.]*

2. This particular shanty is explained as a "halyard shanty of Negro origins" from the West Indies, in Stan Hugill's *Shanties from the Seven Seas* (London: Routledge et Kegan Paul, 1961) p. 522. *[David sang it in a different version than Hugill's, learned from John Townley, who says it is a capstan shanty from the post-Civil War era, and that "Shinbone Alley" was the main street of the "Sailor Town" in St George, Bermuda. David can be heard singing "Bully in the Alley" on the posthumously released tape "'E Liked It All" (available through the CMC Boutique).]*

Dramamuse, la troupe de théâtre du MCC

Dramamuse, CMC's theatre company

3. George F. MacDonald and Stephen Alsford, *A Museum for the Global Village* (Hull: CMC, 1989).

4. [*David refers here to Jay Ingram, whose book,* Talk Talk Talk *(Toronto: Penguin Books Canada, 1992), apparently gives examples of contradiction and support. I was unable to find any exact references.*]

5. Reference to Sullivan in "The Museum and Moral Artifact," *Moral Education Forum*, x (1985), may be in pp. 2-18 [*which he quotes from in paper with Alsford*].

6. MUSE, XI, 3 (Fall 1993), p. 10-14.

7. [*David felt this indoor performance was* substantially different *from the play originally mounted outside the CMC entrance.*]

8. [*See the 1988 document, "Live Interpretation at CMC" by David Parry and Louise Boucher, pp. 33-35 for further exploration.*]

9. [*This was the culmination of a year-long visiting professorship that David held in 1987-88, following an academic year teaching at the Hebrew University in Jerusalem. Both experiences actively expanded David's interest in problems of differing cultural perspectives on the meaning and use of dramatic performance, not to mention how those years challenged him in terms of language!*]

❖ L'interprétation personnalisée et les techniques théâtrales : les enjeux et les défis

Robert Moreau
Agent de projets spéciaux
Lieux historiques nationaux, Parcs Canada[1]
Ottawa (Ontario)

It has become evident to many that cultural institutions such as museums and historic sites are not reaching every level of the population. Many people feel like strangers in these institutions, even refusing to enter them. They do not recognize themselves in the image projected by the museum or the site; they are not receptive to its messages. Over the coming years, in our efforts to reach these people, museums and sites will be exploring new ways of communicating and interpreting. At the same time, with the growing need to generate increasing revenues, museums and historic sites will be encouraged to select popular communications techniques, including theatrical ones. Efforts already under way to use this approach must not be abandoned. With certain modifications, they can become an excellent way of reaching our visitors. However, it must be remembered that they are only a point of departure, and that they must lead to improved communications with our visitors.

Scénario - 1

La famille Tremblay arrive à l'entrée du fort La Paix, un important poste militaire du XVIIIᵉ siècle. Le fort est aujourd'hui un site historique qui commémore la grande lutte dans laquelle se sont engagées les grandes puissances de ce monde, il y a très longtemps, pour la suprématie en Amérique du Nord. À l'entrée du fort, la famille Tremblay fait face à un garde en costume qui crie : «Qui va là? Quel est le mot de passe?» À ces questions, la foule de gens rassemblés à la porte répond : «Vive le roi!» et le garde libère le chemin et dit : « Entrez!»

Immédiatement la famille Tremblay est transportée dans le monde reconstitué du XVIIIᵉ siècle. Les enfants, Nathalie et Éric, se lancent dans l'expérience de voir, de sentir, de toucher et même de goûter à tout ce qui leur est offert. Ils n'hésitent pas à parler aux gens en costume d'époque et à se porter volontaires lors de la démonstration de la marche militaire.

Mᵐᵉ Tremblay suit de près ses enfants dans le site. Tentant de comprendre le monde mystérieux dans lequel elle vient d'entrer, elle participe aux activités d'interprétation et d'animation du site. Avec ses enfants, elle fait la visite guidée du fort La Paix et observe attentivement les différentes démonstrations d'activités historiques.

Pour sa part, M. Tremblay visite le site de façon autonome. N'aimant pas les jeux de rôle, il évite les interprètes en costume qui animent un personnage d'époque. Bien qu'il observe de loin les différentes démonstrations et qu'il écoute de temps à autre les commentaires des guides, il refuse de prendre part aux activités d'animation et recherche plutôt des expositions didactiques qui expliquent l'importance du site.

Après le déjeuner, la famille Tremblay décide d'assister à une représentation théâtrale offerte dans le marché public. Il s'agit de la reconstitution d'une cour martiale basée sur des faits historiques. La pièce a ses effets voulus: l'auditoire est captivé par le drame qui se déroule devant ses yeux. À la fin de la pièce, un interprète signale le dénouement des vrais événements historiques et encourage les gens à poursuivre leur viste du site.

Fatigués, les Tremblay décident de mettre fin à leur visite du fort. Après quelques minutes aux toilettes et à la boutique, ils reprennent le chemin de retour à la maison. Dans l'ensemble, le séjour au site a été très mémorable; ils ont en fait vécu une expérience sensorielle, cognitive et émotionnelle d'un important chapitre de leur histoire. La poupée de Nathalie, le petit canon d'Éric, le livre de recettes et les cartes postales achetés au magasin leur serviront de points de rappel.

Scénario - 2

Après deux heures de route, Paul Nelson et Joanna Johnson arrivent au Grand Rock, un important site historique des États-Unis. Il s'agit en fait d'un des premiers endroits colonisés par les Européens en Amérique du Nord. C'est sur la recommandation de leurs voisins, les Paterson, que Paul et Joanna décident de visiter le site. Lors de leur séjour au Grand Rock l'été précédent, les Paterson avaient été grandement impressionnés par le site. «Ne manquez pas cela», leur signala John Paterson. «C'est formidable! Les gens sont en costume. On vit, on mange et on parle même comme dans l'ancien temps. C'est comme si on était transporté au XVIIe siècle!»

Armés de leur caméra, Paul et Joanna entrent dans le centre d'accueil. Après avoir payé les frais d'entrée, ils visionnent un diaporama de 25 minutes qui explique l'histoire du site et le genre d'expérience qu'ils vont vivre - la reconstitution fidèle de la vie de ce village d'autrefois, basée sur une documentation historique rigoureuse, par des animateurs costumés, qui jouent le rôle de personnages historiques. À la fin du diaporama, les portes du théâtre s'ouvrent et la foule se dirige vers le site. Paul et Joanna suivent le pèlerinage de visiteurs au premier édifice du village.

À l'intérieur de la maison, les visiteurs sont accueillis par un animateur jouant le rôle du personnage historique de John Savage, le leader des premiers colons de cette colonie. Étant parmi les premiers à entrer dans la maison, Paul se retrouve en avant du groupe, face à face avec l'animateur. Ce dernier assume son rôle, regarde Paul dans les yeux, note qu'il est un étranger et lui demande s'il vient d'arriver au village sur l'un des bateaux qui ont jeté l'ancre ce matin. Intimidé par la question et ne sachant quoi dire, Paul ignore l'animateur et ne dit rien. L'animateur se tourne ainsi vers un autre visiteur et lui pose la même question. Celui-ci répond à la question et l'animateur poursuit son jeu de rôle. Se sentant gêné, Paul se faufile graduellement vers la sortie et quitte le groupe.

Pour sa part, Joanna est captivée par le site et ses personnages. Intriguée par la possibilité de dialoguer avec un personnage historique, elle s'approche de l'animateur et se présente comme une anthropologue de l'avenir arrivée le matin pour observer les coutumes du village. Une longue discussion entre Joanna et l'animateur s'ensuit; graduellement, les autres visiteurs quittent la maison pour le prochain point d'intérêt.

Paul décide de poursuivre sa visite de façon autonome. Il observe de loin quelques activités démontrées dans le site. À l'approche de deux animateurs en train de dialoguer sur les pratiques religieuses, il rebrousse chemin. Ne voulant pas être confronté à d'autres animateurs, il n'entre que dans les maisons qui ne sont pas habitées. Après trente minutes, il a tout vu le site et décide d'attendre Joanna au centre d'accueil.

Une heure plus tard Joanna vient le retrouver dans la salle des expositions. Elle lui demande comment il a aimé le site. Paul lui répond qu'il a trouvé les animateurs un peu intimidants et qu'il n'a pas vraiment aimé le site. Satisfaite de son expérience, Joanna mentionne qu'elle a vraiment adoré le site et qu'elle en a appris beaucoup sur les gens qui y habitaient autrefois. Elle ajoute que l'aspect le plus mémorable de sa visite a été les animateurs qui, malgré ses efforts, n'ont jamais abandonné leur rôle.

Scénario - 3

Lors de leur séjour dans la capitale, Alcide et Émelda Landry décident de visiter le Musée de l'histoire. Ayant dû payer des frais d'entrée pour le musée, Alcide, une personne très économe, décide d'en avoir pour son argent et de visiter, par lui-même, l'ensemble du musée. Émelda n'aime pas autant l'histoire que son mari, mais elle le suit fidèlement de galerie en galerie. À l'entrée de la Grande Salle, le vieux couple est accueilli par un guide en uniforme qui les invite à voir une pièce qui porte sur un vrai événement historique. Ayant visité le musée depuis plus d'une heure, les Landry décident de prendre une pause et de regarder la pièce. Mais arrivés dans la salle où se déroulera le spectacle, ils s'aperçoivent que tous les bancs sont occupés. Ils décident alors de regarder la pièce debout près du mur qui longe la salle.

Quelques minutes plus tard, la salle est comble et la pièce commence. Bien qu'il ne voit pas bien le spectacle, Alcide n'ose pas s'approcher des comédiens. Il préfère rester dans le fond de la salle et reposer ses jambes en s'appuyant sur le mur. La présence des comédiens sur la scène ne met pas fin au va-et-vient bruyant des visiteurs dans la salle. En effet, plusieurs visiteurs coupent en avant des Landry en direction de la prochaine salle d'expositions. Graduellement, certains spectateurs décrochent de la pièce et décident de poursuivre leur visite du musée. Soudainement, un nouveau groupe de visiteurs entre dans la salle. On entend des chuchotements de toute part. Ne pouvant plus supporter les interruptions et les bousculades, les Landry décrochent à leur tour et quittent la salle. Alcide et Émelda poursuivent leur visite du musée mais ne retournent pas dans la Grande Salle.

Ces trois scénarios vous semblent familiers ou exagérés? Bien que l'identité du musée et des sites en question ait été cachée, ils ne sont pas fictifs et reposent en fait sur des observations que j'ai recueillies auprès de visiteurs de ces institutions. Je crois que les trois scénarios illustrent bien les avantages et les désavantages de l'utilisation de techniques théâtrales comme moyen de communication dans des musées ou sites historiques. Dans le premier cas, la famille Tremblay vit une expérience enrichissante au fort La Paix. Le site met à sa disposition une grande variété de moyens d'interprétation. Le jeu de rôle par les animateurs et les représentations théâtrales ne sont que deux moyens par lesquels le site transmet ses messages aux visiteurs. Par ces moyens, le site fait appel aux sens créatifs et émotionnels de l'auditoire. En même temps, il offre d'autres moyens de communication plus traditionnels pour les visiteurs à la recherche de l'information factuelle. Il existe donc à ce site une complimentarité des moyens d'interprétation.

Dans le deuxième cas, l'animation de personnification a un résultat mixte : d'une part, Paul est intimidé par l'approche théâtrale et s'éloigne du site; d'autre part, l'approche captive Joanna et semble l'entraîner vers la découverte. Il faut se demander, toutefois, si Joanna n'est pas attirée par la nouveauté de l'animation et si, dans ce cas, le moyen ne domine pas le message.

Finalement, dans le troisième cas, l'approche théâtrale semble correspondre aux besoins des visiteurs. Mais les difficultés techniques interfèrent avec la communication et aucun rapport n'est établi entre les visiteurs et les objets exposés. Puisque le message ne passse évidemment pas, il n'y a dans ce cas aucune transmission de connaissances.

Malgré ces difficultés et les limites évidentes à la communication qu'engendrent l'utilisation de techniques théâtrales à titre de moyen d'interprétation au sein de musées et de sites historiques, nous ne pouvons pas nier la popularité croissante et continue de cette approche dans ces institutions. Il paraît que les avantages, aux yeux de plusieurs, dépassent les problèmes. C'est à cause de cette euphorie apparente que ce texte se veut une douche froide pour l'ensemble des interprètes, des animateurs, des acteurs et des gestionnaires de sites historiques et de musées impliqués dans le débat actuel sur l'avenir de ce moyen de communication muséale.

Je désire exposer, dès le début, ma perspective et mes préjugés à l'égard de ce sujet. Je suis un interprète de carrière et j'aborde cette question avec les yeux d'un interprète qui, d'une part, admire le potentiel et l'impact des techniques et des représentations théâtrales auprès du public et, d'autre part, qui remet en question le caractère interprétatif et éducatif de cet outil de communication dans les musées et les sites historiques. Ce texte, je crois, se distinguera un peu du discours actuel qui se tient au sein de la profession muséale, relativement à ce sujet, par son ton critique de l'utilisation de techniques théâtrales à titre de moyen d'interprétation. Il me semble qu'il y a actuellement parmi nous une tendance dangereuse à considérer les techniques et les représentations théâtrales comme la panacée pouvant guérir tous nos maux de communication avec les visiteurs. Bien que j'admets que des représentations théâtrales peuvent enrichir l'expérience du visiteur au sein de nos musées et sites historiques, il s'agit d'un moyen de communication qui a des limites et qui dans certaines circonstances peut même entraver la communication avec nos visiteurs. Si notre but est de favoriser l'apprentissage chez nos visiteurs, il nous apparaît évident que d'autres moyens d'interprétation complémentaires doivent également être utilisés.

Il y a deux groupes professionnels impliqués dans le débat actuel sur l'utilisation de techniques théâtrales dans le contexte muséal. Des interprètes-éducateurs œuvrent au sein de musées et d'autres institutions patrimoniales et s'intéressent naturellement aux techniques théâtrales et à leur utilisation comme moyen de communication; des acteurs et d'autres professionnels du théâtre pratiquent leur métier dans les milieux non traditionnels - du moins pour eux - que sont les musées, et veulent partager leur amour du théâtre et leur croyance qu'il s'agit là d'un moyen de communication exceptionnel, et cherchent à approfondir leurs connaissances des différents intervenants dans le contexte muséal, dont les interprètes-éducateurs. Bien que ces deux groupes dialoguent depuis quelques années, à nous écouter, je ne suis par sûr que nous parlons tous de la même chose. Notamment, nous ne semblons pas partager la même définition de ce qu'est l'interprétation personnalisée et de ce que sont ses objectifs et son but ultime. D'une part, l'accent est mis sur l'éducation, la transmission de connaissances et l'établissement de rapports; de l'autre, on met l'accent sur la communication par l'imaginaire et sur le divertissement.

Dans le but d'élucider nos discussions, je vais définir l'interprétation personnalisée et revoir brièvement ses caractéristiques et ses objectifs. Je m'excuse auprès des ceux et celles qui n'aiment pas les longs débats qu'engendre souvent la définition de termes. Mais je pense qu'il est essentiel de bien définir les termes afin d'assurer que nous partageons tous les mêmes points de référence et d'avancer le débat.

L'interprétation personnalisée

Bien que l'interprétation existe à titre d'activité reconnue au sein de musées et de sites historiques depuis plus de trente ans, la définition de l'interprétation, telle qu'elle est pratiquée aujourd'hui, n'est pas évidente. L'interprétation est étroitement parentée à l'éducation et à la communication. Il s'agit des deux pôles entre lesquels elle balance. Cette situation contribue sans doute à la difficulté que les interprètes ont à se définir.

Le premier à définir et à établir des principes directeurs de l'interprétation a été l'Américain Freeman Tilden. Dans son œuvre classique intitulée *Interpreting Our Heritage*, Tilden propose en 1957 la définition suivante :

> An educational activity which aims to reveal meanings and relationships through the use of original object, by first hand experience, and by illustrative media rather than simply to communicate factual information.[2]
>
> (Une activité éducative qui a pour but la révélation des sens profonds et des rapports par l'utilisation d'objets originaux, par une expérience de première main et par des médias, plutôt que seulement la communication de faits.)

Selon Tilden, l'interprétation dépasse de beaucoup la simple communication de faits. Il s'agit en effet de la révélation du sens et de la signification d'un lieu, d'un objet, etc. Plusieurs personnes ont tenté au cours des années subséquentes de raffiner cette défintion de Tilden.[3] Malgré ces efforts, elle demeure toujours la base à partir de laquelle la plupart des interprètes définissent leur travail.[4]

Quels sont les points essentiels de la définition de l'interprétation à retenir?

Tout d'abord, l'interprétation a un but éducatif. Elle veut instruire tout en divertissant le public. L'interprétation tient à la révélation des sens profonds et des rapports. Elle cherche à établir un lien entre le site ou l'objet commémoré ou exposé et la personnalité ou l'expérience du visiteur.

L'interprétation s'accomplit par l'utilisation de divers moyens de communication, dont les moyens personnalisés. Ceux-ci varient grandement, depuis les visites guidées aux causeries, les activités d'animation aux démonstrations, les représentations théâtrales aux spectacles historiques, les activités éducatives à l'animation d'époque. Dans chaque cas, l'interprète, l'animateur ou l'éducateur donne de la vie aux expositions et favorise le plus possible le contact direct du visiteur avec l'élément interprété.

En général, les interprètes professionnels ont tendance à considérer les moyens personnalisés d'interprétation comme les plus efficaces. Ce jugement repose sur les grands avantages de cette forme d'interprétation : à savoir, sa souplesse, sa chaleur humaine, son pouvoir d'inspiration et son impact immédiat et profond.

La souplesse de l'interprétation personnalisée réside dans l'interaction immédiate et continue qui s'établit entre l'interprète et le public. L'interprète s'adapte à des auditoires variés et peut répondre à des besoins individuels. Au contraire des moyens médiatiques, l'interprète demeure attentif aux messages verbaux et non verbaux des visiteurs, et peut aller au rythme de la compréhension de son auditoire. Ce genre d'attention aux besoins du visiteur facilite la communication efficace.

L'interprétation personnalisée répond également à un besoin fondamental chez nos visiteurs, soit celui d'un contact humain chaleureux. En effet, des sondages faits auprès de nos publics depuis plusieurs années nous ont révélé que nos visiteurs désirent avoir des relations sociales amicales lors de leur visite.[5] De nos jours, les visiteurs s'attendent à faire quelque chose lors de leurs visites de musées ou de sites historiques. Ils ne se contentent plus de tout simplement regarder des choses ou de lire des textes, ils veulent interagir. Tout en étant attentif aux besoins de son auditoire, l'interprète peut facilement faire participer les visiteurs et les impliquer dans le processus d'interprétation.

L'interprète peut également inspirer son auditoire par son habileté, ses connaissances et son enthousiasme. Il favorise une relation de qualité entre le public et l'objet ou le site contemplé. En ayant recours au connu du visiteur et en lui faisant jouer un rôle actif, l'interprète peut mener le visiteur à une compréhension profonde de l'objet ou du site en question. Il essaie d'engager le visiteur dans un processus d'intégration de la matière afin d'assurer que le message a été bien compris et que le visiteur peut transférer ses nouvelles connaissances à d'autres situations à court, à moyen et à long terme.

L'interprétation personnalisée a un potentiel remarquable. L'efficacité de ce moyen est fondée sur l'expérience vécue. Les recherches en didactique montrent qu'on retient mieux par la pratique que par l'écoute, et par l'écoute que par la lecture. Les interprètes ont davantage le pouvoir d'influencer les visiteurs que des médias inertes, qui par leur artifice peuvent contribuer à éloigner le public de l'essentiel du message. Par l'engagement, le dialogue et la création de rapports, les interprètes peuvent favoriser plus efficacement l'apprentissage chez le public.

Les limites des techniques théâtrales

C'est à la lumière des points précédents sur les objectifs et les caractéristiques de l'interprétation personnalisée que je voudrais maintenant examiner les limites des techniques théâtrales comme moyen d'interprétation.[6] Mes remarques sont fondées sur des années d'observation de cette approche au sein de musées et de lieux historiques.

Les musées et les sites historiques utilisent les techniques et représentations théâtrales pour communiquer avec leurs publics depuis plusieurs décennies. Déjà en 1946, on monte une pièce de théâtre pour communiquer au grand public l'importance de Jamestown, un important site historique des États-Unis.[7] L'utilisation de techniques théâtrales à titre de moyen d'interprétation devient à la mode parmi les sites historiques au cours des années 1970. C'est à partir de ce moment que l'interprétation au sein de ces institutions change avec l'avènement de l'histoire sociale : l'accent des programmes d'interprétation est désormais mis sur les modes de vie. Ceci mène à la mise sur pied de nouvelles approches de mise en valeur, telle que l'approche de l'histoire vivante (*living history* ou animation d'époque), et à la création de nouvelles formes d'interprétation personnalisée, telle que l'animation de personnification (ou l'interprétation à la première personne). Basée sur le jeu de rôle du domaine théâtral, cette forme d'interprétation fait appel à des animateurs costumés qui jouent le rôle de personnages historiques, réels ou typiques, et qui communiquent avec le public comme s'ils étaient réellement des personnes d'autrefois. Plimoth Plantation au Massachussetts a grandement influencé le développement de cette approche et a été le premier site historique à l'utiliser de façon générale pour communiquer avec ses visiteurs. Cette méthode d'interprétation connaît son essor parmi les sites historiques au cours des années 1980.[8]

Pour leur part, c'est à partir des années 1970 que les musées commencent à utiliser des techniques théâtrales pour communiquer avec leurs visiteurs. De façon sporadique, des musées de beaux-arts, de science et technologie et d'histoire utilisent des acteurs en costumes ou des pièces de théâtre pour animer leurs collections.[9] Au cours des années 1980, le nombre de musées qui utilisent des techniques théâtrales continue à croître. Finalement, en 1988, le Musée canadien des civilisations devient le premier musée à avoir parmi son personnel une troupe de théâtre permanente.

L'utilisation de techniques théâtrales dans les musées et sites historiques n'est donc pas un phénomène récent. Les programmes de théâtre sont un moyen de communication original et magique. Le théâtre peut être un merveilleux outil de communication; il capte l'attention des visiteurs comme nul autre moyen et peut garder leur attention pour une période de temps relativement longue. Le théâtre a ainsi le potentiel de mener les visiteurs vers une plus grande compréhension du sujet en question. Il ne faut donc pas être surpris de voir de plus en plus de musées et de sites historiques utiliser cette approche.

Mais telles qu'elles sont mises en œuvre actuellement dans plusieurs musées et sites historiques, les techniques et représentations théâtrales posent de sérieux problèmes, qui mettent en question leur efficacité à titre de moyen d'interprétation. Quels sont ces problèmes?

Tout d'abord, il faut admettre qu'il y a certaines limites inhérentes à l'utilisation de techniques théâtrales en tant qu'outil éducatif. Ayant comme arme principale le drame, cette approche cherche à engager les visiteurs par le biais de l'imagination. Les techniques et représentations théâtrales demandent aux visiteurs de suspendre leur incrédulité et d'utiliser leurs capacités intuitives, métaphoriques, créatives et imaginaires afin de comprendre l'essentiel présenté. Cependant, les visiteurs ne possèdent pas tous le même mode d'apprentissage et n'ont pas nécessairement l'ouverture d'esprit requise pour cette forme d'interprétation. Plusieurs visiteurs, sinon la majorité des adultes, préfèrent un mode d'apprentissage plus direct, qui expose l'information de façon beaucoup plus structurée et rationnelle (voir ci-haut les scénarios 1 et 2). L'utilisation générale de ce moyen de communication peut ainsi facilement frustrer, intimider et même éloigner une importante partie de la clientèle du musée ou du site historique.[10]

Deuxièmement, les représentations théâtrales tentent de communiquer beaucoup d'information aux visisteurs, souvent dans très peu de temps. Les messages à retenir sont généralement implicites. Dans ces cas, le danger réside dans le fait que le visiteur, laissé seul, peut facilement mal interpréter l'essentiel du message à retenir.

Une autre faiblesse de l'approche est qu'elle n'encourage pas nécessairement l'interaction avec le visiteur. Bien que les animateurs ou acteurs essaient d'inclure l'auditoire dans le processus de communication et, dans le cas de représentations théâtrales, demandent presque toujours aux visiteurs de venir les voir à la fin du spectacle s'ils ont des questions, en général il y a très peu d'échange entre le public et les animateurs ou acteurs. Il n'est pas difficile de comprendre pourquoi cela se produit : les visiteurs ne sont pas prêts à interagir avec les acteurs. Depuis notre enfance, nous sommes en fait conditionnés à respecter les comédiens sur scène et à demeurer silencieux lors de spectacles. Pour la plupart des visiteurs, il existe une barrière entre eux et les acteurs. Pareillement aux objets exposés, les acteurs par leur performance deviennent des expositions vivantes, des objets de contemplation et d'admiration auprès des visiteurs. L'idée de franchir cette barrière est aussi impensable dans la tête de la majorité des visiteurs que celle de toucher les objets dans les présentoirs.

Il y a dans toute forme de communication des interférences qui peuvent nuire à la communication et à l'apprentissage. Celles-ci peuvent être les distractions du milieu (les bruits, le climat, l'emplacement peu proprice à la communication, etc.) ou le nombre de participants (un très petit groupe ou un trop grand groupe). Afin d'assurer l'efficacité des moyens de communication, l'interprète doit s'adapter en fonction de diverses interférences. Mais si l'interaction est impossible avec les visiteurs, les interférences seront toujours présentes et entraveront le processus de communication (voir ci-haut le troisième scénario). Même les représentations théâtrales qui se veulent interactives ne réussissent qu'à impliquer les visiteurs de façon très simple, sinon simpliste (voir ci-haut les scénarios 1 et 2). Très souvent les visiteurs ne possèdent pas les informations ou les connaissances du contexte pouvant leur permettre d'interagir avec les animateurs ou acteurs. Dans d'autres cas, ceux-ci ne peuvent pas sortir de leur rôle afin de répondre à des questions contextuelles du public.

Enfin, soulignons le danger de la domination du moyen sur le message. Dans la plupart des cas, la pièce ou la technique théatrale devient l'attrait principal à la fois pour le musée ou le site en question et pour les visiteurs, et non le moyen par lequel on établit un rapport avec l'objet ou le site. Les visiteurs ont un sentiment de divertissement. Ils ont l'impression d'avoir vu quelque chose d'exceptionnel. Ils ont même le sentiment d'en avoir eu pour leur argent. Les commentaires qui sortent de leur bouche à la fin du spectacle ou de la rencontre avec l'animateur sont entre autres : «C'était vraiment intéressant!» ou encore «Ça, c'était le fun!» Mais le visiteurs ne passsent pas nécessairement plus de temps à regarder les expositions pertinentes avant de passer au prochain point d'attrait. Certes, cette approche n'a pas encore fait ses preuves en tant qu'outil éducatif.

En somme, les représentations et techniques théâtrales sont, de prime abord, des moyens de transmission d'information à sens unique. Les visiteurs sont là pour 10, 15 ou 30 minutes et sont traités très souvent comme des vaisseaux vides à être remplis ou des spectateurs à être divertis.

Le but des moyens d'interprétation d'un musée ou d'un site historique est de faciliter la transmission de connaissances et d'engager les visiteurs. Le but n'est pas d'expédier les visiteurs au prochain poste d'intérêt. De la même manière que l'étiquette manque sa cible si elle ne renvoie pas le visiteur à l'objet, la pièce ou la technique théâtrale échoue si elle n'augmente pas la compréhension ou n'élargit pas le champ des expériences d'apprentissage des visiteurs.

La complémentarité des moyens d'interprétation

L'utlisation des techniques théâtrales comme moyen d'interprétation dans les musées et les sites historiques ne se fait donc pas sans embûches. On peut facilement confondre, frustrer et même éloigner le visiteur. Néanmoins, le théâtre et, en particulier, le drame demeurent des moyens privilégiés par le grand public pour apprendre leur histoire. L'historien américain Bernard A. Weisberger affirme que depuis la série télévisée *Roots*, les

Comédienne de Dramamuse, MCC.
Dramamuse actor, CMC

Américains ont une soif sans fin d'apprendre leur histoire par le biais du drame documen-
taire.[11] Une même tendance a été notée au Canada en 1991 lors d'un sondage fait
par la Fondation Bronfmann. Ce sondage a indiqué que les Canadiens voulaient en savoir
davantage sur leur histoire et que l'un des moyens à privilégier était des courtes vignettes
dramatiques.

On ne peut donc pas nier la popularité du drame et du théâtre. Toutefois, dans un contexte muséal, il nous semble qu'il faut ajouter d'autres moyens d'interprétation, à la fois
personnalisés et médiatiques, aux techniques théâtrales afin d'assurer une transmission
efficace des connaissances et des messages de base. Les moyens personnalisés et médiatiques sont des outils de communication complémentaires. La présence de l'un par rapport à l'autre doit être le résultat d'un choix logique. La fin doit justifier les moyens. La
solution réside dans la complémentarité des moyens d'interprétation.

Cette complémentarité peut se faire de différentes façons. Par exemple, un moyen serait
d'employer des guides-interprètes comme intermédiaires entre les visiteurs et les acteurs
ou animateurs. Ces intermédiaires pourraient ainsi recueillir les visiteurs avant la présentation dramatique, introduire le sujet et, à la fin, faire un résumé de la présentation ainsi
que souligner de nouveau les messages à retenir. Les interprètes pourraient également sol-
liciter les questions des visiteurs et y répondre, ainsi que diriger les visiteurs vers d'autres
présentations pertinentes. Puisque ces guides en uniforme seraient visibles un peu partout
dans le musée ou le site, ils seraient facilement reconnaissables et, contrairement aux

acteurs, ils ne seraient pas intimidants. En utilisant les guides-interprètes comme intermédiaires, les musées et sites historiques pourraient ainsi éliminer la barrière qui existe
entre l'auditoire et les acteurs ou animateurs.

Une autre approche serait d'inclure d'autres moyens d'interprétation, tels que des bro-
chures, des audioguides, des expositions didactiques et des présentations audio-visuelles,
dans l'ensemble du musée ou du site historique. Cette approche devrait être guidée par
une stratégie de communication globale qui identifie clairement les groupes de visiteurs
du musée ou du site historique, leurs besoins, les messages à transmettre, les moyens
d'interprétation qui seront utilisés et les expériences que l'on désire offrir à ces visiteurs.

Conclusion

Il est devenu évident aux yeux de plusieurs que les institutions culturelles comme les
musées et les sites historiques ne rejoignent pas toutes les couches de la population.
Beaucoup de gens se sentent étrangers dans ces institutions et refusent même d'y entrer.
Ne se reconnaissant pas dans l'image que projette le musée ou le site, ils ne sont pas
réceptifs à ses messages. Dans nos efforts pour rejoindre ces gens, les musées et les sites
exploreront, au cours des prochaines années, de nouveaux moyens de communication
et d'interprétation. De même, avec le besoin grandissant de générer de plus en plus de
revenus, les musées et sites historiques seront incités à choisir des moyens de communication populaires, dont les techniques théâtrales. On ne doit pas abandonner les efforts
déjà entrepris dans l'utilisation de cette approche. Avec certaines modifications, elles
peuvent devenir un excellent moyen pour rejoindre nos visiteurs. Il faut toutefois se
rappeler qu'elles ne sont qu'un point de départ et qu'elles doivent nous mener à un plus
grand discours avec nos visiteurs.

Notes

1. Les idées et les opinions exprimées dans ce texte sont entièrement les miennes et ne représentent
    pas nécessairement celles de mon agence. Elles sont le fruit de plusieurs années d'observation de
    programmes d'interprétation et d'animation au sein de musées et de sites historiques, et de dis-
    cussion avec des professionnels du domaine.

2. F. TILDEN, *Interpreting Our Heritage*, 2ᵉ édition, Chapel Hill (Caroline du Nord), 1982, p. 8.

3. Voir J. R. DUNN, «Museum Interpretation/Education: The Need for Definition», *Gazette*,
    vol. 10, nº 1 (hiver 1977), pp. 12-16; B. PEART, «Definition of Interpretation», *Interpretation
    Canada*, vol. 5, nº 2 (automne 1978), pp. 3-6; T. RITZER, «One Giant Step Backward for
    Interpretation», *Interpretation Canada*, vol. 10, nº 4 (automne 1982), pp. 12-13.

4. L'association des interprètes professionnels au Canada, Interprétation Canada, s'est inspirée de
    Tilden pour sa définition de l'interprétation. Voir B. Peart, *art. cit.*, p. 5.

5. Voir par exemple, The Longwoods Research Group Limited, *Canadian Parks Service National Marketing Study, Final Report*, 1988, 237 p.

6. Il est important de noter que j'inclus dans le terme «techniques théâtrales» l'utilisation de l'animation de personnification, du drame et de pièces de théâtre, soit historiques ou fictifs. Dans la plupart des cas, ces techniques comprennent également l'utilisation du son, de la lumière, de la musique et de décors appropriés.

7. J.C. HARRINGTON, «Interpreting Jamestown to the Visitor», *The Museum News*, vol. 24, n° 11 (1er décembre 1946), pp. 7-8.

8. Voir J. ANDERSON, *Time Machines*, Nashville, American Association for State and Local History, 1984, 217 p.; R. MOREAU, «Communicating with the Museum Visitor: The Use of First and Third Person Interpretation in Outdoor History Museums of Ontario», mémoire de maîtrise, Université de Toronto, 1988, 160 p.

9. Voir W. AIBEL-WEISS et B. BROWN, «An Interpretive Tool to Meet the Needs of Children and Family Audiences -Theater in the Gallery», *The Museologist*, n° 152 (printemps 1980), pp. 6-9; M. ARTH, «The People Center», *The Museologist*, n° 126 (mars 1973), pp. 12-16; M. BROWN, «One Museum's Drama Experience», *Museum Journal*, vol. 81, n° 4 (mars 1982), pp. 208-209; B.D. ELDER, «Drama for Interpretation», *History News*, vol. 36, n° 6 (juin 1981), pp. 8-11; E.A. ENDTER, «Museum Learning and the Performing Arts», *Museum News*, vol. 53, n° 9 (juin 1975), pp. 34-37 et 72.

10. W.T. ALDERSON et S.P. LOW, *Interpretation of Historic Sites*, Nashville, American Association for State and Local History, 1985, pp. 42-43; P. FORTIER, «Period Presentation and its Development in Historical Parks of Military Significance in Canada», mémoire de maîtrise, Université de Toronto, 1982, p. 61; H. SIDFORD, «Stepping Into History», *Museums News*, vol. 53, n° 3 (novembre 1974), pp. 28-35; T. VANCE, «Developing A First Person Program at a Small Site», *Papers From the ALHFAM Annual Meetings in Denver, Colorado and Williamsburg, Virginia, Washington*, The Association for Living Historical Farms and Agricultural Museums, 1988, pp. 161-180.

11. B.A. WEISBERGER, «American History is Falling Down», *American Heritage*, février-mars 1987, pp. 26-31.

❖ Theatre as a Learning Medium in Museums

Christopher Ford
Senior Lecturer
Bradford and Ilkley College and National Railway Museum
York, U.K.

Cet article remet en question la thèse classique qui pose les musées en lieux de certitude et de connaissance absolue. On y suggère de faire jouer au théâtre un rôle de média d'apprentissage qui permette la réaction individuelle à l'interprétation culturelle, artistique et intellectuelle qu'offrent les musées. On soutient, dans cet article, que le théâtre, dans ces institutions de «savoir absolu», est un puissant média qui aide les visiteurs à développer leur engagement personnel envers le monde qui les entoure, à y réagir et à se questionner sur leur propre conception du monde en regard de celle que les musées leur présentent.

At the beginning of the conference, "The Languages of Live Interpretation," David Parry introduced the idea that the ancient Greek Muses had returned to take up residence in the home bearing their name, the museum. The nine goddesses of music, poetry, dance, and so on, were metaphorically invoked by the recent upsurge in the use of the performing arts and other modes of live interpretation in museum settings.

Certainly in the British Isles there appears to have been a dramatic increase in the use of theatre in museums over the past 10 years or so. Research carried out during 1993-94 (Ford) confirms general perceptions held within the museum community in Britain that the use of a variety of forms of theatre is on the increase.

All museums in the Museums Association (2,175 in total) were questioned by postal survey with a 62% sample responding. Of that sample, 33.2% of museums in the British Isles now employ theatre as a part of their interpretative programme. Importantly, the survey indicates a steady climb in the number of museums using theatre since 1980. Indeed 77% of all museums currently using theatre began this work since that date. Some 10% of them began between 1980-84. A sharp increase was seen in the second half of the 1980's with 27% of all museums currently using theatre beginning in that period. Almost 40% of all theatre in museums has started as recently as 1990. Theatre in museums is a growing phenomenon and, in its current form, represents a new departure in the use of theatre as a learning medium.

National museums appear to be the most likely venue for this new medium (proportionately rather than in raw figures), with 92% of all national museums responding indicating that they use theatre. National Trust, English Heritage and Local Authority museums all hover around having about 50% of their museums involved in using theatre. Independent and private museums seem to be the least likely venues for theatre activity, with only 15-25% of the sample of these museum types using theatre.

Further research is needed, of course, but it is noticeable that the two categories of museum furthest away from state funding, usually operating on a smaller scale and perhaps most vulnerable to financial considerations, use theatre less than other national or local government institutions. Perhaps this is an early indicator that museum theatre is a relatively costly business in raw terms, though it may be a bargain in terms of interpretative value.

The value of theatrical activity in museums will, of course, arise from the clarity of objectives with which museums embark on a policy of using this medium in the first place. This, in my experience, is not so simple a statement as it first appears. Indeed, whilst some museums are able to articulate clearly as to why they are putting theatrical activity into their museum, others are by no means so clear. Conversely, some offer an insight into an interesting tension within the global aims of the museum itself. There is no question that museums in Britain in the 1980's and 90's have had to respond to a shifting social, political and economic climate. Even many state-funded museums now find themselves having to generate significant parts of their income for themselves through visitor entrance fees, counter sales of museum merchandise, providing conference facilities or corporate entertainment, and so on. Other museums, still centrally funded by national or local government, are required to justify their continued funding (and indeed existence) by demonstrating their success, which inevitably turns again to quantitative measures such as visitor figures.

It is not surprising therefore that the inclusion of theatre in the museum programme is at the very least a feature which marketing departments are keen to make the most of. In some cases, there is a distinct impression that the theatre work is heavily influenced by marketing needs rather than by any interpretative direction taken by the museum. In many cases, though, it is probably fair to say that some kind of symbiotic relationship exists between marketing and interpretative departments, and that any theatrical agenda in the museum arises from that relationship. To complete the spectrum, there are also museums where the theatrical activity encapsulates the whole concept of museum operations, with its entire interpretative programme being based on re-enactment or living history of some kind. Obviously, in these cases the presentation of costumed characters and the like is actually so closely bound up with the principal mission of the museum that it would be difficult to consider any representation of the museum which did not highlight these theatrical elements. Such distinctions are necessary in helping to identify the particular role that theatre might play in the museological activity of the museum rather than towards its success as a financially solvent institution.

It is perhaps because of the current vulnerability of many museums that much research exists which will quantify visitor experience in the museum. "Quantify," however, remains the key word, with the majority of research being concerned with how many visitors viewed this or that exhibit; how many enjoyed, were surprised by, were annoyed by, would come again, and so on. Research into what visitors actually thought, felt or learned by viewing exhibitions — and in particular by seeing theatrical activity — remains rare.

Decisions on gallery and general museum designs are currently being generated, partly, at least, by market forces and the need to succeed in persuading families and other visitors that a day at the museum should be a serious alternative to the hugely successful theme parks and other leisure centres in 1990's Britain. Decisions also hinge upon ideological decisions about the mission of the museum with regard to its collection (or site) and its interpretative brief on behalf of the visitor. Let us briefly explore this aspect of museology and then consider specifically the relationship between theatre and the overall museum mission.

Essentially, a museum can be thought of as the trustee of a collection or site deemed to be worth preserving, on behalf of the nation or the community. They are not regarded (by many museums themselves) necessarily as places of learning, though of course learning might take place. They are thought of more as centres of knowledge where, very importantly, the real objects, images or whole buildings are kept, preserved, and exhibited for the public benefit. Whilst museums might employ reconstructions as a method of interpretation, it is in holding the real object that museums differ significantly from centres which are mainly or wholly reconstructions.

It is useful to offer two main categories of museum function. One would include "collecting, documenting and preserving"[1] and is concerned with the holding of the collection for the nation. The other aspect includes "exhibiting and interpreting"[2] and is concerned with making the collection accessible to the nation. We might refer to these as the non-visible (to the public) aspects of museums (holding the collection), and the visible (to the public) aspects of museums (making the collection accessible).

The first category, the non-visible role of museums, concerns us only marginally at this stage, though I expect there to be some implications for researching and preservation in particular when using theatre in museums.

The visible role of museums, however, is highly relevant to the use of theatre in museums and needs to be well understood if we are to explore the potential of any theatre-in-museums movement at this time.

Essentially the role of making the collection accessible to the public involves the museum in two main activities, those of presenting (or exhibiting) and interpreting.

Let us take it that in presenting objects in the simplest sense, museums make it possible for visitors to view the exhibit without any other information, distraction or intrusion into the viewing process. For example, the National Railway Museum might place the steam locomotive Mallard in a location where visitors can see it, walk around it, perhaps view the footplate, but avoid any attempt to explain anything about the engine or its place in railway history.

When interpreting objects, however, let us assume that some attempt is made to help the visitor understand the significance of the object, or even why it is worthy of keeping in the collection at all. Written labels might indicate that Mallard is the holder of the world speed record for steam traction and offer a few details about the Sunday morning in July 1938 when this record was broken — who was driving, and so on. Written labels are one method amongst many of offering interpretations of objects and/or presenting further factual information on the subject. Other methods would include videos; interactive displays; theatre presentations of some kind; reconstructions of settings indicating the use to which objects would be put; fully operational working reconstructions such as a real blacksmith at a forge; the list goes on.

It is in this balance between presenting objects in as simple and objective a way as possible, and interpreting them using any from a whole range of methods, that what we might refer to as "the great museum debate" exists. It is here in this balance that we find the great academic and philosophical debate about museology. What is important here is that theatre lies absolutely centrally in that debate about its visible role of making the collection accessible. This is because theatre is both a means of interpretation and a method of presentation, and we do need to be very clear about the relationship between the two.

Presentation can operate through any or all of the five senses. Theatre of the various kinds has the potential to work through all five. Jorvik (Viking Centre, York) employs the sense of smell, for example. As children prepare and eat their 17th-century style meal at Clarke Hall (Wakefield), the sense of taste becomes a part of the experience. Visitors using the ink pens in the Victorian classroom at Wigan Pier (Wigan) discover through the tactile sensation of scratching away with the pen, as well as through other means of perceiving. Perhaps more obviously, theatre employs sound and vision. We most commonly think of theatre as something which we watch and listen to. We must, however, recognise that theatre is a very flexible means of presentation and potentially can operate at a multi-sensory level in a very short period of time.

At the moment, however, we are concerned with the ability of theatre to "present" in the museum sense of the word. That is, can theatre present in an objective sense, remaining free of interpretation? Can it be an object in a case? I would suggest that it is unlikely that theatre will operate entirely at that level, and indeed will have a tendency to operate away from this mode and towards a more interpretative model. Nevertheless it can be done to some degree. Peter Cheesman, for example, in his community-based documentary theatre in the 1970's followed a philosophy of using the exact words of people offering evidence about life in the Potteries earlier this century. In his play *The Knotty*, about life upon the Staffordshire and Nottinghamshire Railway, he used the exact words of those who had contributed to his oral history research:

> If somebody makes a speech then I insist that the speech is genuine,
> so the audience knows that everything that is said on stage is actually
> said by the person whom the actor is meant to be, so that gives it
> intrinsic authority.[3]

However, even here, Cheesman did alter the order in which things were said, he added music and new words in song, and he set one quotation against another to create new meaning and context. Most importantly he added visual images through the action of the play and evoked an identification between audience and characters, so that the objective evidence of the text became matters of subjective and emotional engagement by the audience.

Identification with characters, events, situations, thoughts and feelings by the audience is the very essence of theatre and storytelling, and I suggest that no matter how factually correct a theatre presentation might be, there is likely to be an element of personal engagement and interpretation present as well.

Having said that, theatre does have the potential to present information in an efficient and powerful way. It can also achieve it in a very simple way.

For example, at the National Railway Museum in York, a glass case near to the Permanent Way exhibition contains a dummy of a railway navvy from the 1840's. The dummy is there to help present the style of dress of navvies of that period. All items are suitably "distressed" as would befit a navvy in dirty working conditions. The case is accompanied by a short label, which reads:

> Thousands of labourers (navvies) worked on the construction of the
> railways in Britain, organised by contractors appointed by the railway
> companies. The work was hard and often dangerous and many died
> through accidents or disease.[4]

The scenery in the case and the label are, of course, aspects of interpretation, as is the dummy itself along with the distressing of items of clothing. Nevertheless it is minimal and serves as a relatively straightforward presentation of navvy clothing.

In *Running the Risk*, Platform 4 Theatre present two navvies. Although nothing is ever said about their dress, they are clothed in exactly the same style of costumes as the dummy with some variations between the two characters. Here the theatre event is presenting the style of dress of a navvy and demonstrates the potential of theatre to present with little interpretation.

Similarly, the opening lines of *Running the Risk* are factual storytelling in both style and content:

> Hello. We're Platform 4 Theatre, and we're here to tell you a story. It's the story of how they built a tunnel about 150 years ago. The tunnel was 3 miles and 13 yards long, which made it more than twice as long as any tunnel that had ever been built before.[5]

Again we see the potential of theatre presentation, in words this time, to offer a straightforward factual account which informs an audience about the length of a tunnel, its comparative size to other tunnels and when it was built. An interesting reaction to seeing a Platform 4 Theatre production, by the Schools Resources Officer of the Midland Railway Centre in Derbyshire, was that the performance "was worth a thousand signs."

Interestingly, there is research which suggests that the optimum length for any written sign in a museum setting is about 80 words. Beyond that, visitors tend to lose interest or concentration and move on.

Running the Risk holds visitors from ages of about 5 years old to elderly visitors for 35 minutes of intense concentration. The performance presents just under 4,000 words to visitors in that time, which is about 50 times the length of acceptable written texts.

This alone indicates something of the potential of theatre as a presentation medium, although it says nothing of the efficiency of the medium in terms of the understanding or retention of the information presented.

Alongside the quantitative research already referred to (Ford 1994), which offers a broad view of theatre in museums in Britain today, another research strand has involved interviewing children about performances and programme content. Children have been aged between 6 and 14, with a total working sample of 42 children so far. This is obviously a small sample to date but indicates some interesting directions which should be pursued further.

The research is concerned with the retention of information offered during performances and also the meanings which the children make of incidents in the play. All of this research has centred around the navvies play, *Running the Risk*.

Retention of specific details such as dates or place-names was generally weak and varied greatly from child to child. Details of the names of people were much stronger as were details about specific tools and jobs undertaken by the navvies.

Explaining what happened at certain points of the play and generally retelling the story were strong features of almost all of the children irrespective of age. Their ability to recount in almost exact detail the action of particular scenes (sometimes with wordage from the script) was greatly increased if they were reminded of the scene by being shown a still photograph of the action. This I consider to be of particular significance and we should remember that theatre is a visual medium with great potential to convey knowledge and meaning via visual means. We need to take care that our visual portrayal has the same academic rigour as our written texts. This also clarifies the whole question of plays having a duality in terms of being appropriate for both adults and children. We can often work through a visual story-line to help children through patches of dialogue not yet accessible to them.

The research seems to indicate that, especially in the context of offering visual clues, theatre is successful in transmitting bodies of factual knowledge. The bodies of knowledge with children seem to be at their strongest when related directly to the story-line or to characters with whom children are identifying. Those familiar with Margaret Donaldson's recent work with Piagetian theories[6] will know that some previous assumptions about the limitations of young children's concept formation were turned on their head once placed in a narrative and personalised setting.

Beyond a simple body of knowledge (facts, dates, names, etc.) children were also able to explain in detail how certain navvying jobs were carried out. They could explain the relationships between various tasks never actually shown simultaneously in the performance. There are strong indications that children were beginning to build interrelated concepts about tunnelling, railway-building, navvies, contractors (usually referred to as "the bosses"). Some detailed line drawings by 7- to 9-year-old children (included) indicate that their concepts about how a tunnel is actually driven through a hill, requiring tunnelling from opposite directions, the purpose of shafts, and so on, appear to be well formed. The dangers of navvying are shown by the representation of navvies tipping out of a basket part way up a shaft. Interestingly, the real basket in the performance never actually leaves the ground. The power of storytelling is that it can form images of reality through fictional recounting, a key point to which I will return soon.

The power of storytelling is that it can form images or reality through fictional recounting. Some detailed line drawings by 7- to 9-year-old children indicate that their concepts about how a tunnel is actually driven through a hill, requiring tunnelling from opposite directions, the purpose of shafts, and so on, appear to be well formed. The dangers of navvying are shown by the representation of navvies tipping out of a basket part way up a shaft. Interestingly, the real basket in the performance never actually leaves the ground.

Theatre, then, does appear to have the potential to present knowledge or information in a way which is relatively free of interpretation. Let us turn now to the other possible function of theatre and consider its potential to interpret information in order to help visitors understand the meaning or importance of the knowledge they are gaining. A key feature in presenting a factual story through theatre is that it inevitably involves identification with one or more characters. As mentioned with reference to Cheesman (above), we tend to view the story in the context of the lives of the characters. The great human capacity to identify with the experience of others offers great potential for interpretation of events in human terms.

In *Running the Risk*, well-documented facts are presented. The names of the characters (Gypsy Joe and Fighting Jack) are typical of documented navvy names. The jobs undertaken in the play (digging, blasting, running barrows along narrow planks, ascending shafts over 500 feet in height in baskets which sometimes tipped up, throwing navvies into the dark) are all real events. In fact, no significant event in the play or detail of day-to-day living as a navvy is unsubstantiated by factual record. Lodging these events in a story, however, where the audience become ever more involved with the personal experience of Gypsy Joe, results in audiences not simply absorbing the facts of navvy life but in them increasingly questioning the justification for such existence. They become interpreters of the story and the place of navvies in railway history in their own right. They tend to develop personal opinions about the events and frequently wish to discuss these with the actor/interpreters after performances.

Of course this view of theatre as both a means of interpretation and a method of presentation brings us back to considering the museum debate about the balance to be established between the two. It will also serve to explain the caution with which some museums might regard some kinds of theatre. In plays offering a particular frame on events, as *Running the Risk* does, do audiences need to be clear that it is only one view and not the whole story? Certainly, I would prefer some kind of clarification of this for visitors, along with encouragement that they debate the matter further themselves.

A brief example to demonstrate the very fine line between presentation and interpretation will emphasise the care with which we should use theatre in museum settings, especially in the context of the museum debate mentioned earlier.

At an early part of *Running the Risk*, one actor repeats accurately an extract of the speech, as reported by newspapers of the day, made by John Parker, MP at the banquet to celebrate the opening of the Woodhead Tunnel. A top hat and tails are worn and a glass of red wine is held aloft as the MP (and Chairman of the Railway Company) speaks his lines:

> It's only fair to say that the magnificent work of the new tunnel is further evidence to the ingenuity of mankind. And we must praise especially the work of the chief engineer, Mr. Joseph Locke, and his assistant, Mr. Purdon. I think we can all agree that the tunnel was a very stiff job. I propose a toast to the engineers.[7]

This relatively straightforward presentation of the banquet is what I would regard as a safe presentation in museum terms. It offers images of the dress and the actions of John Parker, and represents as faithfully as possible the words reported at the time.

At the end of the play, however, some of the lines are repeated over the dead body of Joe, one of 32 navvies killed during the building of that tunnel. The actor tells the story of Mr. Purdon's evidence before a Select Committee investigating safety when building railways. The speech reports that Mr. Purdon himself had been quite open in saying that he regarded some safety measures as a waste of time and not worth the delay for the sake of saving a few lives. This aspect of the speech is true enough and taken from

Select Committee reports of the period. However, the last few seconds of the play place the interpretation of the playwright heavily upon the story of Woodhead Tunnel:

> Meanwhile, in Sheffield, the Chairman of the Sheffield, Ashton and Manchester Railway drank a toast to the health of Mr. Purdon. After all, the Woodhead Tunnel had been a very stiff job.[8]

During these last few lines the actor/interpreter has put on his top hat and tails and, whilst raising his glass of wine, places his booted foot upon the dead body of Joe.

The actions in the final seconds of the play are quite deliberately laden with meaning and it is unlikely that a visitor would take that image as one of victory and triumph so much as one of exploitation and a disregard for human suffering. There is no doubt in my mind that *Running the Risk* is very heavily laden with interpretative features.

Again, the research with children referred to above (Ford 95) seems to bear this out. All of the children in the group were able to relate the navvy's lives to their own and had firm opinions about what it was like to be a navvy. Generally speaking, the younger children thought it might be quite fun because of the dancing and singing and "parties," but that it was also very hard and dangerous. Overall, they did not want to be navvies. Opinions about the "unfair" treatment of the navvies by "the bosses" were also virtually universal across the sample.

Older children in the group extended these interpretations to include ideas on exploitation, cheap labour, the benefits of working rather than starving, and the recklessness of the navvies themselves. On the whole, older children did not want to be navvies either (because of the dangers), but neither would they wish to be like the contractors. They did not agree with the attitude of the contractors in the play, and felt that they would personally wish to have more admirable values and a greater regard for human suffering.

Some older children were able to express clear views on the play itself, to realise that it was told from the navvies' point of view and that there was more to the whole story than the play had shown.

The flexibility and the power of the theatre medium which I have attempted to indicate here is interesting in its own right, but becomes especially important to this research once we set it in the context of the museums themselves. Any debate on theatre in museums is not a lively or outspoken debate (as seen at Liverpool in 1991) simply because it is about using theatre. It is so important because it is part of a deeply rooted debate about museum practice in general and in particular about the balance between presentation and interpretation towards which museums strive.

Bearing in mind the delicate balance between objectivity and informed interpretation, it is important to recognise one of the principal features of theatrical activity. Crucial to using theatre as a learning medium is the constant recognition that theatre is in essence a fictional activity. In the context of theatre in museums we can regard theatre as a "fictional activity that helps to illuminate/define real experience."[9] No matter how elaborate re-enactments might be, no matter how extensive the reconstruction and peopling of entire villages, no matter how accurate the costuming, character research, language, incident portrayal, and so on, theatrical events are not actually real. I realise that in this I state the obvious but, for two reasons, I do not apologise. One is to do with the understanding of the theatre event by the visitor and the other is to do with the understanding of theatre, especially as a learning medium, by the museums.

One of the simplest and yet most revealing questions asked of children during research surrounding *Running the Risk* was whether they assumed that anything they saw or found out in the museum (including the theatre shows) would be true. The vast majority simply replied "Yes." Further discussion confirmed that most young people (in this small sample) in the 9-14 age range felt that museums were essentially places of fact and knowledge.

Discussions with actor/interpreters in museum sites are equally revealing but this time indicate a divide between those who clearly recognise theatre as a fictional activity and wish the visitor to know this, and those who feel that the pretence must be somehow hidden from visitors in order to make the event more "real." Those who attended the "Go Live" conference on theatre in museums at the National Museum of Film, Photography and Television in Bradford (England: 1993) will remember Eric the Viking. A fearsome-looking Viking character provided the focus for discussions about "What does he do at the point of meeting a visitor on the museum gallery?" The suggestion of "Tell them you're an actor" from the conference floor was a hotly debated point and was disliked intensely by some. More recently I have been fascinated by the explanation to myself and an adult colleague by two actor/gallery characters in a major London museum about why they wouldn't perform in role for us. If we'd been children it would have been alright, but because adults are "really hopeless at role-playing" (London 1995) they would just tell us what they would have done if we'd been children! The intention had been that both actors would have portrayed an individual female character each, both from around the turn of the century (1900). They would have spoken to us in first-person role about their lives, one a domestic housemaid, the other an aviator. As visitors we were not actually expected to be in role ourselves, but simply to accept that they were in role and go along with it. The whole activity would take place on two separate galleries close to exhibits relevant to their respective stories, rather than in any kind of dedicated theatre performance space. Actor/gallery characters and visitors share the same space in close proximity and it seems to be that the difficulties experienced by many adults (and in turn the actors) in dealing with this encounter have led to this curious age-related differentiation in visitor experience.

Other museums, on the other hand, demonstrate absolute clarity with their visitors that the theatre event is a part of the museum experience and that it is theatre, re-enactment, living history, or demonstration. What they are clear about, is that the event is not actually real.

The importance of these observations lies in an understanding of the need for clear contracts between participants when embarking upon theatrical or dramatic activity. This is not simply a point of academic interest within theatrical circles but is one of the most fundamental principles in understanding theatre as a learning medium and therefore of great importance to the museum community. Essentially, we can view drama or theatre as a form of play, particularly in the early years of learning sense of the word. Playing of course has a range of recreational, social and emotional functions to offer us, some of which overlap with a view of play as a way of learning. As a learning medium play does offer us a rich source of experience beyond our daily living. By engaging in play situations and behaving for a short period "as if" that situation were real, we can derive, under the correct conditions, real insight into what that situation might actually be like.

Amongst the necessary conditions is the clear understanding by all participants that:

   i)   they are playing and that this is not actually real;
   ii) they are emotionally and physically safe during the playing;
   iii) they will be able to stop or change the playing if they become
        uncomfortable with it.

Young children tend to be experts in this field and these, along with other conditions, can frequently be observed in their day-to-day playing, especially role-playing, at home, school and elsewhere.

Most adults do not have the opportunity for regular role-playing and lose their proficiency in some of the necessary skills, but those skills generally remain dormant rather than disappearing. I am not surprised that the actors in London found that adults are not at home with role-play. What does surprise me is that they do not seem to be addressing the issue and re-creating the correct conditions under which adults will feel at ease with engaging in, or even simply watching, role-play.

If theatre is to be a viable medium in museums then these conditions of playing cannot be ignored. To do so will not simply put adults (and actors) off engaging in fictional activity in the technical sense, but will actually undermine the whole potential of theatre as a learning medium at all.

We should remember that many adults will be familiar with going to the theatre or cinema or their child's school play and that the notion of watching a theatrical event in a group (rather than alone at home with television) is probably familiar to most. What is important here is that the whole ritual of going to the theatre is in itself a form of contract which projects adults into the play situation. We understand our role as an audience and understand the role of the actors. There are certain social rules which govern the event and, generally speaking, adults find little difficulty with the idea of becoming involved in what is a fictional situation on stage. Even though audiences are absolutely clear that the whole event is fictional, it is not uncommon for people to be amused, frightened, sentimental, to laugh or to cry. In other words, far from the knowledge that we are in a theatre stopping us becoming deeply engaged it actually allows us to become engaged, and possibly even to come away from the event challenged in our thinking and feeling about the events portrayed. We have entered the "as if" and for a short time lived through a situation via the lives of the characters.

Theatre which takes place in a museum will not usually offer the natural signals to visitors that they are entering a fictional playing situation and that normal theatre rules apply. In simple terms, most people probably go about their daily lives (including visiting museums) assuming that what they are experiencing around them is real. Why should they think any other? Events which are bizarre or out of the ordinary generally put people on the defensive and result in avoidance, retreat or confrontation. Spectrum Theatre (National Museum of Science and Industry: London), at an early stage of their experimentation with gallery characters who approached visitors unexpectedly, found that very many adults in family groups instinctively put their children in-between themselves and the actor. Actors responded by addressing the children for the rest of the encounter. Adults expressed negative views in subsequent research and did not enjoy being approached in this way. Children were more at home with it, probably because they are still in a period of their lives where play is an important and much used way of living (as mentioned earlier).

It seems to me that clarity of contract between the museum and visitor is essential in opening up the full potential of this medium. If visitors feel at ease with the theatrical event then we can genuinely take the visitor way beyond the immediate experience of the collection or site alone. We can engage visitors at a thinking and feeling level with the core matter of the museum mission itself. Visitors at least become highly motivated meaning-makers, with the collection becoming a matter of importance to them personally rather than them only remaining passive observers of other people's lives, times and places. At best, visitors may become personally involved in the stories, demonstrations, explanations and events portrayed through theatre to such an extent that they do not simply become interested in the museum mission, but that the museum mission becomes a part of their lives taken away with them in newly accommodated concepts, attitudes and feelings.

In the British Isles at present there appear to be five principal modes of theatrical activity. What is important here is that the best examples of each style demonstrate a range of contracts each appropriate to that particular style. Establishing ways of clarifying the "rules of playing" with visitors will vary. The crucial point is that the fitness of theatre style for the purpose of fulfilling museum objectives should be fully considered and appropriate strategies employed.

In brief, theatre in British museums seems to fall into these categories, bearing in mind that some museums use a variety of these techniques simultaneously.

Scripted Plays

Generally speaking these events involve set piece scripted plays of between 20-40 minutes in length. They are performed usually by a team of no more than five actor/interpreters. Contracts are clear for the visitor who easily recognises the medium and can quickly fall into being an audience for a play performed by others. There are opportunities for a vast range of styles, and plays can range from being essentially didactic, information-giving stories to engaging audiences at a feeling level in the characters portrayed or issues raised during the performance. Museums are able to plan for a known script and presentation taking place in a defined space to be part of a broader interpretative brief of a gallery or exhibition. Visitors are clear both before, during and after that it is a play and that they can join in if they wish.

Visitors in Role

Some museums are based on visitors themselves entering role-play alongside one or more actors or facilitators of some kind. These are frequently targeted at school groups where the organisation of visitors arriving to enter role, often in costume, is easy to manage. Having said that, there are some museums where adults visit knowing that they can, for example, "go back to school" in the Victorian classroom. Again, contracts are clear with the rules of playing being established beforehand. In the best of these examples visitors know that they can stop the role-play if they wish to and that there will be time to talk about what happens "in the play" when it is over. This style does seem to offer the possibility of reflection and the opportunity to make sense of the drama in a way which I have yet to see done so effectively through other styles. Problems do arise if visitors are not aware that they will be expected to respond in role during their visit and agree to this.

Comédienne de Dramamuse, MCC
Dramamuse actor, CMC

Gallery Character/First-Person Interpretation

This approach usually involves a single costumed character being present on gallery next to, and sometimes directly interacting with, particular exhibits. The medium is flexible and time-efficient making it possible for a team of two or three actor/interpreters to cover as many different galleries simultaneously. Interactions are invariably initiated by the actor and these can take visitors by surprise. Some museums make it clear on entry or at the point of contact with the character that this role-play will be happening and indicate that visitors are free to interact or not. Others leave it as a surprise and it is in these cases that the kinds of confusions indicated earlier seem to occur. At best, gallery characters offer fascinating personal insights into artefacts or sites and invest the object with meanings not apparent through viewing alone. At worst, visitors, confused by the unexplained presence, spend much of their time establishing the rules of playing. Visitor and actor alike are often frustrated at the boundaries imposed by the character him- or herself and are unable to engage in conversation outside the direct life experience of the character. For example, even if the actor does know the answer to a visitor question, he/she sometimes cannot offer it because it happened after the character died. To work really efficiently through this style does require an outstanding level of knowledge, understanding and skill on the part of the actor/interpreter and raises questions about the required qualifications, status (and perhaps salary) of such people within the museum.

Third-Person Interpretation

In a sense, these activities cannot be regarded as drama, role-play or theatre, even though they may at first appear to be exactly this on a large scale. The use of costumes and arte-facts, the involvement in authentic tasks on or near exhibits or even across large sites such as whole villages appears to be theatricality of a high order. Yet, on closer examina-tion these interpreters never actually enter a role of any kind nor do they ask visitors to accept them as such. The best examples involve careful explanation to visitors about the place of costumed demonstrator/interpreters on the particular gallery or site. The crucial feature here is that all identification with the character remains in the third person and because of this all interaction between interpreter and visitor remains in the here and now. The event never becomes fictional, the visitor-interpreter agenda remains open and the opportunities for visitor engagement with the museum mission are many, with fact-finding being high on incidence surveys.

Re-enactment of Specific Events

These events usually occur on a grand scale. They can occupy vast sites or smaller dwellings and can involve anywhere between two or three up to several hundred actor/participants. The great majority of museums using re-enactments stage them as one-off events (maybe annually) and generally use 50-150 people in re-creating the event. Visitors are clear that they are an audience and know the rules of playing much in the same way as with the scripted play. Empathy with the nature of the original incident is high on the agenda, with a focus on the atmosphere of the event often rising above particular bodies of knowledge about it.

Given that one in three museums in the British Isles (research sample: Ford 1994) are now using theatre as part of their interpretative programmes and that the trend seems to be ris-ing, and given the range of styles employed, it seems that theatre in museums is in a healthy state in the U.K.

There are many fine examples of museums using the theatre medium to help achieve set objectives within broad interpretative programmes. Theatre style in many cases seems to be consistent with what the museum hopes to get from it. Other cases, however, seem to be confused. The theatrical events are sometimes being driven by a marketing agenda and not particularly well matched to the interpretative brief. In other cases, any interpretative brief is undermined because the operation is essentially theatrically driven with little re-gard for the conditions under which people will feel at ease enough to engage with the event and learn through it.

The potential for engaging with the mission of the museum through theatre does seem to be immense and has not yet been fully realised by some museums.

The research with groups of children referred to earlier seems to indicate that young people at least are retaining specific knowledge and developing broader concepts through the theatre medium.

Theatre, though, can also engage people at a personal level. Again, the research with children indicates that visitors can be encouraged to form their own opinions about events, artefacts, people and places through engagement with theatre.

To embark fully on theatre programmes of the latter category, however, would represent a radical departure for some museums from the approach of offering a defined interpretation of their collection or site. Once we represent the lives of people, their aspirations, failures, triumphs or compromises, then we invite a response from the visitor which is every bit as human and individual as the protagonists themselves. This represents a form of engagement which is far deeper than the push-button interactive displays sweeping through museums at present. We do not have to stand for long on many interactive galleries before we will see visitors with "button fatigue" wearily setting exhibits in motion only to drift away before the programme has completed. It is the electronic equivalent of the "80-word guideline," and in the days of the split-second image on television, it has limitations in holding attention for long.

What theatre offers is a form of engagement which is able to reach in a deeper sense the hearts and minds of each individual who becomes involved through watching or participating. At the centre of theatrical activity is its relationship to real human living. The sign next to the navvy dummy at the National Railway Museum in York, saying that "many died through accidents or disease," is objective, perhaps clinical, maybe an insult to those who did die. More importantly, the statement is stripped of all human experience and the visitor has little contact with the anonymous figure in question. Place that event in the context of a story, however, where the visitor becomes engaged with a real person who has a name, who feels the cold and hunger and pain, who sings and dances and gets drunk, then we have a very different visitor experience on our hands. When they discover through the story that Gypsy Joe seems to die a violent death because of the deliberate decision of a contractor who went on Parliamentary record as saying that it was not worth using the slower safety methods for the sake of saving a few lives, then the visitor is not dealing anymore with an anonymous figure lost in the grandness of railway history. The visitor is now able to work from the standpoint of their own expertise, that of being human. They can readily empathize with pain and cold and hunger. They can have their own opinion about the contractor's decision. They can begin to weigh up the fantastic achievements of the engineers, the contractors, the financiers and the navvies in creating a transport revolution with their bare hands virtually overnight, against the human cost. It is then a small step to look at their own world here and now and find parallels in which they are personally involved.

After the final performance of *Running the Risk* at the Canadian Museum of Civilization, one of the CMC actor/interpreters came to say that he "felt solidarity with workers from a different age." The universality of human experience is revealed.

The museum is brought to life by theatre, not only in the obvious sense of having characters and demonstrations and plays, but in the sense that it enables visitors to appreciate the museum in the context of this universal human experience. Surely a global aim of finding out about our past and present through museums of every kind is not only to find out about that part of history or nature or science or technology. It is to help us to understand ourselves and our world here and now.

To present our past or our present as a carefully categorised and quantified phenomenon is not to preserve our culture but to deny it. It is an act of cowardice through which we become observers of a sanitised and safe world rather than active participants in it.

Many of the artefacts held in our museums represent important fields of knowing about ourselves. In this context the need for objectivity and impersonal truth is of course valid. There is a crucial place for coming to understand the fixed laws which we believe govern our universe and all that happens within it. There is the need for clarity and unambiguous fact. But these artefacts also represent some of the greatest achievements of humankind at the same time as revealing the fallibility of established truths. If we do not see those achievements against the background of human endeavour, triumph, defeat, folly, and glory, then how can we measure their greatness? How can we really value our past and our present? How can we continue to strive for our own future, if we fail to recognise ourselves in the actions of others?

Jacob Bronowski, scientist and philosopher, in his book, *The Ascent of Man,* reflected on the horror of Nazi death camps, of which his own parents were victims.

> This is where people were turned into numbers. Into this pond were flushed the ashes of some four million people. And that was not done by gas. It was done by arrogance. It was done by dogma. It was done by ignorance. When people believe that they have absolute knowledge, with no test in reality, this is how they behave. This is what men do when they aspire to the knowledge of gods.
>
> Science is a very human form of knowledge. We are always at the brink of the known, we always feel forward for what is to be hoped. Every judgement in science stands on the edge of error and is personal. Science is a tribute to what we can know although we are fallible. In the end the words were said by Oliver Cromwell: "I beseech you in the bowels of Christ, think it possible you may be mistaken."
>
> We have to cure ourselves of the itch for absolute knowledge and power. We have to touch people.[10]

Theatre is all about touching the hearts and minds of people. It is about those moments when the lives of the portrayed characters and those of the observers fuse into one and at that moment alternative truths are revealed.

I do not, of course, associate in any way museums with the extremes of Bronowski's particular example above. Nevertheless, one feature of museums is the objectivity of their mission. I would suggest that the potential of theatre to help visitors also engage at a personal level with that mission should not be overlooked.

We have the opportunity through theatre to help visitors become active meaning-makers of both the objective world around them and the personal world within. They can develop a deeper understanding of the lives of people different to their own. They can come to understand the nature of our own development through a medium which is perhaps unique in its capacity to make sense of human behaviour.

In the end, the reason that visitors will return to the museum is because they see a part of themselves in it. The biggest investment that museums can perhaps make in terms of visitors, is to ensure that visitors feel a personal investment in the content of the museum. Theatre as a learning medium can probably contribute significantly to such a goal.

References

1. Museums and Galleries Commission
   Guidelines for a Registration Scheme for Museums in the United Kingdom
   (London. HMSO. 1989)

2. Museums and Galleries Commission
   Guidelines for a Registration Scheme for Museums in the United Kingdom
   (London. HMSO. 1989)

3. Chris Cade
   Taped Interview with Peter Cheesman. 6.6.89 New Victoria Theatre. Stoke-on-Trent
   Appendices in Final Dissertation MA Educational Theatre — Devising for Documentary Theatre
   University of Leeds. 1989

4. National Railway Museum
   Great Hall Final Text
   (York. National Railway Museum. Not published. 1992)

5. Chris Ford
   Running the Risk
   (York. Platform 4 Theatre. Not Published. 1993)

6. Margaret Donaldson
   Childrens' Minds
   (Fontana Press. 1978)

7. Chris Ford
   Running the Risk
   (York. Platform 4 Theatre. Not Published. 1993)

8. Chris Ford
   Running the Risk
   (York. Platform 4 Theatre. Not Published. 1993)

9. Jonothan Neelands
   Making Sense of Drama
   (London. Heinemann. 1984)

10. Jacob Bronowski
    The Ascent of Man
    (London. Book Club Associates. 1973)

❖ Les formes d'interprétation personnalisée et la mise en exposition : les contextes de sociabilité de l'appropriation

Raymond Montpetit
Directeur, maîtrise en muséologie,
Université du Québec à Montréal
Codirecteur, Groupe de recherche en histoire et théorie des expositions (GRHITE)

This reflection positions live interpretation vis-à-vis the definition of an exhibition and of interpretation in general. Live interpretation forms can be understood as major components of the sociability of the visit; they encompass not only the interventions which the designers intend for visitors, but also the interactions which occur between visitors, and which contribute to the active process of understanding and appropriation during a visit. Live interpretation is thought of in relation to seven different types of museographic exhibition: symbolic, taxonomic, analogue, immersion, thematic, narrative and demonstrative. Each of these types is a potential favoured form of live interpretation, focusing on appropriate use by visitors. The general hypothesis is therefore that an exhibition is a place where one form or another of customized interpretation is practised, because it gives rise to interaction and interpersonal development of the senses as a way of accessing its proposed content and meaning.

Je voudrais traiter de «l'interprétation personnalisée» en relation avec la «mise en exposition», en proposant quelques réflexions sur l'exposition, sa nature et sa réception, parce que c'est là, à mon avis, au cœur de ce qu'implique le geste d'exposer à l'intention d'un public de visiteurs, que naît le pourquoi de notre recours, de plus en plus fréquent, aux techniques et moyens d'interprétation en général, et à l'interprétation personnalisée en particulier, qui est l'une des formes que l'interprétation peut revêtir.

En premier lieu, je rappellerai quelques définitions de l'exposition et aussi de la notion centrale d'interprétation, afin de voir comment les moyens dits «d'interprétation personnalisée» s'y inscrivent et servent les objectifs que poursuit l'interprétation en général. En second, je proposerai un bref examen des types d'interprétation personnalisée qui ont cours en contexte muséal et qui vont de pair, je crois, avec les diverses formes muséographiques d'expositions développées dans l'histoire de la muséologie. Il en ressort que doter une exposition d'un volet «interprétation personnalisée» qui oriente son appropriation, n'est peut-être pas un geste aussi nouveau qu'on le pense.

Tout comme, dans le monde antique grec, la montée de la démocratie a vu surgir une discipline, la rhétorique, qui enseigne les méthodes pour «persuader et convaincre par la parole», on constate que la démocratisation croissante des musées s'accompagne, elle aussi, d'une forme de discours qui est, pour ainsi dire, la rhétorique muséologique. Ce discours, vous l'aurez reconnu, est celui de l'interprétation, qui emprunte une gamme de supports divers, dont la personne humaine elle-même, pour atteindre les visiteurs d'exposition et communiquer avec eux.

1. L'exposition et les moyens d'interprétation

Que fait-on quand on expose des objets matériels, comment cela peut-il faire sens, à quelles conditions et pour qui? L'exposition est de plus en plus vue comme un moyen à part entière de communication, et quand elle a recours à l'interprétation, c'est pour mieux s'acquitter de ses missions et atteindre les objectifs qu'elle s'est donnés au départ.

Une consultation du mot «exposition» dans le *Grand Robert*, par exemple, met en relief ces champs de significations :

Exposition : au XIIᵉ siècle, du latin *expositio*. Action d'exposer, résultat de cette action.

1° Action de mettre en vue.
2° Présentation publique de produits, d'œuvres d'art; ensemble de produits et d'œuvres d'art exposés; lieu, emplacement où on les expose.
3° Figuré. Action de faire connaître, d'expliquer quelque chose.
4° Situation d'un édifice, d'un bâtiment, par rapport à une direction donnée. Orientation.
5° Action de soumettre quelqu'un ou quelque chose, à l'action de...

Cette définition suggère quelques traits caractéristiques de l'exposition, dont déjà plusieurs pointent vers la nécessité de la doter d'un volet «interprétation» :

L'exposition concerne la **vue**.	Perception
Elle est un geste qui a trait au **public**.	Communication
Elle est un lieu et un rassemblement d'**objets**.	Espace / matière
Elle se propose d'**expliquer** ce qu'elle montre.	Raison
Elle prend **position**, oriente, installe une perspective.	Opinion
Elle **affecte** les visiteurs et les soumet à son action.	Persuasion

L'exposition se veut le plus souvent, un agent actif, elle s'adresse aux visiteurs et opère sur eux. Elle montre un ensemble d'objets, réunis en un lieu et les ordonne en aménageant sur eux un point de vue, orientant ainsi comment ceux qui la visitent et contemplent les objets recevront son propos dans un certain parcours.

Voici quelques définitions, proposées par des muséologues, du mot «exposition» ou *exhibition* en anglais, et de deux autres notions connexes, celle de *display*, qu'on pourrait traduire par «étalage» ou par l'action de «faire étalage de», et celle de *exhibit*, qui correspond à une unité, à un élément faisant partie d'une exposition et qui se traduirait par le néologisme «expôt».

Exhibition

An assemblage of objects of artistic, historical, scientific, or technological nature, through which visitors move from unit to unit in a sequence designed to be meaningful instructionally and/or aesthetically. Accompanying labels and/or graphics (drawings, diagrams, etc.) are planned to interpret, explain, and to direct the viewer's attention.[1]

Exhibit/display

An exhibit is a display plus interpretation; or, a display is a showing, an exhibit is showing and telling. Therefore, an exhibit should not be thought of as a single object, but rather as a deliberate interpretation of a subject or a grouping according to a theme . . . The term "exhibit" carries the connotation that something has been added to the objects shown (interpretation) in order to accomplish something of importance (education in the broad sense).[2]

Exhibition

Exhibition should be defined as "showing for a purpose," the purpose being to affect the viewer in some predetermined way.[3]

Exhibition

In the case of most exhibitions, objects are brought together not simply for the sake of their physical manifestation or juxtaposition, but because they are part of a story one is trying to tell. The "context" of the exhibition confers upon them a "meaning."[4]

Display/exhibit/exhibition

The word "display" will generally refer to a presentation of objects for public view without significant interpretation added. "Exhibit" will usually mean the localized grouping of objects and interpretive materials that form a cohesive unit within a gallery. "Exhibition" will be used to allude to a comprehensive grouping of all elements (including exhibits and displays) that form a complete public presentation of collections and information for the public use.[5]

Plusieurs composantes matérielles se conjuguent dans l'espace d'exposition, pour se faire les supports d'une communication intentionnelle envers les visiteurs. Aussi, si une partie du sens tient aux caractéristiques des objets perçus isolément et en eux-mêmes, une autre strate de sens relève de leur mise en commun dans une distribution spatiale particulière qui est celle du contexte spécifique d'une mise en exposition.

Exhibition

An exhibition is a means of communication aiming at large groups of the public with the purpose of conveying information, ideas, and emotions relating to the material evidence of man and his surrounding, with the aid of chiefly visual and dimensional methods.[6]

Exposition

L'exposition, c'est l'action de mettre en valeur, à destination de tout public, un ensemble de biens mobiliers, immobiliers ou fongibles, selon un programme précis et dans un espace déterminé, sous toit ou à l'air libre, à l'aide de moyens variés, visuels essentiellement.[7]

On définit donc l'exposition comme un «montrer qui ordonne, suggère, démontre et/ou raconte aussi quelque chose», ce qui exprime bien son caractère de moyen intentionnel de communication et ses objectifs de faire que ce qui est montré ait du sens. L'exposition repose sur une volonté de faire voir et de dire quelque chose; en montrant des choses matérielles, elle opère **un placement d'objets dans un espace de visibilité** et, le plus souvent, planifie un **déplacement programmé des visiteurs le long d'un parcours orienté**. Elle rend ainsi du sens accessible à ceux qui la visitent au moyen d'une déambulation attentive à ce qui est donné à percevoir et à lire.

À cette dimension de contemplation / déambulation s'en ajoute une autre : elle a trait non plus aux rapports **visiteurs-objets**, mais bien aux **relations interpersonnelles** et aux échanges qui ont cours, dans l'espace d'exposition, entre des personnes. En effet, la production de signification mise à la fois : 1° sur la **perception** de ce qui s'offre matériellement, et donc sur les actes que nécessite le décodage de ce perçu, et 2° sur l'**interaction personnelle**, à savoir sur ce que font et sur ce que se disent les personnes qui se trouvent dans l'exposition.

La demande faite sur les visiteurs est complexe et variée; considérons, par exemple, cette énumération d'actions que les visiteurs peuvent être invités à accomplir dans une exposition : 1. voir, 2. percevoir, 3. se mouvoir, 4. lire, 5. participer, 6. s'émouvoir, 7. s'imaginer, 8. éprouver, 9. communiquer, 10. apprendre, 11. s'approprier, 12. changer. Certains de ces gestes sont toujours requis, d'autres sont optionnels, étant tributaires du type d'exposition et des muséographies employées.

Les activités d'interprétation, dont l'interprétation personnalisée, entrent bien en action dans cet au-delà du «montrer» dont les concepteurs d'exposition sont préoccupés; elles interviennent en appui aux objectifs de *démontrer*, de *raconter*, d'*expliquer* et quelquefois de faire *participer* et de *simuler*, que les concepteurs d'exposition poursuivent, quand ils prennent conscience que les objets montrés risquent souvent de rester, pour une bonne partie du public d'aujourd'hui, des témoins matériels muets et non compris. Le besoin que nous sentons de plus en plus fortement d'avoir recours à des moyens d'interprétation dans nos expositions, repose sur la distance qui sépare les objets montrés, 1° du propos particulier que telle exposition veut tenir à leur sujet, et 2° des références nécessaires pour que les visiteurs puissent procéder à cette production orientée de signification.

Toute exposition réalisée met en jeu beaucoup plus que l'ensemble des objets de collection — œuvres d'art, objets archéologiques ou historiques, spécimens naturels — qu'elle contient. Elle compose et installe un espace polymorphe, multisensoriel et public, un environnement stimulant dans lequel les visiteurs pénètrent, se laissent prendre en charge, à la fois physiquement et intellectuellement, pour vivre une expérience à plusieurs niveaux et, le plus souvent, interagir et échanger entre eux. Plusieurs travaux récents pointent dans cette direction, affirmant, par exemple, que «le dispositif médiatique de l'exposition s'identifie à l'ensemble de l'espace de réception. Avec lui, l'exposition dépasse le cadre d'une relation entre l'individu et l'objet, devenant un véritable dispositif communicationnel entre un public et une présentation»[8] ; si, «pour le visiteur, l'environnement de l'exposition est le média primordial de communication»[9] , nous ajoutons que cet environnement est aussi peuplé des autres visiteurs qui le parcourent, avec ou en même temps que moi, et quelquefois encore, de personnes qui m'interpellent.

De telles considérations conduisent à repenser comment opère, en contexte expositionnel, la production de sens dans laquelle les visiteurs sont engagés, et à prendre en compte le caractère socialisé des interprétations que les visiteurs mettent de l'avant dans leur effort de comprendre. Ce faisant, il devient manifeste que le rôle des interactions entre individus est important dans le processus actif de compréhension et d'appropriation. Du côté de la réception, «les actes interprétatifs sont des actes illocutoires par lesquels les visiteurs donnent collectivement un sens aux exhibits»[10]

Ainsi, les formes d'interprétation personnalisée ne s'arrêtent pas à celles que les concepteurs mettent en place, mais se prolongent dans les interactions que les visiteurs ont entre eux, au sujet de tout ce qu'ils perçoivent dans l'espace global de l'exposition et de la façon dont cela a du sens pour eux.

En résumant, notons que les activités d'interprétation personnalisée se situent sur les deux versants de la mise en exposition, tant dans la planification et la production, que dans la réception et l'appropriation :

> 1° d'une part, du côté *production*, ces activités font partie des moyens qui s'offrent aux concepteurs pour rejoindre et impliquer ses publics;
>
> 2° d'autre part, du côté *réception*, elles interviennent dans les pratiques de sociabilité par lesquelles les visiteurs interagissent, se racontent et s'expliquent ce qu'ils voient et s'approprient les contenus de l'exposition.

Examinons maintenant quelques définitions de l'interprétation, pensée en tant que moyens ou activités dont se servent les concepteurs pour atteindre les publics visiteurs; plusieurs de ces définitions sont bien connues dans la muséologie nord-américaine. Mais en les relisant, nous resterons attentifs à ce que ces moyens interprétatifs agissent aussi dans la sociabilité que les visiteurs partagent entre eux.

Commençons par rappeler la définition classique donnée par F. Tilden.

Interprétation

L'interprétation est une activité éducative qui veut dévoiler la signification des choses et leurs relations par l'utilisation des objets d'origine, par l'expérience personnelle et des exemples plutôt que par la seule communication de renseignements concrets.[11]

Un effort planifié pour créer à l'intention du visiteur, une compréhension de l'histoire et de la signification des événements, des personnes et des objets qui sont associés au site.[12]

Interpretation is a communication process designed to reveal meanings and relationships of our cultural and natural heritage to the public through first hand involvement with objects, artefacts and landscape or site.[13]

L'interprétation est un processus qui vise à communiquer au public la signification ainsi que la valeur du patrimoine naturel et culturel, en impliquant directement l'individu avec les phénomènes pour le rendre conscient de la place qu'il
occupe dans l'espace et le temps.[14]

Méthode de sensibilisation qui consiste à traduire, pour un public en situation, le
sens profond d'une réalité et ses liens cachés avec l'être humain, en ayant recours à
des moyens qui font d'abord appel à l'appréhension, c'est-à-dire qui mènent à une
forme vécue et descriptive de la connaissance plutôt qu'à une forme rigoureuse-
ment rationnelle.[15]

Cette définition, précise et englobante, est celle que je préfère, parce qu'elle met en relief le
fait que l'interprétation, en contexte muséal autant qu'en contexte naturel et culturel *in
situ*, est avant tout une manière de communiquer et un mode suggéré d'appropriation.

"Interpretation" is the act or process of explaining or clarifying, translating, or presenting a personal understanding about a subject or object.[16]

Plusieurs de ces définitions caractérisent bien un mode de relation qui s'instaure entre les
visiteurs et les contenus — objets et messages — que présente l'exposition au moyen
d'une gamme de supports. Le placement dans l'espace de choses à contempler n'étant plus
vu comme suffisant, l'exposition cherche, par l'interprétation, à interpeller le public et à
faire un pas vers lui. L'objectif est de gérer la relation qui s'établit entre les visiteurs et l'exposition, d'attirer et de retenir leur attention et d'orienter les idées qui circuleront et que
les visiteurs échangeront à son propos. Pour ce faire, on aménage des modalités d'accès au
sens de ce qui est montré et des suggestions d'appropriation, en mettant en place des dispositifs facilement décodables par tous, parce que reposant sur des références familières
que l'on sait partagées par la majorité des visiteurs.

Si pour certains, tout l'appareil informatif et explicatif qui s'ajoute aux objets exposés
fait partie des moyens d'interprétation, d'autres muséologues insistent sur le fait que la
simple information, écrite ou orale, fournie aux visiteurs, n'est pas encore de l'interprétation véritable : interpréter demande plus, c'est actualiser, c'est provoquer l'émotion,
animer, révéler, impliquer et rendre ce qui est communiqué sur un niveau autre que celui
de la pure intellection. Si l'interprétation tend souvent vers les simulations et les recréa-
tions contextuelles, qui plongent les visiteurs dans un «faire comme si» stimulant pour
l'imaginaire, c'est parce qu'elle cherche à s'adresser à la personne entière et non à sa seule
intelligence : «Interpretation is getting people to think about what it all means, about
their part in it all.»[17]

L'interprétation est en une modalité de présentation centrée sur l'implication du public :

We present the materials we want the visitor to know in an informational style, or in an interpretative style. The difference between the two styles is not what we present but how we present it. Informational styles simply dispense the facts, the way a field guide lists and describes species, for example. But the interpretive style reveals a story or larger message [...] to help the visitor relate to that message.[18]

L'interprétation narre les objets, elle les active et les présente de façon à encourager leur appropriation dans une expérience de visite profitable. Pour réussir, elle traite l'information qu'elle transmet, afin que celle-ci puisse éveiller des échos, évoquer des références connues chez les visiteurs et ainsi être intégrée à leurs expériences et à leurs univers mentaux. Grâce à ces dispositifs et activités, objets et informations sont repris et présentés dans une dynamique apte à provoquer une appréhension qui fait appel à l'identification et à l'émotion, tout autant qu'à l'intelligence rationnelle.

L'interprétation en général et l'interprétation personnalisée viennent donc appuyer l'exposition et ses objectifs, en particulier dans ses tâches d'expliquer, d'influencer et de guider l'appropriation des visiteurs, en impliquant ce qui est montré dans une trame particulière de références qui est productrice de sens.

Résumons cela dans un tableau :

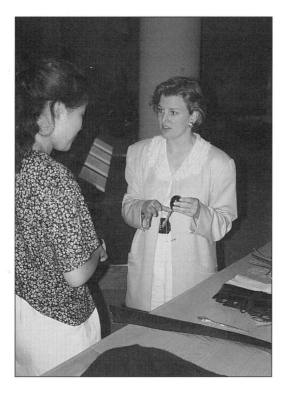

Animatrice au MCC
CMC animator

68

Exposition et interprétation

Espace physique	Espace mental
1° Des **objets** sont réunis par le collectionnement; certains sont sélectionnés pour **exposition**. 2° Ces objets supportent un **ordre** que leur agencement dans l'espace incarne et suggère.	
	3° Pour saisir l'ordre sous-jacent et les significations qu'il porte, il faut des savoirs et des **références**.
L'interprétation intervient à la fois dans l'espace **physique** et dans l'espace **mental**.	
4° Elle repose sur des **supports** interprétatifs matériels, installés parmi les artefacts exposés,	
	5° et sur les **discours** de personnes qui informent et interprètent ce qui est montré.
6° Ces prestations orales peuvent prendre la forme d'une **animation** ou d'une **démonstration** à observer à même l'espace de l'exposition.	

Discours, animation et démonstration constituent les principales formes d'interprétation personnalisée qui ont cours dans l'exposition.

L'interprétation, qui installe une relation dispositif-visiteurs ou personne-à-personne, peut prendre pour objet un artefact, un ensemble d'artefacts ou même un site entier; elle opère en inscrivant ces réalités dans une trame capable de les rendre signifiants pour les visiteurs, dans l'expérience de visite qui est la leur.

> The goal of interpretation is understanding, good interpretation will help visitors understand what the site can reveal about the importance of people and events connected with it, about a way of life, or about the cultural tastes of the past. It consists of what is shown, said, or done that will help those visitors experience a personal involvement and a sense of identification with their heritage. It includes not only the person-to-person relationship between visitor and interpreter, but also the visitors' learning experiences through museum exhibits, audio-visual de-

vices, labels, interpretative markers, living history programs, craft demonstrations, and publications.[19]

L'interprétation personnalisée comprend donc tout ce qui prend appui sur une relation interpersonnelle entre un **guide-animateur** et les **visiteurs**, et **entre les visiteurs** dans la sociabilité de la visite. Quand ces échanges misent presque exclusivement sur l'ordre du discours, tout se passe dans l'espace mental des paroles et des idées; mais il arrive aussi que l'interprétation personnalisée joue plus sur le visible et le concret; elle prend alors place, avec une certaine théâtralité, dans l'espace d'exposition, donnant lieu à des *animations* ou *démonstrations* offertes parmi les autres éléments exposés. De telles interventions constituent une composante humaine qui contextualise, dynamise et personnalise le propos que tient l'exposition au sujet de ce qu'elle donne à voir.

Le tableau suivant rend compte de la place de l'interprétation dans le fonctionnement des expositions dites interprétatives.

Exposition interprétative

Espace perçu	Activités interprétatives	Sélection thématique	Résultat : appropriation
Les OBJETS exposés	sont pris en charge par des moyens d'INTERPRÉTATION *matériels* ou *personnalisés*	qui font émerger des thèmes intégrateurs et des trames narratives.	Un sens est suggéré explicitement aux visiteurs; il est véhiculé en faisant appel aux références et aux émotions partagées, s'intégrant ainsi au vécu de chacun par le biais de l'expérience de visite.

À l'intérieur des expositions interprétatives, la contemplation des objets exposés se fait dans un contexte pro-actif, où sont en opération des moyens d'intervention planifiés qui mettent explicitement de l'avant des liens entre les artefacts et tissent autour d'eux des réseaux de sens capables de rejoindre les visiteurs en misant sur des références communes et des expériences partagées. Voyons plus en détail comment cette dynamique d'appropriation fonctionne dans diverses formes d'expositions.

2. Les formes muséographiques et l'appropriation

Toutes les expositions ne s'offrent pas aux visiteurs de la même façon; elles sont installées selon diverses logiques muséographiques et appellent, en retour, différents modes d'usage et d'appropriation, qui mettent en action diverses formes de relations interpersonnelles. Sans faire ici un historique détaillé de la mise en exposition, il est certain que celle-ci a pris, à travers le temps, des formes variées, et qu'encore aujourd'hui, nous pouvons visiter des expositions aux «principes muséologiques» bien différents.

Quelles sont, muséographiquement, les formes typiques que prennent les expositions, comment se présentent-elles aux visiteurs qu'elles se proposent d'accueillir et avec lesquels elles communiquent? En examinant ces formes et en identifiant quelques grands types, il me semble qu'on pose, en même temps, la question des genres d'appropriation que ces types d'expositions rendent possible et appellent, à la fois, pour favoriser la transmission des contenus présentés.

Je dirais que le travail de «mise en exposition» obéit à deux grandes logiques : il met en place des expositions exogènes ou référentielles, et des expositions endogènes ou interprétatives, en fonction d'une part, de comment elles fonctionnent comme lieu de transmission de sens et, d'autre part, en fonction du mode de réception qu'elles exigent des visiteurs. Sous ces deux grandes logiques, on retrouve sept types de muséographie d'exposition qui, avec différentes fréquences, ont encore cours aujourd'hui. Mais tous ces types ne jouissent pas d'un même degré de popularité, principalement parce que certains ne réussissent à s'adresser qu'à des visiteurs «connaisseurs» dotés de compétences et de références particulières, alors que d'autres sont mieux conçus pour un usage «grand public» et favorisent un accès plus démocratique à leurs contenus et propos.

Définissons ces deux grandes logiques et leurs sept composantes muséographiques.[20]

I - Les expositions exogènes ou référentielles sont celles où la disposition des choses montrées repose sur et fait référence à un ordre préalable qui structure la présentation et qui doit être connu et reconnu par les visiteurs.

Quatre types de muséographie entrent dans cette catégorie; les deux premières se réfèrent au savoir, les deux autres renvoient au réel :

1° **La muséographie symbolique :** les relations de similitudes
2° **La muséographie taxinomique :** les rapports de classes
3° **La muséographie analogique :** les images du réel
4° **La muséographie d'immersion :** les simulations intégrales

II - Les expositions endogènes ou interprétatives sont celles où la disposition des choses montrées est générée par les besoins de la mise en exposition elle-même et rendue explicite dans son dispositif; où l'ordre et la logique retenus sont fonction des objectifs de communication avec les visiteurs et du «discours» que tient l'exposition.

Trois types muséographiques entrent dans cette catégorie :

5° La muséographie thématique : l'intégration sous un thème
6° La muséographie narrative : l'intégration dans une histoire
7° La muséographie démonstrative : l'intégration dans une action

L'exposition a toujours ordonné les objets collectionnés dans un espace aménagé pour les recevoir, les conserver et les rendre compréhensibles, d'abord au collectionneur lui-même, puis à ses pairs et aux autres visiteurs admis à les contempler. L'hypothèse générale qui me guide est donc que l'exposition constitue bien un lieu où se pratique une forme ou une autre d'**interprétation personnalisée**, car *les visiteurs prennent en considération les objets montrés et tout l'environnement de l'exposition, grâce à une interaction et une élaboration interpersonnelle de sens; ces rapports interpersonnels sont des agents producteurs de significations.* Un examen attentif montre que les différents types d'expositions se prêtent à diverses formes d'interprétation personnalisée, car les dispositifs muséographiques adoptés influencent la nature des actions requises des visiteurs et donc celle des discours interprétatifs qui s'imposent pour encadrer la réception souhaitée. Voyons ces sept types de présentations pour mieux comprendre les genre d'interprétation personnalisée qui s'y pratique.

Les sept types muséographiques d'expositions

I. Les expositions à logique exogène et référentielle

1° La **muséographie symbolique** : cette forme de muséographie dispose les objets montrés en fonction de leur interprétation dans un réseau de correspondances et de rapports, établis par un savoir symbolique préalable, partagé par les visiteurs.

2° La **muséographie taxinomique** : cette forme de muséographie dispose les objets selon le travail classificatoire d'un savoir scientifique; ils sont montrés selon leur place ou rang, dans une distribution sérielle, comme les genres et les espèces, les matériaux ou les styles.

3° La **muséographie analogique** : cette forme de muséographie présente des ensembles d'objets disposés dans l'exposition comme ils l'étaient dans leur contexte d'origine. Elle installe alors des «images», des «scènes de vie» qui font référence, par ressemblance, à une situation réelle que les visiteurs reconnaissent, comme à l'origine de la présentation.

4° La **muséographie d'immersion** : cette forme de muséographie dispose aussi les objets en conformité avec leur contexte d'origine; mais elle place les visiteurs physiquement dans un espace de simulation intégrale, qui leur permet d'entrer dans la scène et d'expérimenter concrètement l'environnement de la situation traitée.

> C'est de l'analogique avec en plus, une inclusion dans le «faire comme si».
>
> II. Les expositions à logique endogène et interprétative
>
> > 5° La **muséographie thématique** : cette forme de muséographie regroupe les objets montrés en fonction d'un thème intégrateur donné et les ancre dans ce thème.
> >
> > 6° La **muséographie narrative** : cette forme de muséographie raconte une histoire; elle installe les objets en fonction d'un récit -avec épisodes, personnages actions et dénouement - selon le rôle qu'elle leur confie dans ce récit.
> >
> > 7° La **muséographie démonstrative** : cette forme de muséographie distribue des objets parmi des dispositifs où ils figurent dans des démonstrations dynamiques, afin d'expliquer leurs causes, leur nature ou leur fonctionnement.

Chacun des sept types muséologiques d'expositions entraîne un type particulier d'interprétation personnalisée, il se prête de préférence à un type d'appropriation qui fait intervenir des interactions entre personnes, dans le but d'expliciter une certaine signification qui forme le message transmis par l'exposition. Chaque type encourage donc par son dispositif, un genre d'interaction et de relation interpersonnelle, 1° entre le personnel du musée et les visiteurs, et 2° entre les visiteurs eux-mêmes qui doivent recourir à leurs références et partager certaines de leurs compétences à l'occasion de leur passage dans l'exposition.

Les expositions sont des dispositifs organisés en fonction de ce visiteur au comportement «idéal». Elles favorisent certains usages et donc certains visiteurs, précisément ceux qui sont capables d'entrer en relation avec sa distribution et ses contenus, selon le rapport qui convient à la logique adoptée.

Voici comment les sept types de muséographies déjà identifiés se relient à des formes d'interprétation personnalisée et misent sur une sociabilité qui correspond à l'appropriation encouragée par les dispositifs en place.

Type # 1 : la muséographie symbolique

La disposition spatiale reprend et incarne un ordre fondé sur des rapports de similitudes et des harmonies qu'une certaine vision du monde découvre entre les objets collectionnés. Les principes d'agencement qui régissent les choses montrées relèvent de cette interprétation de leurs affinités.

L'interprétation personnalisée que ce dispositif appelle est l'échange et la discussion entre connaisseurs et intéressés. Le contexte régulier de sociabilité est celui où un collectionneur, souvent présent, parle avec des visiteurs, dans une réciprocité et un partage de connaissances. On assiste à des réunions d'études et à des visites guidées centrées autant sur les actions de collectionnement que sur les objets eux-mêmes exposés ou entreposés.

Type # 2 : la muséographie taxinomique

La disposition spatiale reprend et incarne un ordre fondé sur les catégories classifica-toires des savoirs disciplinaires (celles de la géologie, de l'histoire de l'art, de la biologie, de l'anthropologie, de l'ethnologie, de la paléontologie, de la botanique, etc.) La mise en espace obéit aux rapports régissant les définitions et les concepts qui structurent la théorie et classent les objets.

L'interprétation personnalisée que ce dispositif requiert est celle de l'échange, de l'enseignement disciplinaire et de l'étude des objets de la collection. Professeur et étudiants discutent des spécimens et de leurs apports au savoir disciplinaire. Le bon usage demande ou bien que le visiteur connaisse le système scientifique que l'exposition matérialise, ou bien qu'une interprétation personnalisée, de type didactique, intervienne pour fournir les clés de compréhension.

Type # 3 : la muséographie analogique

La disposition spatiale retenue pour ces installations d'objets respecte l'agencement de contiguïté fonctionnelle et spatiale qui prévalait hors musée. Les objets sont disposés en «scène de la vie», comme ils étaient dans le contexte original d'où ils proviennent, et offerts, en tant que tout cohérent, à la contemplation.

L'interprétation personnalisée que ces ensembles analogiques suggèrent repose sur le pouvoir d'évocation de ces scènes pour les visiteurs; ceux-ci font appel à leurs con-naissances pratiques et à leurs «souvenirs» pour commenter la scène. La réception demande qu'ils identifient ce qui est vu et l'intègrent à leurs connaissances. Des acteurs peuvent intervenir pour animer ces scènes de personnages d'époque.

Type # 4 : la muséographie d'immersion

La disposition spatiale des muséographies d'immersion obéit à une logique de la simulation; elle installe les éléments montrés, authentiques ou reproduits, dans une scénographie réaliste qui reconstitue le lieu et les conditions d'une «expé-rience» offerte aux visiteurs. Plongés au centre du dispositif, ils peuvent non seulement contempler la scène, mais y pénétrer et vivre l'environnement intégral reconstitué.

L'interprétation personnalisée qu'engendre l'immersion fait appel aux expériences pratiques des visiteurs; dans ces environnements globaux, les formes d'interprétation doivent contribuer à l'effet de la simulation. Le dispositif se prête bien aux dramatisations théâtrales et aux jeux de rôles avec acteurs-interprètes. La réception exige la participation active du visiteur : il doit imaginer, jouer le jeu, s'identifier à la situation et faire l'expérience que propose la simulation.

Type # 5 : la muséographie thématique

La disposition spatiale prend en charge les artefacts selon le rôle qu'elle leur confie dans le traitement du thème intégrateur de l'exposition. Elle met l'accent sur certains objets principaux et sur les seuls aspects de ces objets qui sont pertinents à la trame thématique retenue.

L'interprétation personnalisée commandée par cette logique contribue à faire que le développement thématique et son articulation soient rendus bien manifestes pour les visiteurs. Des guides-animateurs peuvent assumer une partie de la transmission de la trame interprétative et compléter oralement les supports écrits. La réception exige attention, écoute et lecture ordonnée des supports qui communiquent les thèmes.

Type # 6 : la muséographie narrative

La disposition spatiale de ces muséographies obéit à une logique narrative, celle du *story telling;* elle distribue les artefacts et les autres éléments exposés, selon leur rôle dans un parcours qui suit les phases successives de l'histoire racontée.

L'interprétation personnalisée que réclame une telle muséographie, concerne la transmission des éléments — personnages et actions — de ce récit. Les interactions servent la narration par laquelle l'histoire prend appui sur les objets et les intègre à son déroulement. L'intervention de «conteurs» demande que les visiteurs écoutent, s'identifient aux personnages, suivent leurs actions et imaginent comment les objets montrés sont impliqués dans l'aventure racontée.

Type # 7 : la muséographie démonstrative

La disposition spatiale de ces muséographies aménage des lieux d'interaction dans lesquels les objets montrés figurent comme éléments d'une démonstration didactique, présentée au public.

L'interprétation personnalisée sur laquelle ces muséographies reposent, demande l'intervention de démonstrateurs qui expliquent des aspects du propos de l'exposition et utilisent certains objets pour en démontrer la nature, ou le fonctionnement. La réception demande la compréhension des processus explicatifs et peut exiger la participation des visiteurs. Il arrive que la démonstration fasse aussi appel à l'analogie et à la simulation, pour ajouter un aspect théâtral aux explications transmises.

Les formes d'interprétation personnalisée varient donc selon le type d'exposition où on les retrouve; elles sont toutefois dédiées à quatre fonctions principales :

1° *l'information* : l'interaction personnelle renseigne sur les caractéristiques des objets (ou site) et sur leur sens; mais une telle information n'est pas encore de l'interprétation, à moins qu'elle n'aille au-delà de l'informatif, pour réussir à convier l'imaginaire, à démontrer des dynamiques et à impliquer le visiteur dans le propos tenu;

2° *la socialisation* : l'interaction mise sur les relations internes du groupe de visiteurs, elle a pour but que les visiteurs se stimulent et s'entraident dans la visite, qu'ils se sentent «à l'aise» dans l'espace muséal et concernés par les choses et les thématiques proposées à leur appropriation;

3° *la narration* : l'interaction regroupe les visiteurs autour d'un narrateur qui raconte une histoire dont personnages et actions concernent le site et les artefacts;

4° *la simulation* : l'interaction est axée sur une dramatisation et l'interprète devient un personnage dans une histoire. Ce jeu peut être un spectacle à regarder, le *living history* des Américains, ou bien prendre une forme plus participatoire d'animation collective et d'expérimentation.

Comprendre le fonctionnement des types d'expositions et comment s'y inscrit l'interprétation personnalisée exige d'accorder une grande importance aux relations humaines qui y ont cours. L'interprétation personnalisée est une forme «dirigée» de relation interpersonnelle. Du point de vue des institutions muséales, il s'agit d'une intervention qui, en liaison avec les objectifs de l'exposition et les usages que réclame son dispositif, vient compléter la communication avec les visiteurs; elle oriente les perceptions, enrichit l'expérience de visite et influence la production de significations. Du point de vue des visiteurs, l'interprétation personnalisée inclue non seulement les rapports au personnel spécialisé du musée, mais aussi les interactions avec les autres visiteurs, qui participent avec eux à dire le sens de ce qu'ils découvrent et à assurer une appropriation des contenus. C'est sur ce fond de sociabilité que s'érige, en bonne partie, la richesse de l'expérience vécue dans l'exposition.

Je résume mon propos dans ces deux tableaux, le premier sur les logiques muséo-graphiques exogènes, le second sur les logiques endogènes.

Types de muséographies d'exposition	Formes d'interprétation personnalisée	Compétences requises pour l'appropriation
Les logiques exogènes :		
1. Muséographie symbolique	Discussion, analyse et partage entre connaisseurs. Interaction entre pairs.	Connaître et percevoir les similitudes et les associations symboliques.
2. Muséographie taxinomique	Discussion, analyse et partage entre scientifiques et visiteurs. Interaction maître-élèves.	Comprendre la logique conceptuelle des théories classificatoires.
3. Muséographie analogique	Observation, partage d'expériences entre spectateurs. Interaction acteurs-public.	Reconnaître la scène et la relier à ses expériences de vie.
4. Muséographie d'immersion	Observation, partage d'expériences entre ceux qui pénètrent dans l'environnement. Interaction environnement-public, avec ou sans acteurs.	Participer, imaginer, jouer le jeu, éprouver physiquement ce qu'offre l'environnement simulé.

Quant aux trois muséographies endogènes, elles se résument ainsi :

Types de muséographies d'exposition	Formes d'interprétation personnalisée	Compétences requises pour l'appropriation
Les logiques endogènes :		
5. Exposition thématique	Prise de connaissance des thèmes et messages transmis à l'intention des visiteurs. Interaction guide-public.	Saisir le propos et les relations entre les objets exposés et les thèmes structurant la présentation.
6. Muséographie narrative	Élaboration d'une histoire avec personnages et actions reliés aux artefacts. Interaction conteur-public	Écouter et comprendre l'histoire racontée et imaginer le rôle qu'y jouent les artefacts.
7. Muséographie démonstrative	Démonstration active menée devant les visiteurs. Interaction démonstrateur-public	Saisir les processus explicatifs et leurs rapports aux objets.

Aujourd'hui, nous connaissons, par des enquêtes, les caractéristiques déterminantes qui motivent le choix d'une activité de temps libre chez nos publics visés; les gens fondent leur décision de visiter sur :

— le caractère valorisant de l'activité;
— le confort physique et psychologique anticipé;
— l'occasion de vivre des interactions sociales;
— l'occasion d'apprendre;
— l'occasion de vivre une nouvelle expérience;
— l'occasion de participer activement.

Nous pouvons donc constater que la présence d'activités d'interprétation personnalisée répond à plusieurs de ces facteurs positifs de choix; quand elle est réussie, cette forme d'interprétation contribue à plusieurs titres, à doter l'institution d'occasions que les visiteurs recherchent et souhaitent trouver dans leurs activités de temps libre. La volonté affirmée de placer le visiteur au centre des préoccupations des concepteurs, de même que le désir d'accroître la fréquentation, devraient assurer le maintien et le développement, dans nos sites et musées, de ces interventions interprétatives personnalisées.

Notes

1. George Ellis BURCAW, *Introduction to Museum Work*, AASLH, Nashville, 1984, p. 6.

2. G. Ellis Burcaw, op. cit., p. 115.

3. Michael BELCHER, *Exhibitions in Museums*, Leicester University Press, Smithsonian Institution Press, Leicester, Washington, 1991, p. 37.

4. Peter VERGO, «The Reticent Object», *in The New Museology*, Reaktion Books, London, 1989, p. 46.

5. David DEAN, *Museum Exhibition. Theory and Practice*, Routledge, London, 1994, p. 3.

6. Jan VERHAAR et Han MEETER, *Project Model Exhibitions*, Reinwardt Academie, 1989, p. 26.

7. En collaboration, *La muséologie selon Georges Henri Rivière*, Dunod, 1989, p. 265.

8. Jean DAVALLON, «Le musée est-il véritablement un média?», *in Publics et musées*, n°2, décembre 1992, p. 108.

9. Ross J. LOOMIS, *Museum Visitor Evaluation: New Tool for Management*, AASLH, Nashville, 1987, p. 160. Nous traduisons.

10. Manon NIQUETTE, «Pour une analyse de la réception et du partage social des connaissances», *in Publics et musées*, n°5, janvier-juin 1994, p. 87.

11. Cette traduction est tirée de *Vagues. Une anthologie de la nouvelle muséologie*, vol. 1, M.N.E.S., Mâcon, 1992, p. 248-249. En anglais, voir Freeman Tilden, *Interpreting our Heritage*, University of North Carolina Press, 1977, p. 8.

12. Définition adoptée par l'American Association of Museums.

13. Définition proposée par Interpretation Canada, 1976.

14. Définition proposée par l'Association québécoise d'interprétation du patrimoine (AQIP), 1980.

15. Voir *Néologie en marche*, «Interprétation du patrimoine», n°38-39, Québec, 1984, p. 61.

16. David Dean, *op. cit.*, p. 6.

17. J. Mark SMITH, «Interpretation & Philosophy» *in Interpscan*, vol 20, n°4, hiver 1992-1993, p.5.

18. John VEVERKA, *Interpretive Master Planning*, Interpretation Publication and Resource Center, Falcon Press, 1994, p. 19. L'auteur en vient, dans le même sens, à définir une «exposition interprétative» ainsi : «An exhibit is interpretative if it makes the topic come to life through active visitor involvement and extreme relevance to the everyday life of the viewer.» *op. cit.*, p. 125.

19. William T. ALDERSON, Shirley Payne LOW, *Interpretation of Historic Sites*, AASLH, Nashville, 1987, p. 28.

20. Voir aussi notre article «De l'exposition d'objets à l'exposition-expérience : la muséographie multimédia», *in Les muséographies multimédias : métamorphose du musée*, Musée de la civilisation du Québec, Québec, 1995, p. 7-14.

❖ The Language of Live Interpretation: Making Contact

John A. Veverka
John Veverka & Associates
Dansville, Michigan

Pour être efficace en communication didactique, l'interprète doit en connaître autant sur la psychologie des visiteurs que sur le sujet qu'il interprète. Entrer en rapport avec les visiteurs doit faire que ceux-ci comprennent le message ou l'histoire qu'on leur «interprète». Cet article donne des idées d'interprétation pour les visiteurs de musées, qui tiennent compte de leurs besoins d'apprentissage. Une stratégie de planification didactique partielle sur le développement de thèmes didactiques, sur des objectifs didactiques mesurables et sur l'analyse des visiteurs y est élaborée.

Interpretors[*] must speak many languages. Not particularly foreign languages, but rather the language of the everyday person. Depending on the site or resource they are working with they may be called upon to speak:

- the language of children
- the language of rural visitors
- the language of urban visitors
- the language of "experts"
- the language of local residents
- the language of tourists, and more.

In interpretive terms, this means that they must *relate* to the everyday lives of everyday people. To help the interpretor do this there are a few general concepts and principles of "recreational learning" that may come in handy. This paper will look at not only how to speak the conceptual "language" of the visitor, but how to make actual "contact" with your message or story.

Understand Your Visitors

To be successful with live interpretation the interpretor should know as much about how visitors learn and remember information presented to them as they do about the resources or artifacts they are interpreting . It has been my experience that most museum

---

[*]   Interpretor is spelled with an "or" to distinguish the person from a foreign language translator.

interpretors are well trained in the materials of the museum or historic site, but receive little or no training in "visitor communication strategies." Here are a few general learning concepts and principles that may be of use in preparing and delivering your live interpretive program.

Is museum theatre really the "last" form of truly popular theatre?

Conceptually, the programme represents a broad synthesis of the kinds of ideas developed in the successful full-time programme at the Science Museum of Minnesota and individual theatre projects at other museums, combined with various approaches to first-person and theatrical or quasi-theatrical interpretation at a multitude of heritage sites.

A current statement of objectives might be as follows:

(a) To stimulate emotional and intellectual interest in and response to the Museum's collections and exhibits.
(b) To provoke argument (but not to argue a point).
(c) To pose questions (but not to provide answers).
(d) To show what needs to be thought about (but not to state what needs to be done).
(e) To show that the interpretation of history and culture depends partly upon whose perspective you choose in the story you are telling.
(f) To show that an artefact, a social interaction, or a transaction may have many meanings, some of which may not yet have occurred to anyone.
(g) To show that some of these meanings may not yet have existed, and may perhaps not exist until some time in the future.
(h) To explore and to celebrate the similarities which join us in the human community, and the differences between us which make us fascinating to each other.
(i) To reveal "the other" in ourselves, by showing the familiar in unfamiliar ways, and the unfamiliar in our own back yard.
(j) To provoke laughter and tears, to excite, to startle, to shock, and occasionally to horrify the visitor, but above all to make sure that his or her visit is never "ordinary."
(k) To demonstrate and embody the idea that the experience the Museum offers is immensely enjoyable, stimulating and fun.

If there is an over-riding theme in these propositions, it is that theatre at the CMC should be about *surprise* and *provocation*, with the further objective that it stimulate questions in the visitor: questions about the artefacts, the exhibit, the visitor's own attitudes, and particularly about the nature of the museum experience itself.

Source: Jeanne Cannizzo and David Parry, "Museum Theatre in the 1990s: Trail-blazer or Camp-follower?" in *Museums and the Appropriation of Culture* (London: The Athlone Press, 1994), p. 45.

Learning Concepts

1. We all bring our pasts to the present. Try to find out how the visitors' knowledge or experience level relates to your story or resource. Have they recently been to other museums or historic sites? If so, which ones? Were those past visits good experiences?

2. First impressions are especially important. Make sure that the first impressions the visitors have of you and your program are outstanding! This may be your greeting of the visitors at the start of the program, your appearance (are you in costume or uniform?), the visual look of the program starting point or other non-verbal cues.

3. Meanings are in people, not words. If I were to say the word "tree," what tree would come to your mind? We all have our own "visual dictionaries" and personal interpretations of words. When you describe an artifact or other resource in a lecture, what do the visitors visualize? Make sure that you have the appropriate visual aides with you to avoid "meaning" differences between you and the visitors. Be aware too that most technical terms are new for visitors. Be sure to define them — don't take it for granted that the visitors know what they mean.

4. Simplicity and organization clarify messages. The chief aim of interpretation is provocation NOT instruction. During an interpretive program your job is not to make the visitors experts in history, science, art, etc. Your job is to inspire them to want to learn more. Keep the program simple, focused, and fun.

Learning Principles

Here are a few general learning principles that will help with the live interpretation program planning and presentation.

1. People learn better when they're actively involved in the learning process.
2. People learn better when they're using as many senses as appropriate.
3. People prefer to learn what is of most value to them at the present.
4. Learning that people discover for themselves generates a special and vital excitement and satisfaction.
5. Learning requires activity on the part of the learner.
6. People learn best from hands-on experience.

With these concepts and principles in mind, you should also remember the following. Visitors remember:

10% of what they hear,
30% of what they read,

50% of what they see,

90% of what they do.

Planning for Contact

To help insure its success, *every* interpretive program should be planned. Planning steps would include the following.

1. WHAT? What is the main theme of the program? A theme is expressed in a complete sentence, such as "The logging history of Northern Minnesota still affects each of us here today." Another theme might be "The early settlers of the Rouge River Valley found creative ways to farm the valley." The interpretive program then "illustrates the theme to the visitor."

2. WHY? Why are you giving the program? What are your objectives for the live interpretation? The following are the three kinds of objectives that are needed in planning an interpretive program, with an example of each.

> Learning Objectives. At the completion of the program 60% of the visitors will be able to describe three innovative farming tools invented by Rouge River Valley farmers.

> Behavioral Objectives. At the completion of the program the majority of the visitors will want to look at the tools in the museum collection.

> Emotional Objectives. By the completion of the program the curiosity and interest level in the visitors will be raised so that they will be motivated to want to look at the museum collections, and attend other live interpretive programs sometime in the future.

Remember, objectives are measurable. They are also tools to help you focus on just what you want your program to accomplish. As you consider the theme or topic for your live presentation, and have written the objectives you want the program to accomplish, there are two very important questions you must ask yourself about your program.

1. **Why would a visitor want to know that**? This is an important question for you to answer about the information you are planning to present. If you can't think of several reasons why a visitor would *want* to learn the information in your program, you have a problem! This is where you RELATE to the visitor — give them a reason to attend the program.

2. **How do you want the visitor to use the information you are interpreting to them**? If you don't want them to use the information, then why are you doing the

Comédien de Dramamuse, MCC

Dramamuse actor, CMC

program? The answer to this question will become your behavioral objectives for your program.

You don't want to spend a lot of time giving answers to questions that no one is asking!

3. **WHO**? Who are the visitors coming to the program? What is their age, knowledge level, interest level, etc. How much time do they have? What do you think some of "their objectives" for attending your program might be? Do they have any special needs (visual or hearing problems, handicaps, etc.)?

Considering the What?, Why?, and Who? parts of your live interpretation program will help you focus your time and efforts. The answers to the two questions above will help make sure the program is relevant to the visitor, not just the curators or resource experts.

The Three Bs

Interpretors are in the BENEFIT business. Your interpretive program should be planned to illustrate to the visitors (and agency managers) three benefits. You should consider how the program will help:

Benefit the site or resource. For example, will the program help reduce damage to historic structures, or help keep visitors on designated trails?

Benefit the visitor. How will attending your program benefit the visitors? What's in it for them? The answer to this question is what you use to advertise the program.

How will your program benefit the agency you work for? More memberships? More gift-shop sales? A better political "image"?

What is the Product of Your Product?

In doing live interpretation it is easy to get caught up in the "interpretation" and forget what our real product is. By selling "the product of the product" you put the idea of your program in a context that the potential user knows and understands (relates to). For example, in the commercial world:

Are you selling drills, or holes?
Are you selling cosmetics, or "hope"?
Are you selling new cars, or status?

What is the product of the product for your live interpretation?

Are you selling looking at artifacts *or* valuing the cultures/people that made them?
Are you selling looking at rooms of furniture *or* pride in the people that made and use them?
Are you selling "collections" *or* the benefits to all people in the saving and conservation of historic materials?

To Make Contact . . .

We know from years of interpretive research that the "live interpretor" is the most powerful of all of our interpretive media and opportunities. The interpretor can instantly "read" an audience and make adjustments in the program to help relate to the different audiences they may encounter. They can look into the visitors' eyes and grab the visitors' imaginations and emotions. They can take a boring topic and make it come to life for the visitors. But to be successful, live interpretation requires that the interpretor think about and plan for its success. Being successful with any live interpretive program requires the interpretor to identify what *success* means. The successful interpretor will need to understand how the visitors learn and remember information, and how to provoke, relate and reveal the story to them. They will have a focused message (theme) and objectives that they are going to strive to accomplish. They never stop trying to improve their program

Comédienne de Dramamuse, MCC
Dramamuse actor, CMC

and trying new ways of inspiring the visitors. The reward the interpretor receives from his or her work really cannot be put into words — a deep sense of satisfaction, pride and more. The reward the visitors receive from the interpretor's efforts are equally as powerful. For when a trained, focused, and inspirational interpretor meets with visitors hungry for inspiration, something special happens. They make contact and the journey begins.

References

Ham, Sam H. (1992). *Environmental Interpretation: A Practical Guide for People with Big Ideas and Small Budgets.* North American Press, Golden, CO.

Tilden, Freeman (1957). *Interpreting Our Heritage.* The University of North Carolina Press, Chapel Hill.

Veverka, John A. (1995). *Interpretive Master Planning.* Falcon Press, Helena, MT.

❖ Les techniques théâtrales... un atout pour l'animateur

Monique Camirand
Consultante à l'animation et à l'éducation muséale
Paroles en jeux, inc.
Montréal (Québec)

Many sites or exhibition centres are increasingly opting for theatrical interpretation to capture the public's attention and imprint themselves on its memory. The question is, should an actor or an interpreter be hired to play an actual, symbolic or imaginary character? If the choice is an interpreter, it then becomes essential to provide that individual with basic training in theatre techniques which will enable him or her to develop skills related to voice, gesture, appearance, emotions, costume, performance and staging. Without this training and regular follow-up, the interpreter risks failing to ensure the credibility of the character with the public, thus marring the quality of the interpretation.

Un des principaux rôles de l'animateur est de faire découvrir un sujet d'ordre historique, scientifique, artistique ou autre. Dans un contexte d'exposition ou d'interprétation, une panoplie de moyens sont mis en place pour appuyer les propos de l'animateur. Son défi... faire vivre son sujet et l'esprit des lieux afin de capter l'attention des visiteurs et de marquer leur mémoire.

Les techniques théâtrales peuvent devenir un atout important pour aider l'animateur à relever ce défi. Entre autres, l'animateur apprendra à varier son ton de voix et sa gestuelle en fonction de l'espace muséal où il se trouve et du message qu'il désire transmettre aux visiteurs; il se déplacera d'un objet ou d'un lieu à un autre, après avoir réfléchi à une mise en scène qui met en valeur le sujet mais aussi la place du visiteur; s'il présente une animation théâtrale, il se préparera à incarner un personnage réel, symbolique ou imaginaire pour accueillir les visiteurs, raconter un fait vécu, faire la démonstration d'une technique ou encore simuler la réalité du passé. Cette forme d'animation théâtrale se vit à proximité du public et favorise l'interaction entre l'animateur et le visiteur, entre le sujet et l'objet, contrairement au spectacle qui se vit habituellement sur scène sans interaction directe avec les spectateurs.

Plusieurs sites ou centres d'exposition désirent avoir recours à cette forme d'animation théâtrale qui attire les visiteurs de tout âge. Cependant, quelques questions se posent : Doit-on engager un comédien ou un animateur pour jouer un personnage? Quel

Animatrice au MCC
CMC animator

programme de formation devons-nous offrir pour assurer un travail de qualité? Devrait-il y avoir un suivi après la formation?

Une réflexion s'impose pour pouvoir faire des choix judicieux. D'une part, le comédien de formation connaît les principales techniques théâtrales pour faire vivre un sujet. Par contre, il n'est pas un spécialiste du contenu ni, dans bien des cas, de l'animation et de l'interaction avec un public. D'autre part, l'animateur est souvent sélectionné parce qu'il connaît le contenu et qu'il possède les qualités requises pour réaliser une bonne animation mais... il n'est pas comédien.

Le programme de formation devra donc combler les manques de l'un ou de l'autre. Aujourd'hui, dans le cadre de ce symposium, notre choix s'arrête sur l'animateur. Dans le cadre de sa formation, il est alors essentiel de consacrer plusieurs heures aux techniques théâtrales pour lui permettre de développer les principales aptitudes reliées à la voix, aux gestes, au regard, aux émotions, au port du costume, à l'interprétation, à la mise en scène. Sans cette formation de base, l'animateur risque de manquer de confiance devant l'ampleur de la tâche pour assurer la crédibilité du personnage face au public. On ne s'improvise pas comédien du jour au lendemain. Il faut comprendre les techniques, les pratiquer, les intégrer et les répéter dans l'espace muséal avant de se présenter aux visiteurs. Un animateur motivé a de fortes chances de réussir, surtout s'il se sent épaulé pendant et après sa formation.

Le suivi est aussi important que la formation pour assurer un travail de qualité. Selon les moyens matériels ou financiers et la disponibilité du personnel, le suivi peut se faire de différentes façons. L'idéal est de filmer l'animateur sur cassette vidéo, sans oublier les réactions du public afin d'obtenir une vision globale de la réalité. Si cela est impossible, il serait important d'enregistrer la période d'animation sur cassette audio pour entendre et «sentir» le personnage et écouter les propos des visiteurs. Une autre façon, très simple, est de demander à une ou deux personnes (collègues, personne-ressource en théâtre, superviseur, etc.) d'observer l'animation théâtrale dans sa globalité.

Ce suivi, qui relève davantage de la formation continue que de l'évaluation, permet d'identifier à partir de critères préétablis les points forts et les points faibles de l'animation. Ainsi, durant la période estivale, il peut y avoir trois suivis : un premier en début de saison pour observer le jeu et les réactions du public et apporter les modifications requises en fonction de la réalité; un deuxième, quatre ou cinq semaines plus tard pour vérifier l'intégration du personnage et la qualité d'interaction avec les visiteurs; un troisième, un mois avant la fin de la période estivale pour permettre à l'animateur de conserver sa motivation jusqu'à la fin de la saison en se lançant des défis personnels et professionnels car il y a toujours place à l'amélioration.

En somme, après plusieurs années d'expérience en animation, nous constatons que les techniques théâtrales sont un atout majeur pour l'animateur car ses principaux outils de travail sont : sa voix, ses gestes, sa posture, ses émotions et sa qualité de présence avec le public. Il peut maîtriser son sujet mais avoir de la difficulté à le communiquer, à le faire vivre, à le mettre en scène. Pour y arriver, il faut être formé et surtout avoir un laps de temps raisonnable pour pratiquer avant d'être en mesure d'offrir une animation de qualité qui rendra la visite inoubliable.

The task of interpretive theatre, like all interpretation, is to communicate ideas and to get audiences thinking about a subject. Some exercise of imagination, or suspension of disbelief, is helpful. But if the principal impression with which visitors leave is that they have just witnessed the reincarnation of real people from the past, then form has overwhelmed content and interpretation has failed. From this perspective, it is not so very significant if interpreters' speech does not reproduce the language or dialects of the characters they represent, or if costume and sets are replicas rather than original artifacts. Although the whole issue of visitors' ability to distinguish between what is real and what is simulated in museum presentations is complex and deserves more attention, structured theatre is a form of presentation familiar to, and so not deceiving of, most visitors.

Theatre is not the best interpretive technique for every topic, every exhibition, every visitor. It is one more addition to an expanding toolbox which includes static and interactive exhibits, labels, pictorial materials, audiovisual presentations or effects, hands-on, computer games, audioguides and the spectrum of other live interpretation techniques. Although the interpretive strategies of a museum will be influenced by the philosophical, cultural and social concepts of which it is founded, it is wise to have as wide as possible an array of interpretive tools at one's disposal. As museums become increasingly aware of the diversified interest, learning styles, tastes and behavior of their visitors, the value of a variety of specialized communications media becomes clearer. No one interpretive technique is inherently superior, although we still need a better understanding of the relative educational effectiveness of the options in a given situation.

Source: Stephen Alsford and David Parry, "Interpretive Theatre: A Role in Museums?" *Museum Management and Curatorship*, 10, 1 (March 1991), p. 16.

❖ To Be or Not to Be in Character? That is the Question

Richard H. Pickering
Director of Special Projects
Plimoth Plantation
Plymouth, Massachussetts

L'histoire vivante racontée à la première personne est populaire auprès des visiteurs, mais elle n'est pas appropriée à tous les musées d'histoire. Les établissements doivent se demander si le jeu de rôles constitue le meilleur moyen d'interprétation de leur site et s'il remplit leur mission éducative. Ils doivent examiner les relations de travail entre les chercheurs, les interprètes et les conservateurs, parce que c'est la collaboration entre ces trois catégories de travailleurs qui assurera le succès d'un programme à la première personne.

First-person living history is popular with visitors, but it is not appropriate for all history museums. The historic site and the institution's mission may best be served by reenactments on video, static exhibits and third-person interpretation. The following remarks offer some criteria for museums considering a role-playing program. They are based on my eleven years of experience with Plimoth Plantation, a private, non-profit living history museum located 45 miles south of Boston in Plymouth, Massachusetts. Established in 1947, the museum exhibits include three open-air sites: the 1627 Pilgrim Village, Hobbamock's (Wampanoag Indian) Homesite and *Mayflower II*. Plimoth Plantation's on-site programming employs both first- and third-person interpretation.

The role-players in the reconstructed Pilgrim Village and aboard *Mayflower II* take on the identities of actual residents of 17th-century Plymouth. They dress in reproduction period clothes and speak in the dialect of their character's home region. Roles range in status from single person to housewife, servant to master. Together, these roles depict the social life of a village which knew both enlightenment and superstition, success and failure. This precise community portrait is possible because of extensive genealogical research, a wealth of documents describing the Pilgrims' first years in New England, and the burgeoning scholarship on Colonial British America.

First-person interpretation, because of its humanity, is the most effective way of dispelling myths about the Pilgrims as dour, repressed Puritans. By immersing the visitor in a markedly different spiritual and emotional climate, interactive role-playing heightens awareness of the contrast between modern and medieval world views.

Hobbamock's Homesite represents the encampment of a Native American family who lived along the brook near the Plymouth settlement. Here, the interpretive staff, despite their costumes and activities, do not assume character roles, but explain the exhibit from a 20th-century perspective. Myths about the Indians are commonplace. Many visitors arrive with preconceptions and stereotypes about Native American cultures; these would be impossible to discuss if the Homesite interpreters were role-playing. There are additional communications concerns. Few Wampanoag spoke English in 1627, so conversations with visitors would have to be translated. Also, the recovery of their Native language requires further research. Linguists still do not fully understand Wampanoag syntax and pronunciation.

Here are a few things to discuss when considering a role-playing program.

First-person living history is always informative and entertaining, but its practitioners must ensure that it is responsible. How many curators, each evening as they drift off to sleep, make a silent wish that their velvet ropes shall never disappear? As museum professionals, we must share their dread that original sites, exhibiting original objects should be used for demonstrations. The re-creation of daily activities, one of living history's most vivifying elements, is unthinkable in the delicate world of original artifacts. Reconstructed environments, filled with reproduction objects, are most appropriate for living history and first-person interpretation. In this context, historical characters can be shown interacting with the everyday objects of their lives. Also, visitors may sit on furniture, touch textiles and heft tools without causing a preservation crisis.

Some sites are too extensive to be staffed as working communities. The expense would approach Hollywood proportions. The stories that some museums tell demand too much historical time as well as geographical space for effective role-playing. While not impossible in a first-person format, the depiction of generational change is better suited to theatre settings, guided tours and static exhibits. Many visitors are confused simply moving through an unfamiliar museum space without adding the concept of change over time.

When considering the use of role-players, living history museums must evaluate the accuracy and visual seamlessness of their material re-creation. No matter how breathtaking the character interpretation, environmental anachronisms may undermine visitor trust. This issue of trust is of particular importance if the first-person experience is a total immersion and the historical presentation is not mediated by a third-person guide. The popular reputation of a museum is sustained not only by painstaking research, interpretation and reconstruction, but by the visitor's pleasure in her inability to find flaws in the representation of the materials and mentality of a past world.

A single inaccuracy can lead the visitor to question the validity of the entire experience. Means and message are inseparable when the historic presentation is totally first-person. One of the programmatic goals of first-person living history is the suspension of distrust as well as the suspension of disbelief. Deserved trust is the chief defense against critics who accuse living history sites of being little better than theme parks. With disbelief suspended, any visitor may enjoy a re-created community as a fantasy world, yet when intellectual distrust is overcome, the thinking visitor tacitly acknowledges the scholarship behind the representation.

The museum which presents the past through unscripted role-playing places heavy demands on its research staff and its interpreters. Museum theatre and guided tours shape visitor questions to a greater degree than is possible with improvisational first-person, though in the latter format the conversations between characters and visitors do have repetitive elements. "What do you do for a living? What are you cooking? Are you married? How many people live in this house? Where do you go to the bathroom?" Once these basic questions are answered, then more personal interests begin to shape the interaction. A visitor may want details on midwifery, religion, world affairs, sports, embroidery, crime, animal husbandry, sexuality or tooth pulling. The list of possibilities is endless. It is imperative that interpreters' needs drive institutional research because they are the chief means whereby a living history museum touches the public. While a role-player should not be afraid to say, "I don't know," when confounded by a question, a masterful interpreter is widely read in his period and prefers to say, "I don't know," when that response punctuates the intellectual limits of a character's mentality.

A successful role-playing program is supported by (1) training manuals that distill recent scholarship in all subject areas necessary for creating a persona within the historical context, (2) ongoing research memos in areas of need as identified by the interpretation staff and (3) the active involvement of researchers in helping role-players build their characters. One exciting element of this visitor/interpreter/historian relationship is the democratization of research. No area of inquiry (as long as the question posed is appropriate to the period reconstructed) is outside the realm of the museum's representation.

An unscripted first-person interpretation program offers tremendous challenges to a museum's research and reproduction abilities, yet when that format is the best means of fulfilling the institution's educational mission, the ceaseless process of learning and revising becomes rewarding in itself.

Outdoor historic sites at their best often confront the normal expectations of visitors with a kind of shock, an environmental surprise that can provide those moments of cognitive dissonance in which true learning about the historic context can occur. I would argue that in the museum theatrical moments . . . — despite the lack of the real offending substance and smell — can create through good performance those same windows for learning. In other words, can provide moments, and sometimes extended periods, when surprise disarms the visitor and opens the way for genuine, felt connections with the context, the object, and the people — and for the assimilation of other interesting and surprising information.

In *Le vase brisé*, in fact, there is a good deal of such information for the taking. Quite apart from the details of public sanitation and daily life in the tavern, the visitor is introduced to the complex web of urban regulations that plagued the lives of the citizens of New France every bit as much as their modern equivalents plague our own lives today. In the counter-accusations which follow the tavern keeper's initial charge, the barrel maker accuses her of selling liquor illegally to the native population (incidentally raising in the visitors' minds a current as well as an historic social problem). She then accuses him of eating meat in Lent. This of course is also against the rules for him as a good Catholic — a bit of information that many visitors will undoubtedly know. But he then produces a further surprise: no, he says, it was *beaver* flesh, and therefore legitimate:

M. Barolet : ... mon bon monsieur, cette viande mangée qui tant tracasse la gueuse n'était que du castor!

Mme Aubry : Et alors?

M. Duchemin : C'est que voilà, madame, le castor est permis.

Mme Aubry : Et pour quelle raison?

M. Duchemin : La queue de l'animal, par l'Église, est classée amphibie.

Mme Aubry : Et alors?

M. Barolet : C'est ni chair, ni poisson!

M. Duchemin : On peut en consommer tous les jours de l'abstinence.

Mme Aubry : Il faut être jésuite pour distinguer cela!

M. Duchemin : Dame Aubry, trois cents livres pour injure à l'Église!

Source: "Surprising the Visitor: Interpretive Theatre at the Canadian Museum of Civilization," conference proceedings of the Museum Education Association of Australia, September 30 to October 4, 1991.

❖ Music, a Language of Interpretation

Scott Mair
Evergreen Co-op
Calgary, Alberta

Écrire une chanson est un geste très personnel. Certains écrivent la musique d'abord, puis ajoutent les paroles. D'autres font le contraire. Et d'autres, comme moi, écrivent les deux en même temps. Il n'y a pas de bonne ou de mauvaise manière d'écrire une chanson. Ce que je livre ici, c'est ce qui a marché pour moi, et j'espère que cela marchera pour vous aussi. La musique est vraiment l'outil d'interprétation individuel le plus puissant qui soit.

Music has always been part of interpretation: an interpreter and their guitar at sunset; a moving sideshow soundtrack; a camp-fire sing-a-long. With good reason. There is no single more powerful tool available to interpreters than music.

Music evokes mood. Every time I hear Connie Kaldor sing *Wood River*, I cry. I can't help it. They're good tears, tears that come with a warm fuzzy feeling, and there's nothing I can do, or want to do, to stop them. I'm sure you have songs like that: that always make you smile; that inspire; that bring a touch of melancholy. Could you imagine a movie without music — much of your emotional response to a movie is facilitated by the music. As interpreters we help our visitors develop an emotional attachment to our natural and cultural resources, imagine the power of your interpretive message when it's linked to a song that evokes a complementary mood.

Music can instantly set a time and place. I'm embarrassed to admit it, but whenever I hear the Knack singing *My Sharrona* I'm instantly transported back to Moose Lake Provincial Park in my first summer as an interpreter. As soon as the opening chords of *Buddy, Can You Spare a Dime* sound, I'm primed for a program on life during the Great Depression. Letting the music establish the setting frees you valuable words for more important work.

Music helps establish character. Certain characteristics just naturally attach themselves to certain styles of music. Who's ever heard of a laid-back march? Again, why waste words describing the *characteristics* of your interpretive program characters when music can do it instantly? For example, the American elk is the only member of the deer family whose antlers sweep back (like duck-tail hair of the '50s); he's a musician (bugling to attract the ladies), and wants as many mates as he can handle. Is there any mammal that personifies the '50s Elvis image better? Elvis the Elk is a character already defined by a whole genre of music.

Music changes pace. A song can go from happy to sad in an instant, without seeming contrived (try that with text). A song can infuse your audience with energy or calm a raucous crowd.

Music is a tool for teaching. Advertisers know the power of music. Why can we remember a commercial jingle after one listen, but have to struggle for days to learn the helminth taxonomy of the salmonid hind gut? After one listen to *I was a Teenage Tapeworm*, you too will be convinced of the teaching potential of music. The information essentially piggybacks on the music into your memory. When visitors leave your program singing the songs, you've taught them something.

Music attracts audiences. For the first three years following a switch to a more theatrical style of programming we routinely attracted 32% of our available campground audience to our evening programs. The year we began including more music in our programs (1988), our attendance jumped 5 percentage points. And each following year we've continued to add an additional 5 points to the percentage of our campground users attending our evening programs. This year, our programs should attract over 60% of the available campground audience. Coincidence? I think not!

The power of music. Much of the reason why music is such a useful tool for interpreters is because its an integral part of our popular culture, part of our shared experience. This common ground can form the foundation for us to build learning experiences upon.

Music is versatile. It can be used in any style of interpretation — theatrical or traditional. It can be used at prop talks and on guided walks, in theatres and classrooms, in costume, with puppets, or in uniform. And best of all, they can have a life beyond the program they were written for: a song written to describe calypso orchids can fit into programs on spring; a song developed for a theatrical event can be just as effective on CD, CD-ROM, video, etc.

I think most of music's power may rest with how it interacts with our brains. Considering the rhythms of our lives — our breathing, heartbeat, brainwaves, the circadian variations of hormonal levels — is it any wonder we respond so viscerally to musical rhythms?

Music also involves higher brain functions, typically being processed by the right cerebral cortex in non-musicians and by the left for musicians (who analyze the time signature, key, poly-rhythmic variations and whatever else musicians do when they listen to music). When you add lyrics, more areas of the brain become involved as grammar, syntax and symbolic meaning are processed. Listening to music is a multidimensional neurological activity that involves divergent parts of the brain. The potential of linkages between so many different parts of the brain may explain the versatility of music as an interpretive tool.

Using Music

If music is so great, why aren't more interpreters using it? Many people think you have to be a *musician* to use music. If you play the guitar, you have to play well. If you sing *a cappella*, you have to have a good voice. To some extent this is true. It's no fun listening to someone croak their way through a song. But standing up and playing an instrument or singing without accompaniment are not the only ways to use music interpretation.

Using copyright-cleared music to set the mood can work just as well for an interpretive program as it does at the movies. Played behind the inspirational part of your program, moving music can add power to your message. If you can turn on a tape recorder, you can use music to accentuate your program.

It doesn't take a lot of practice to play *Old Suzzanah* on the harmonica, but it will add so much to the feel of your program — especially if you're playing a Klondike prospector. Even if you hit a few clunkers it's probably truer to the playing style of a real sourdough than a virtuoso performance would be. With a little practice, folk instruments like penny whistles, ocarinas, bamboo flutes and Jews harps are surprisingly easy to coax a tune out of. And for that matter it's not all that difficult to learn to strum a cord or three on the guitar.

If you insist you're totally inept with instruments, not to worry; there are thousands of songs out there waiting to have lyrics rewritten to convey your message. Your voice isn't sweet enough to carry the tune unaccompanied? Karaoke to the rescue — hundreds of songs with rich musical accompaniment to help keep you in key and on the beat, without the burden of someone else already singing on the tape. If you're still not sure about the quality of your voice, sing in character. A quick viewing of the Muppets will show you how *off* you can be and still get away with it. Still insist you can't sing? Rex Harrison made a whole career out of not singing. Talk the lyrics. If it's good enough for Rex and Lorne Greene (remember Ringo?), it can work for you too. If worst comes to worst, there's rap. No singing talent required there, you have to be BAD.

> *Don't let your attitude intrude, on your singing mood,*
> *Anyone can do it, I ain't bein' rude.*
> *You can make a million reasons, some for every season*
> *To stop from makin' noise that is really pleasin'.*

In the end it's up to you, decide what you can do,
But if Scott can do it, hell man, you can too!

Writing Lyrics

The lyrics are what separate interpretive songs from all other songs. If they don't teach, they're not interpretive. The information must be foremost. Before you even sit down to write, you have to have a very clear idea about the information you want to be conveyed in the song. One simple trick is to write down exactly what pieces of information you want to get across. As you include them in the song, cross them off the list. It's simple, but it works.

Once you've itemized the information, are there elements of the story that must be advanced in the song as well? Does your song on damselfly ecology and behaviour also have to promote the story of Daphne and Danny, two crazy nymphs in love? Does your song on bear identification also have to set up the tone for your section responding to attack situations?

If you're rewriting lyrics to an established song, the format of the song is already decided: the rhyme scheme, the beats per line, the beats per bar. For an original song all this information must also be established before you begin to write (more about this later), but some writers find it useful to rewrite the lyrics to an existing song and then write new music based on these new lyrics. The structure of the original song provides a foundation for them to build their song upon.

You're ready to go once you have the interpretive songwriter's single most useful tool: the rhyming dictionary! Yes, such things exist (it was a surprise to me too), and no, you're no less of a poet for using one (interpretive lyrics can in no way be confused with real poetry).

After I've decided on the basic style of the song (blues, operatic, country, etc.), the tempo and rhythm, what information has to be conveyed and perhaps even the rhyme scheme, I scribble down the first line that comes to mind that meets all these parameters. Often it suggests a whole series of lines and the song writes itself. But if it doesn't, I look up the last word I've written. *"Orange, orange . . . what rhymes with orange?"* In some cases you have to start again. Eventually you'll get a line that fits with the song, and has lots of potential rhymes to build your song from.

A few more tips to keep in mind:

- Don't be a rhyme slut. It rhymes or it doesn't. Don't force it.
- Use multi-syllabic rhymes whenever you can. Overuse of simple, monosyllabic rhymes makes your lyrics predictable and less interesting to listen to.

- Give your audience a reason to concentrate on what the lyrics say. Humour is a good motivator. Because an audience is most likely to listen to the first two lines of a verse, if they are funny, it encourages your audience to listen to the next two lines.
- Make sure your rhyme schemes are readily apparent. As the audience anticipates the upcoming rhyme, when the word is finally said it has greater impact and is more likely to be remembered.
- Try to have information in every line you write. You'll be surprised how easy it becomes to write lines that are informative and entertaining at the same time.
- Listen to the way your lines sound. Do they have rhythm, energy and colour even without the music?
- Increase the instructive value of your songs with repetitive choruses and echo lines (where the audience repeats the line back to the performer).
- There are no hard and fast rules. Anything can work. But *be ruthless* in your evaluation to ensure that it does.

Writing Music

When you write lyrics to other people's music, you have to concern yourself with copyrights. You are using someone else's intellectual property for which you legally require their permission. Writing your own music is an option that is not as daunting as it appears. The structure of a song and the characteristics of different styles of music provide a foundation that you need only embellish to complete your song. It may not be quite as easy as that, but the difficulty of the task is not the greatest obstacle in the songwriting process — your attitude is. Saying, *"I can't write a song,"* is the only impediment in your way. If you enjoy music, you can write songs.

Let's look at a song and see what we're up against. A common song structure is a four-line verse with a two-line chorus repeated between each verse. The two chorus lines usually rhyme with each other and the verse lines can rhyme in a variety of combinations. Theoretically each line of the chorus and verse can have a different melody, which would mean you'd have to write up to six lines of music, which are repeated with each verse and repetition of the chorus. Six lines of melody doesn't seem nearly as difficult a task as writing a whole song did a few moments ago.

However, six lines of melody is the *most* you'll have to write. In many songs each line of the verse and chorus repeats the same melody, so you may have to write only *one* line of melody. Even I can do that!

Each style of music also has a structure that can help you build a song. When you hear a song on the radio, how do you know it's a country song? Even if you don't know anything about flats and sharps, minor keys, 7th chords and time signatures, it's not hard to tell a country song from heavy metal, and opera from rhythm and blues. Best of all you don't have to really understand the structure to use it. Intuitively, you already know how to recognize various musical styles. Try singing songs you already know in styles that they're not normally performed in. How about *Don't Let Your Babies Grow Up to Be Cowboys* in an operatic style, or *What a Friend We Have in Jesus* as a heavy metal tune?

The information you are trying to get across will help you determine the musical style to use. Clearly, a song about elk, or at least a song about Elvis the Elk, should be in a '50s rock and roll style. What Elvis talks about in the song will further define the style. Clearly, *Don't Mess Around with an Elk in Rut* is not a crooning ballad. What I do at this point is to sing some of the songs that represent the style I think is appropriate for this song (e.g., *Heartbreak Hotel, Don't Be Cruel*). Singing these songs, mixing them up, throwing in some of the lyrics I think might work almost always leads me to a few melody lines that set up the rest of the song. My musician friends do essentially the same thing, but on their instruments.

A few tips to keep in mind:

- Happy, upbeat songs are much easier for audiences to listen to, and consequently are more effective at conveying information.
- Listen to lots of music and think about what makes it distinctive.
- Practise singing songs you know in styles they're not usually performed in. Not only is it a lot of fun, but it will help you write in a greater variety of styles too.
- There are no hard and fast rules. Anything can work, but be ruthless: ensure that it does.

Writing a song is a very personal thing. Some people write the music first and add the lyrics later. Others do it the other way around. And some people, like myself, have to do them both at the same time. There is no right and wrong way to write a song. What I've given you here are some things that have worked for me and I hope they'll work for you too. There really is no single more powerful tool available to interpreters than music.

❖ Language Issues and Commissioning a Theatre Piece: The Producer's Challenge

Jennifer Grace
Formerly attached to the National Capital Commission in Ottawa
Vancouver, British Columbia

Les participants à cet atelier ont discuté de ce que signifiait desservir des visiteurs dans diverses langues. Deux projets d'interprétation de la Commission de la capitale nationale (CCN) ont servi d'exemple pour alimenter la discussion. Il s'agit de *Scènes de la capitale* et d'*À vous de juger*. Les moyens employés pour atteindre le public étaient différents dans ces deux programmes parce que les objectifs en étaient différents. *Scènes de la capitale* a été conçu d'abord pour éveiller l'intérêt envers l'histoire alors qu'*À vous de juger* était un programme éducatif.

In this workshop participants discussed the various means of serving a linguistically diverse audience. Two National Capital Commission interpretation projects were used as examples to stimulate discussion: *Capital Vignettes* and *You Be the Jury*.

Canada's Official Languages Act was passed in 1969, giving Canadians the right to be served in the official language of their choice by the Federal government. Consequently, the National Capital Commission provides bilingual services to visitors to the National Capital Region. This, however, poses some challenges when staging a piece of theatre.

The program's objectives will in large measure dictate what type of approach is most effective and efficient. In the case of *Capital Vignettes*, a program of historical sketches performed for visitors to Parliament Hill, the program's main objective was to entertain and inspire interest in Canadian history. As inspiration was more important than education, it was possible to stage a play with dialogue that some members of the audience might miss. *Canada Comes of Age/Le grand jeu Canadien* was such a bilingual play. While unilingual audience members would not get all of the dialogue, the play was largely visual and was amusing whether or not you attended the whole performance and whether or not you understood every word. An alternative approach was adopted with *Ici Radio Canada*, a play which recounted the history of French-language radio in Canada. Given the theme, which worked in French but not in English very well, a separate play about the same historic time period but about a slightly different topic was staged in English.

You Be the Jury was an interpretation project with a different objective and thus a different approach. It was developed to teach young Canadians about Canadian history and their Canadian heritage. *You Be the Jury* was a participatory theatre program which involved the audience directly in the play, a technique that works well with the 12- to 14-year-old target age group. The educational objective and participatory format made full comprehension of the dialogue imperative. Staged indoors, to groups of schoolchildren who made advance reservations, two separate versions of the play were written and performed on different nights. While this is the most expensive option in terms of both scriptwriting and production of the play, it was a very effective means of reaching the program's objective.

Obviously, program objectives are not the only factors to be taken into account when choosing a means of reaching a linguistically diverse audience. The availability of bilingual/multilingual scriptwriters and actors is a major factor. Moreover, the cost of separate version plays can be prohibitive. Can you afford a bilingual cast or possibly two separate casts? What can you afford in terms of props and set? The remainder of the workshop revolved around a discussion of these equally important variables.

❖ Dramamuse, la troupe de théâtre du MCC ... sans paroles

❖ Dramamuse, CMC's theatre company . . . without words

Études de cas

PART TWO

Case Studies

❖ The Nepean/Powerhouse Museum Performance Research Project

Gordon Beattie
Senior Lecturer and Director, Theatre Nepean, University of Western Sydney
Director, Nepean/Powerhouse Museum Performance Research Project
Sydney, Australia

Cet article examine l'expérience acquise ces quatre dernières années dans un projet de recherche en spectacles mené par le département d'art dramatique de l'University of Western Sydney, Nepean, et le Powerhouse Museum de Sydney, en Australie. Plusieurs types de spectacles dans les musées y sont décrits en regard de l'expérience menée.

This paper will examine the Live Interpretation Performance Research Project carried out over the last four years with performance students from the Theatre Department at the University of Western Sydney, Nepean and the Powerhouse Museum in Sydney. The initiative for this project came from staff in the Community and Education Division and their Director, Jane Westbrooke. They were interested in the way theatre might be able to be used to challenge the reception of the museum by its patrons. The project provided us with the opportunity to experiment with performance possibilities in the museum with each year's project informing the next. Over the last four years we have been on a major learning curve about live interpretation in museums. This paper will outline some aspects of that learning curve. How could we use theatre in the museum? How could the museum be used in creating theatre?

How could the museum be used in creating theatre? The two starting points we used to answer these questions were first, the museum's physical structure, that is, its architecture and space, and second, the particular exhibitions.

The Powerhouse Museum is part of the Museum of Applied Arts and Sciences, established in 1879; it consists of the Powerhouse Museum, the Sydney Mint Museum and the Sydney Observatory. The performance research project concentrated on the Powerhouse Museum. The museum's physical structures could be described as post-modern Turbo Rooms of the old Ultimo Powerhouse. The buildings themselves are exciting theatrical spaces, which range from very intimate rooms, through to large almost overwhelming spaces, with sweeping ramps and corridors, balconies, overhead walkways, voids and escalators.

The first four performances I would like to describe are those which set out to celebrate and disrupt the spaces of the museum. These projects were developed by the performance students under the direction of Gordon Beattie. In project one, students were asked to experience the museum as if they were first-time patrons. What was the experience of entering the museum from Harris Street? What are the sounds you hear in the Museum? What does it feel like? What are some initial impressions? The performers then discussed this experience and a number of points emerged. First, in relation to sound, on entering the museum there is a distinct change in the sounds you hear from the traffic noise of Harris Street to an apparent quiet. It is an apparent quiet because if you listen carefully and as you move through the museum you can hear the sounds of the museum: the sound effects of the steam train, the sound of machinery, recorded voices, the regular playing of the steam organ on the old carousel. Second, in relation to the spaces was that the various balconies and walkways allowed a large number of opportunities for people to stand and watch, not just to look at particular exhibitions, but also to look at the museum itself and at other people looking.

A number of performances emerged. The first was, with large groups of performers, *Living Toys*; *Swimming Routines* was the second, with small groups of performers. *Living Toys* was a performance with 36 people, which set out to explore the reverberations of voice through chant and song in the spaces of the museum. The group was divided into four groups of "toys." The groups collaborated to compose separate vocal chants and physical movement patterns for each group. The chants, while being distinctively different, were composed to harmonize and mix like the rounds of a children's song. During the performance each group started from a different point in the museum; in the Turbo house, the entrance and the upper balconies. At a particular time, the groups began to chant and move to a central meeting point. The museum filled with voices that echoed and resonated throughout the museum. The patrons encountered different groups as they passed by or heard them in the distance. Wherever the spectators turned they were surrounded by sound, coming from the walkways and from around corners. The usual sounds of the museum were displaced by the singing. As the groups gathered and descended to the meeting place, the balconies and observation points were filled with patrons drawn by the sounds of the toys as they met in celebration. A number of observations were made by staff from the museum after the performance: for a few minutes after the performance many patrons just stood and listened; the sounds of the museum became heightened after the chanting stopped; they felt that after the performance people listened to the museum differently; during the performance they felt that the reverberating vocal sounds increased people's curiosity, this was reflected in a general excitement amongst the patrons.

The second performance that emerged from a similar process was the Ester Williams and Busby Berkly massed swimming routines. This was a very amusing and simple routine where two groups of 15 people dressed in old-fashioned bathing costumes and caps mimed formation swimming through the museum, discovering particular objects of fascination in the exhibitions. This routine was particularly successful in focusing on the different spaces and the different places they could be viewed from. The swimmers moved in formation throughout the museum, appearing on escalators, around corners and on walkways. Similar to this routine, in that the performances were not designed to reflect or draw attention to an exhibition, but to surprise and amuse, were two performances with small groups. The first was a flock of ballerinas who danced their way through the museum in an adoring fashion, and the second was a group of auctioneers who stylistically and in "auction speak" (nonsensical gibberish) sold off items in the museum including parts of exhibitions, security guards and members of the public.

The four performances described above illustrate some of the ways we used performance to highlight the physical structure of the museum without focusing on particular exhibitions. The focus was on performers moving through and intersecting the spaces in ways that disrupted, surprised and amused.

The second and key starting point for making theatre in the museum was the exhibitions. When we enter the world of the exhibitions we enter the world of curators, research, library, security and education staff. As performers we were entering a world of different languages and expectations. Initially it was a juggling act to satisfy or allay both fears and expectations about a mob of energetic performing-arts students running rampant in the museum. The first year was particularly important in laying the groundwork for future years. For both the performers and the museum staff it was moving into new territory. In the past the museum had employed performers with set scripts, or performances that had been viewed or recommended to staff for holiday programs. In these projects we were going to be creating characters from scratch, through working with the curators, research and improvisation. There was a nervousness from the museum staff that there was not a script that could be read. We had to learn to articulate our processes. We ended up with excellent cooperation from Education, Curatorial and Library staff.

The performers as well as the museum staff had to develop a language to explain their processes. The actors' main experience had been with fairly traditional theatre spaces and with a traditional audience-performer relationship. One of the first decisions we made was that we would not work from a set script but create characters 1. who were directly related to or derived from an object or part of an exhibition; 2. who directly related to a theme or entire exhibition; 3. who directly related to the interactive public exhibitions and that rather than a traditional show-and-tell, where the audience are passive observers, characters would be developed that would directly interact and talk to and with the patrons of the museum. The starting point for the development of characters was not to be a script, it was to be the objects in the exhibitions. This was another challenge for the performers, whose usual starting point was a set script. To stimulate the performers' thinking in this area, I appropriated the notion of Objects as text and developed this notion in my introduction to the use of objects as and with texts.

Every object in an exhibition has been selected by a curator for a specific intent. An object is contextualised by where it is placed in relation to other objects, labels and other written materials, and/or other visual or audio texts in the exhibition. Every object has texts surrounding it (both intentional texts and unintentional texts). This area is worth expanding. An intentional text is a text which is provided by the curator and designers, a simple example would be a label next to an old biscuit tin: AN ARNOTTS BISCUIT TIN 1945, which is exactly what it is. Where that tin is located in an exhibition, for example in a reconstructed 1940's domestic kitchen, provides other information. These are intentional texts, they are quite specific and at the same time quite general in their representation of the 1940's domestic kitchen. Unintentional texts are provided by the patrons themselves, based on their experience. To a young person, the 1940's kitchen could simply represent a primitive underdeveloped technological relic from the past, while to an older person, the 1940's kitchen could evoke nostalgic memories and, as a specific example, in the case of the biscuit tin, very specific memories of special occasions such as Christmas, when there was a tradition of giving biscuits as presents (a luxury during a time of shortage). Every object, therefore, has texts surrounding it. These are the stories of the objects and the stories of the people who are associated with them, the people who made them and how they were made; the people who owned them, the journeys the objects had made are the traditional theatre starting points for analysis for texts of who, what, where, when with the addition of how and why. Once the performers started to think this way and research the objects with the curators and in the library, the potential for different characters exploded. As a result of this research the performer would gain considerable knowledge about the object and the basis for developing a character. An object surrounded by invisible text could be a wonderful key to the imagination.

Over the four years of the project a number of different audience-performer styles of interaction emerged.

1. A solo character who is in a specific location who is discussing specific things to do with the location and objects in the exhibition or reconstructed historical location. For example, a pharmacist in an old pharmacy talks to the patrons about their ailments and

his remedies from the time, or a brewer in the old brewery exhibition talking about methods of brewing, his life and times. The interaction is direct: one on one or one to a small group, with the character providing information to the patrons and telling stories. I regard this as quite a traditional approach, one employed by many groups in re-creations of historic villages such as Old Sydney Town and Sovereign Hill Ballarat, where individual performers demonstrate activities in costumes of the times or re-enact scenes of various authenticity from a particular time.

2. Characters who have no or very little interaction with the public. Some interesting and more problematic characters and interactions came from this group. Two examples: the first is a couple with a fur-clothing fetish, dressed outlandishly in very expensive furs; they moved through the museum looking for the fashion-design section arguing the advantages and disadvantages, look and feel of leopard, mink and fox. They were attention-seeking and riveting to watch, but not really suitable for a family audience. The second was what I describe as The Hallucination of the Mirror. In this performance the object of attention was a massive, polished wooden sideboard with intricately carved Asian motifs round the frame. The two performers, as white female Christian missionaries, stared into the mirror and recalled the stories of their plight as if the stories were being played out in the mirror.

3. Characters who have maximum interaction with the audience. These characters provide some information, however, unlike the characters described above, the characters in the third category are seekers of information. They need the public to provide information, or to interpret aspects of the museum for them, either from what they already know or from the intentional text of an exhibition. The patrons of the museum are now active interpreters of the museum, the role of information giver usual associated with the performer has now been reversed. I would like to give two examples. Two scientists who are fused together in an accident and completely hopeless are searching for answers to some problems in the interactive science area. The two scientists come up with the most outlandish hypotheses as to why things work the way they do and challenge the patrons to come up with better solutions, which, of course, they do. Two sculptures of 17th-century explorers come to life and find themselves lost in the museum. They are carrying an old out-of-date map with very little of the east coast of Australia marked on it. The interaction with the patrons provides the opportunity for the patrons to explain to the explorers the rest of the map of Australia and the wonders of modern science and technology.

The reversal of roles technique, where the museum is being actively interpreted by the patrons of the museum in situations that have been constructed by the performers, is one which has emerged over the last two years and one which we will be continuing to explore with the research project. This particular technique provides the opportunity for some patrons of the museum to interact with the museum in new ways, allowing voice to be given to some of the unintentional texts of an exhibition. While the notion of an "unintentional text" may be relevant where the patrons' participation is one of passive observation or interaction with technical gadgets, with the introduction of this type of live interpretation we may very well be able to design exhibitions whose very purpose is to give voice to and discover these now intentional texts.

❖ Theatre in Museum Education (TIME)

Rosemary Linnell
Director of TIME
Steyning, U.K.

Le théâtre est un système, dans l'éducation muséale, qui réunit la compétence et l'expérience à la fois des éducateurs et des comédiens de formation. S'ils travaillent de concert à la planification et à la prestation de programmes théâtraux conçus minutieusement, le musée peut être sûr de profiter d'un intérêt soutenu tandis que les comédiens peuvent donner la mesure de la problématique humaine, dans sa forme et avec ses tensions, du sujet. Les enfants sont toujours les maîtres protagonistes de la pièce et ils y participent comme si l'aventure qu'elle présente leur arrivait. Les comédiens dirigent invariablement des discussions, après le spectacle, qui font le lien entre les rebondissements de la pièce et les artefacts du musée.

All museum education departments, I suppose, are concerned to bring objects to life, to give them a context and a value as examples of a culture that is not the same as our own. It is for that reason that museums employ interpreters to provide a living context to the building, the gallery or the objects.

But just as there are degrees or levels of involvement in any interpretive programme, there are also degrees or levels of depth in the learning available when using actors in a museum. The method described here is one where the theatre element is most pronounced, where the visitor (usually a school class) is an active participant in the whole programme, and where the museum education department and the acting company work together from the beginning.

First, a little history of how TIME began. The company was first developed in England as part of the education policy of the Inner London Education Authority. It offered an outreach service to London schools as an adjunct to the TIE (Theatre in Education) work of the Curtain Theatre in London's East End. The first programme was developed with the Tower of London and soon spread to other museums in the capital. When the Education Authority was dissolved the service was disbanded and had it not been for the support of the individual museum education departments, the whole idea would have foundered. At the present moment, however, there is a great deal of interest in the methods that the company uses and this has led to the formation of an independently funded operation with a regular schools programme throughout Britain as well as visits, workshops and training sessions in Canada and Europe. (Throughout this chapter the acronym TIME, which is also the name of the company, will stand for Theatre in Museum Education.)

There is a fundamental difference between using actors as interpreters and a fully-fledged theatre experience. There is also a difference between a theatrical performance and participation in a carefully planned situation involving actors and theatrical practice. They all have their place and serve different conditions and purposes. The best way to explain what those differences are is to start from the beginning and go through the entire process of setting up and operating a TIME programme.

In the main, TIME programmes are designed for school groups. There has been a welcome move in recent years to include family and interest groups in specific, booked events and this could well be the way forward for companies such as ours.

The process starts with the museum, and by museum let us also mean centre of historical interest. They have a collection, perhaps a special exhibition with a specific focus. School groups are likely, or need to be encouraged, to visit as part of a curriculum study . . . not as a fun day out. The museum will probably provide teachers' notes and/or a worksheet, or an introductory talk with, perhaps, handling objects, but they may feel that the children will need help to focus their attention, and to understand the topic. Few teachers have time to spend on travelling to special workshops, even in a city like London, so how can the children gain the necessary background and be motivated to want to learn more about the significance of the objects rather than just study them?

Send for the actors! Or rather for the director of the company. Because what is needed here is a blend of two or three separate skills. The museum education department know their clientele, they know the subject and the way in which they would like to put it across; the actors know how to develop character and situation and how to shape a story and to communicate on a variety of levels other than the purely intellectual. The director's job is to construct a piece of theatre that will allow those two partners to use their skills to the best advantage.

By employing an acting company to do all the planning and operating of the drama, the museum education department is able to draw on the expertise of outsiders who may bring a fresh way of seeing things. Naturally there are risks and this is why TIME never comes with a ready-made package, but always asks who the programme is intended for, what teachers want when they bring a class to the museum, what the museum feels is lacking in the facilities already provided and where drama could perhaps add a further dimension. The operating of a two-week-long, specific and pre-booked programme also releases museum staff from the day-do-day teaching of school groups and, provided they take time to observe and discuss with the actors, they can be free of responsibility; it also

At first glance, theatre might seem to be incompatible with a museum's essentially educational mission. We think of it today principally as a vehicle for entertainment, forgetting that, historically, it was always intended to educate as well as entertain. For centuries — even as far back as the roots of theatre, in dramatic ritual — it has been a vehicle for communicating society's values, for addressing ethical issues, for moral education and for influencing the attitudes or behavior of its audiences. It can thus be considered a very traditional teaching method, and most modern theatre still aims at communicating messages which are educational, whether they supply the answers or merely pose the questions. Again historically, theatre does not merely supply information, it contextualizes information (or objects) intellectually, emotionally, socially, politically, spiritually and aesthetically.

Source: Stephen Alsford and David Parry, "Interpretive Theatre: A Role in Museums?" *Museum Management and Curatorship*, 10, 1 (March 1991), p. 13.

means that several hundred schoolchildren can be gainfully employed in a controlled environment at certain times of the year when, perhaps, galleries are being rearranged or curriculum demands are overstretched.

Whereas interpreters represent these characters who first handled or lived with certain objects and can tell a story or interact with visitors, theatre adds a whole plot, and can (in our case certainly must) pose a moral dilemma and tackle an issue of some importance. The actors are not themselves the main characters in the story, the children are. They are the ones who must solve the dilemma, make decisions and abide by them, taking responsibility for their actions.

The topic having been decided and the issues sorted out, the next step is to choose a moment of crisis or a turning point in history when a group of people found themselves having to make fundamental decisions. Much of our work at the present time is centred around the Second World War because of various anniversaries and because of the curriculum, therefore it is certain that these moments of crisis are going to be life-and-death occasions, but in any period there are going to be moments of importance to someone, even if the matter is purely local or even domestic: for example, children who had become apprentices to Thomas Culpeper, the herbalist, were faced with the distraught grandmother of a sick child. If their questioning revealed symptoms that suggested plague, what should they do? Report her to the authorities behind her back, tell her what must be done and trust her to go herself, visit the child and risk spreading infection, or palm her off with a palliative and keep quiet? Whatever their decision, they had to find the best possible way of handling the woman as well as the situation.

Once the plot and the issues are determined, then the role of the children is paramount. Since children themselves do not often make fundamental or national decisions, their role in the drama is usually that of adults, and often adults who are in a position of authority. In order to take on the role, they will have to be in possession of everything that entitles them to that position; they will need to undergo a period of training and even some sort of test in order to demonstrate their authority. In order to negotiate with William of Normandy for a charter (a copy of which was in the museum) the Witan of England met and were sworn in. They then spent some time studying the evidence of the Bayeux Tapestry before having to tell Edith, widow of King Edward and mother of three sons killed in the battle, how the situation lay. Strict chronology would argue that the tapestry was produced some years later, but the needs of a dramatic situation suggest that near-contemporary sources, presented as an integral part of the story, are more vivid than giving the children the facts beforehand.

In TIME programmes our young fellow actors are participants and audience simultaneously. The situation causes them to learn and also motivates further learning. It is a beginning not an end. The element of entering the unknown is important and yet we always make sure that they meet us as actors and understand that this is fiction. They do not need preparation in school beforehand, although we always check how much knowledge of the topic they have by sitting on the floor with the children before starting the play and talking to them about what they understand by the topic.

Theatre as a means to learning is probably the most important area of our philosophy. Perhaps we take it too seriously, but a visit to a museum and participation in a TIME programme should never be just a fun outing, or the drama seen as a frivolous undertaking: for that reason the children do not act out a familiar situation, they are not performing to anyone and they do not dress up. The whole exercise is an intense learning process that stimulates the emotions as well as the intellect.

Having determined the role of the young people, we have next to decide our own. We work in teams of two or three. Three is ideal since there is more likelihood of the issues being addressed directly and not seen as a conflict between two opposing characters. In the present financial climate, however, we find ourselves having to design programmes on a very restricted budget. Our characters are hardly ever recognisable historical personages or the main protagonists in a situation. They are often real people, although sometimes the topic and the issues are best approached through an invented character. We often think of them as being door-openers. When the young people are ready to move from one stage of the drama to the next, the actor's character will usher them along to take up the next responsibility.

Sometimes a costumed character is important to the children, as in the Norman Conquest drama. Queen Edith was a halfway role and therefore the actress wore dark trousers and shirt but put on a full-length, purple cloak to meet the Witan. The members of the Witan, the council of England, wore golden badges of office, a device which allowed them to take solemn oath, to feel the dignity of their position and to use a formal and increasingly powerful style of language appropriate to their role, the period and the situation. When a deputation from the Witan first met William of Normandy, they were hooded and could only hear his voice. When the whole group finally returned either to swear allegiance or to offer war, they saw him on a raised dais in full costume, spotlit in a darkened room and drawing a huge sword on which the young aetheling — or the queen on her own behalf if the Witan would not submit — swore the oath of fealty. This is the sort of occasion where theatre practice is paramount; the use of solemn ritual, costume and "props," and above all the ability of professional actors to build belief in the situation lend a degree of excitement, climax and even danger that remains with the participants for a long time.

Reality and historical accuracy are absolutely vital, yet in the drama the young people are free to change the course of history. How can the two be reconciled? Strangely enough history usually repeats itself. Given enough time to build up to the decision-making moment and given the firm establishment of historical circumstances, the number of options open to the young people are limited. If, in the heat of the play, a choice is made that is different from the historical one, then in the obligatory debrief discussion with the actors at the end, the reasons for such differences can be explored in a very satisfying way. Sometimes teachers are upset if their nicely liberal class puts a German Jewish refugee into an internment camp. Yet that was the decision made by the British Government during the war, and that, given the circumstances under which the children operated, was the hard-fought decision that they came to in almost every one of some fifty performances. It is in the debrief that any notes for follow-up work and suggestions for further study and books to read can be given to the class and the teacher.

Theatre allows the participants to become involved in the sort of hot-potato issues that are difficult to handle in school, and the distancing effect of a historical setting allows for empathy rather than twentieth-century thinking to develop. By allowing plenty of time for discussion at the end, parallels may be drawn with our own situation, it is surprising how often the daily news points up how little difference there is between human behaviour in the distant past and today. A group of adults in Norway became very angry about having been trapped into an agreement with the Hanseaic league, their (own-language and very heated) discussion ranged over religious tolerance and the rights and wrongs of joining a European community — issues that were entirely relevant to their own politics but totally within the bounds of the historical dilemma.

Theatre also allows the use of handling objects, copies or simplified versions of the real thing to be made available to children. A facsimile of a Royal Decree can be torn in pieces by a Catholic dissenter in the Gunpowder Plot to the horror of the participants, but a new one can be produced for the afternoon's performance.

Professional acting companies, and especially the younger actors, are usually excited by the opportunity of creating such a complete characterization without a script and shaping a drama through introduction to climax and beyond, with that most perceptive of groups, a class of children. TIME programmes also offer work in a notoriously under-employed profession, so from a theatre company's point of view the connection is a valuable one, the museum staff need to be aware that the actors must be fed with all the background material available in a form that they can absorb quickly. Access to specialist libraries is fine in the later stages of preparation but at the beginning, when a focus is being sought, a children's book or school textbook is more useful. The museum should be able to determine the viewpoint from which they wish the topic to be approached, but the actors should be able to choose the theatrical shape and focus of the drama. This usually means an early meeting, especially with a new collaboration, because setting-up and preparing all the material and rehearsing the actors does take time. Mostly we run programmes for two solid weeks, which is what most museums can afford Equity rates for, and what is a reasonable period of engagement for the actors. Any less is not economic, and longer usually ties up rooms and/or gallery space for longer than is practicable. There are usually two sessions a day, each session occupying two hours (allowing for briefing, discussion and a minimum hour-and-a-quarter's drama).

By avoiding the use of any script the children are able to contribute fully and communicate with each other and the actors on their own terms. The timing and sequence of events is, however, very strictly worked out beforehand and an hourglass becomes one of our most useful props. "Before the sands of time run out" is a frequently used phrase in our dramas. By putting pressure on the children and by compressing events into dramatic rather than real time they can stretch their abilities and surprise both themselves and their teachers. A theatre piece has to have a beginning, middle and end and there has to be a satisfactory conclusion, so that the children's efforts are valued and seen to have achieved something worthwhile. Teachers are usually given the role of chroniclers or clerks so that they are part of the situation and not seen as a critical audience. To help them fulfill their role as observers, teachers are given clipboards and notes that describe the sequence of events and the children's anticipated responses at each stage of the drama (although the responses may prove to be untypical). One of the most satisfactory moments in any TIME programme is when the participants betray a heightened degree of righteous indignation and demand restitution of perceived wrongs and injustices.

Such concentration and involvement in the reality of a historical situation is best when it can happen behind closed doors. Gallery events are naturally more diffuse. There is often a very good reason why actors in costume and groups of children talking freely and perhaps getting worked up about something should be excluded from a public gallery; yet the whole purpose of the work is to bring gallery objects into focus. What we try to do is either include a visit to the gallery as part of the drama or end the session by taking actors and children to view the real thing, out of role but with the drama fresh in their minds. If it is to be part of the drama then the actual journey from one room to another cannot be too long or the children, especially the young ones, will lose the focus and become excitable children again. It is often more satisfactory to allow a cooling-off discussion first and then the gallery visit can prove to be a highly motivated learning experience.

Seven- to twelve-year-olds usually find dramatic reality easy to sustain. They are used to each other's company and have a sense of security in pretending. After a move to a new school at thirteen, new rivalries may hamper their ability to be sensitive to drama and therefore they may take longer to operate satisfactorily and may have to work in smaller groups. Older pupils can be inhibited and therefore need a different approach. We usually start with a more academic approach where they are given a task of some complexity to tackle and are allowed to respond to ideas and situations without being asked to assume a very distinct role. For example, in a programme about propaganda, fifteen- and sixteen-year-olds worked in groups designing words to go with First World War pictures to be used in a recruiting campaign. When they then met a "Tommy" who was supposed to offer the right sort of heroic image that might serve as a role model, they could identify with his suppressed feelings about the horror of life in the trenches, probe further and question him, and when challenged to go back to producing patriotic posters could show the same involvement in the fictional situation as if they had been acting in role. The time for discussion at the end tends to be longer with older students than with the younger ones, who are often exhausted by the drama itself.

Although our experience of working with family and casual visitor groups is limited, the potential is obvious. The only restriction is that they have to agree to spend a certain time on the activity, and that the programmes are usually of shorter duration. Three generations coming together on a drama about evacuation in the Second World War led to some very moving moments and the children who were asked, at the end, to record grandma's stories were as impressed as their own mothers at thoughts and feelings that had sometimes never been told before. The older women usually said that the drama had allowed them to speak of their experiences in a way that they had not thought possible and the museum was able to add a whole new section of personal and local history to the exhibition.

Naturally TIME programmes are not infallible. There are some young people for whom acting as if they were someone or somewhere else is wellnigh impossible. We have met whole classes where the ethos of the school is against drama of any kind, either because the children are too undisciplined to work seriously, or, and this is more difficult, where the school itself regards the development of the imagination as of little value and actors as objects of ridicule. Why such highly competitive academic establishments book a TIME programme we can never be sure, but they have provided the very rare occasions on which we have ever had to interrupt the drama in order to negotiate a resumption of work. For the most part, however, it has proved to be a very satisfactory way of intensifying appreciation of museum visits.

Some years ago a study was set up by the Institute of Education in London to evaluate the learning that took place as a result of a TIME programme. By setting up control groups and testing the results of three different approaches to the history of the Gunpowder Plot, an educational psychologist found a universally high degree of ability, in the children who had taken part in the drama, to recall as well as to understand facts and issues and to relate ideas to their own as well as to a bygone age. Not surprisingly they had also been the most articulate and stimulated groups, although all the children were of very mixed ability. Even the simplest version of this form of inactive learning, when it is based on a blend of factual truth and imaginative honesty seems to provoke greater awareness in the young people than even the best storytelling or practical work can do. The collaboration between museum education staff and actors seems to bring out the best in both and above all in the young people who participate with them in this form of living history.

❖ À Pointe-à-Callière, l'animation théâtrale pour faire du musée un lieu convivial au quotidien

Ginette Cloutier
Directrice, Animation-éducation
Pointe-à-Callière, Musée d'archéologie et d'histoire de Montréal
Montréal (Québec)

From its opening in May 1992, the mission of Pointe-à-Callière, Museum of Archeology and History of Montreal, has been to be open and accessible to the public at large, and above all to be user-friendly. The very concept of its museography, based on human beings and not just objects, and the installation of a sizeable reception and interpretation team throughout the museum so that real people interpret the remains and greet visitors, demonstrate the museum administration's desire to make it a user-friendly, welcoming place. It is worthwhile for disciplines such as archaeology and history to be humanized so that they can be made manageable.

Une mission d'ouverture et d'accessibilité

Dès son ouverture en mai 1992, Pointe-à-Callière, Musée d'archéologie et d'histoire de Montréal s'est donné une mission d'ouverture et d'accessibilité au grand public et surtout de convivialité. Le concept même de sa muséographie axé sur les humains et non seulement sur les objets, et la mise en place d'une importante équipe d'accueil et d'animation dans tout le musée pour que ce soit des humains qui animent les vestiges et accueillent les visiteurs démontrent la volonté de la direction du musée d'en faire un lieu convivial et accueillant. Les disciplines comme l'archéologie et l'histoire ont avantage à être humanisées pour être apprivoisées.

L'animation... un rôle déterminant pour des visiteurs hétérogènes

Des études de clientèles menées par Locus, Loisir et Culture pour le projet du Biodôme ainsi qu'une évaluation de l'exposition permanente **Lumière** présentée à La Villette (France) démontrent que «...l'animation est la meilleure façon de répondre aux attentes d'une clientèle hétérogène - écarts d'âge, diversité des origines, degré de scolarité variable, intérêt plutôt tiède pour l'histoire et l'archéologie traditionnelles - qui préfère une approche chaleureuse, variée, adaptée à ses besoins.» De manière générale, les études de clientèles démontrent que l'animation figure parmi les quatre ou cinq facteurs les plus appréciés de la visite des musées. Inversement le manque d'animation et d'information sont spontanément les principaux facteurs d'insatisfaction. L'étude sur le musée de La Villette indique que l'absence d'interaction avec les guides-animateurs est le principal élément de déception chez les visiteurs.

L'animation joue donc un rôle déterminant dans la décision des visiteurs d'effectuer des visites répétées. Elle augmente le rayonnement du musée et favorise une évolution positivede la fidélité des visiteurs.

De l'animation à l'animation théâtrale

La Direction Animation-éducation du Musée a élaboré un premier concept d'animation théâtrale qui sera mis en place dès l'ouverture du musée en mai 1992 et sera interprété par les guides-animateurs. L'animation théâtrale proposée s'inspirait fortement d'un concept d'animation déposé par Camirand, Bournival, Michaud à la demande de Pointe-à-Callière en mars 1992.

Monique Camirand de Paroles en Jeu a grandement influencé et modifié les approches d'animation pratiquées jusque-là dans les musées. Son document *Animer dans un contexte d'exposition,* réalisé en collaboration avec Marie-Thérèse Bournival, et les nombreuses formations qu'elle donne sur l'animation ont enrichi les formes d'animation ainsi que le rôle des guides-animateurs. «Le guide-animateur doit jouer un rôle polyvalent; guide, interprète, hôte, animateur, comédien, éducateur et doit utiliser toutes les formes, techniques et outils d'animation pour le servir.» Le guide-animateur est d'abord un communicateur, celui qui a le contact direct avec les visiteurs, celui qui a un message à transmettre, certes, mais surtout celui qui a pour mission de faire vivre aux visiteurs une expérience totale (cognitive, émotive et sensitive), et conviviale qui leur donnera le goût de revenir au musée.

C'est sur ces bases que le musée a défini et mis en place son premier concept d'animation théâtrale : des capsules théâtrales d'une durée de cinq minutes chacune, intégrées quotidiennement à la visite du musée et animées par les guides-animateurs qui «évoquent» des personnages historiques ayant vécu sur le site de la Pointe-à-Callière. Les accessoires sont simples, minimaux afin que le guide-animateur puisse, en un tour de chapeau, revenir rapidement et facilement à son rôle de guide-animateur. On ne parle pas ici d'animation historique, technique d'animation qui consiste à faire revivre une période de l'histoire par le biais de gens en costume d'époque dans le rôle de différents personnages. Les capsules théâtrales se font en costume contemporain et «évoquent» des personnages historiques à l'aide d'accessoires, des chapeaux par exemple. Elles servent à créer la surprise, à changer le rythme de la visite et à interpeller l'imaginaire et l'émotion des visiteurs pour apprivoiser l'histoire.

Les applaudissements de la majorité des visiteurs lors des capsules théâtrales nous confirment leur intérêt. L'effet de surprise et d'émerveillement est créé, les visiteurs apprécient. Cependant, d'autres types de visiteurs, les «spécialistes» ou les universitaires, et parfois les adolescents, boudent ce type d'animation, laissant les guides-animateurs inquiets, dans la crainte d'être ridicules et en manque de moyens pour réagir et contrôler la situation devant les réactions plutôt froides et même cyniques de ces visiteurs. Résultat : malgré la satisfaction de la majorité des visiteurs, les guides-animateurs retiennent surtout les expériences négatives et sont de moins en moins enthousiastes à animer ces capsules théâtrales.

Trois ans de recherches et d'expérimentations pour la mise en forme de l'animation théâtrale

Personnifier le personnage dans un costume de guide-animateur et passer du rôle de personnage historique au rôle de guide-animateur en l'espace de quelques secondes semble chose difficile pour les guides-animateurs du musée. Nous avons donc expérimenté au cours des trois dernières années différentes formules, tels les contes, puis les récits où le guide-animateur raconte la vie du personnage au lieu de la personnifier, et enfin la lecture d'édits et d'ordonnances avec le ton du huissier-crieur. Nous avons adapté les personnages et les textes selon le type de visiteurs. Ainsi des formules similaires pour les familles, enfants et aînés, d'autres pour les adolescents; quant aux spécialistes... peut-être leur esprit analytique appréciera-t-il un jour? Nous avons fourni aux guides-animateurs des scénarios et des textes écrits par des comédiens et des metteurs en scène et adaptés par les guides-animateurs. Nous avons choisi plus de personnages historiques féminins pour aider la performance de nos guides-animateurs, qui sont en majorité des femmes. Une formation intensive en animation théâtrale, pose de voix, jeux dramatiques, exercices d'improvisation, présence constante d'un metteur en scène, formation collective et individuelle ont contribué à améliorer le rendement et la performance des guides-animateurs en animation théâtrale.

Au fil du temps, nous avons également modifié le portrait de l'équipe en choisissant quelques guides-animateurs ayant une formation de base en art dramatique. Ceci, afin de contribuer à maintenir dans l'équipe, un certain équilibre entre les individus pratiquant des approches d'animation cognitives et les autres plus émotives et théâtrales, permettant aussi un transfert de compétences entre les individus : ceux ayant une formation de base en sciences humaines et ceux ayant une formation de base en art dramatique.

Malgré cette amélioration de leur performance théâtrale, plusieurs guides-animateurs du musée manquent de conviction et ne voient pas l'intérêt des capsules théâtrales, des contes ou des récits pour apprivoiser l'histoire et l'impact positif chez les visiteurs.

L'animation théâtrale en costume d'époque

L'animation théâtrale en costume d'époque quoique plus traditionnelle demeure fort appréciée du grand public et c'est une formule d'animation théâtrale beaucoup plus facile à interpréter pour les guides-animateurs. Au cours des dernières années, le Musée a conçu et réalisé dans le cadre de son programme d'action culturelle des animations théâtrales historiques, telles que «Le marché public dans l'ambiance du XVIIIe siècle» et «Parcours nocturne» qui sont interprétées par des guides-animateurs «volontaires». Une performance théâtrale de taille animée par les guides-animateurs depuis trois ans soit l'événement «Qui est le vrai Père Noël» viendra sûrement marquer la voie que prendra l'animation théâtrale à Pointe-à-Callière. Cette animation de personnages traditionnels de Noël - Babouchka, Melchior, Befana, saint Nicolas et Santa Claus - en costume d'époque, que nous travaillons depuis trois ans avec tous les guides-animateurs, les a enfin convaincus de l'intérêt, de la richesse et du plaisir à jouer cette forme d'animation. Jouer dans un costume de théâtre entouré d'un décor semble les sécuriser et inspirer leur personnage.

Les guides-animateurs sont enfin émus et émouvants. On est loin de la formule initiale où le guide-animateur en costume contemporain avec un seul chapeau évoque les personnages du passé. Mais puisque l'important est de les faire revivre pour mieux apprivoiser et se rappeler le passé, «Guides-animateurs, revêtez-votre costume d'époque et faites revivre dans ces vestiges Louis Hector de Callière, le huissier, le commis, Élizabeth Bégon et Sarah Wurtele pour le plaisir de tous».

❖ The Languages of Science: Live Interpretation in Science Museums, Technology Centres and Discovery Places

Susannah Daley
Head of Theatre and Live Interpretation
National Museum of Photography, Film and Television
Bradford, U.K.

La compagnie de théâtre Action Replay du National Museum of Photography, Film and Television de Brandford, en Angleterre, utilise le théâtre pour abolir la barrière des langages que constituent la science et le musée. Le besoin, en particulier, de traduire une situation en quelque chose d'agréable où tous les humains se reconnaissent peut être abordé par le biais d'une convention théâtrale où des signes culturels, des symboles et la langue que la plupart des gens comprennent sont utilisés.

Action Replay was created as the resident theatre company for the National Museum of Photography, Film and Television in 1989 by the then Head of Museum Colin Ford, and Susannah Daley.

The company's mission is to provide visitors with theatrical interpretations of the history, science and culture of photography, film and television. In 1993 the Museum opened the Spotlight Gallery, a mixed-media performance and exhibition space, used by the actors for family visitor and educational theatre programmes. The National Museum of Photography, Film and Television is part of the National Museum of Science and Industry.

Action Replay, National Museum of Photography, Film and Television

The language of Science is made up of numbers, signs and symbols and is used by scientists to communicate effectively and efficiently between each other. Like many other disciplines, Science has its own shorthand, which in effect acts as a code! To the lay person, this code can be as impenetrable as an unknown foreign language. How many of us could look at Albert Einstein's writings on the theory of relativity and understand the significance of the numbers and symbols in our everyday lives? Like any unspoken language, Science requires interpretation, we must crack the code before we can begin to understand the message. Just as a language interpreter acts as a medium for the translation of foreign languages to the native tongue, so science museums are attempting to act as mediums for the "public understanding of science." However, generally speaking, museums are still shouldering the burden of "Empirical Truth." Visitors are inclined to believe information presented in museums constitutes irrefutable fact (see paper by Chris Ford, National Railway Museum).

As established institutions, museums suffer inherent language barriers due to the historical nature of their role as academic centres of scholarly research; they are only just beginning to present a multifaceted view of the world as for far too long they have been reliant on the opinion of the resident "expert." The cultural impact of Science is too big and too widespread to be ignored, it cannot stand in isolation, it is intertwined with History, Geography, Economics, Design, Fashion, Leisure, Folklore and everyday human interaction. Attempts are being made by science museums to break down the multi-layered codes carried in both subject and medium through new-style exhibitions, demonstrations, publications, video and audio presentations and increasingly through Live Interpretation. Theatre is a responsive medium that can form a bridge from the most unintelligible scientific equation to relevant information, allowing the visitor to experience "illumination." I'm not suggesting that every museum visitor is theatre literate, however, in general terms theatre uses a code of visual and cultural symbols, signs and language that most people are familiar with. Museum visitors know how to act as audience; we live in a tele-visual age where most people understand the convention of the character, soliloquy, the passing of time and changing of place. Visitors willingly "suspend their disbelief" in order to make sense of what they see.

Theatre gives us the means to translate the language of Science into the language of shared culture. It is not always enough to know what something does, it often leads to a better understanding of an object or a principle if one knows how or why it was invented or discovered. We say that "Need is the Mother of Invention" — the understanding of that need is often pivotal to the understanding of the object/principle. In order for people to relate to an object they must have a connection to it. Theatre is the medium by which we can most easily and readily identify that connection. We stop dealing merely with the object itself and begin to explore people's reaction and relationship to it. Museum objects can be seen as the "Hardware of History," what actually connects people as humans is the "Software."

At the National Museum of Photography, Film and Television, Action Replay Theatre tell the story of John Logie Baird, a sickly child who missed a lot of school and who tinkered with odd bits of junk at home until he managed to produce what we now know as television pictures. To show an audience of schoolchildren a boy not much older or younger than themselves, working on "barmy" experiments with very ordinary everyday objects, is to hold a mirror to them, they recognise the character — maybe their tinkering in the garden might turn out to be the start of something big. To show them a theatrically devised horse-race with Mechanical System ridden by Logie Baird and Cathode Ray Tube ridden by Marconi with the prize of broadcasting for the BBC, is to relate to something within their cultural sphere. It demystifies the "inventor" and re-codes the information into a digestible form but most importantly of all, it relays a common human experience. The history of Science can often be anecdotal, Live Interpretation allows characters to share their thoughts, feelings, hopes and anxieties to provide an audience with a human story as well as logical fact. An industrial museum may tell us that the "Spinning Jenny" revolutionised the textile industry because of its speed — but the theatre performance might show us what a Spinning Jenny is, tell us who made it and why, exactly how it revolutionised the textile industry and the effect that it had on the workers of the textile cottage industry. The point becomes not one of the object but one of the people surrounding the object. Theatre is providing access to the unheard voices of Science.

The language of Science has been too frightening to too many people for too long and has been coupled with the language of museums, which has been too limited and too narrowly focused. Theatre and Live Interpretation are providing museums and visitor centres with a language that is easier for its audience to decode and can provide an entertaining and meaningful translation.

❖ Theatrical Techniques in a Science Museum

Mitzi Hauser

Education and Research Writer

National Museum of Science and Technology

Ottawa, Ontario

De l'usage de techniques théâtrales dans un musée de sciences et méthodes pour incorporer des spectacles «aux expositions».

Trois manières d'écrire la pièce :

1 - pièce complète, écrite par les comédiens;

2 - pièce improvisée, genre de démonstration libre : interprétation de personnages historiques, interprétation de textes écrits par des spécialistes du contenu;

3 - mélange des deux genres - une formule gagnante, spécialement pour les expériences en science.

Trouver l'histoire cachée

Ce pourrait être un artefact particulier qui parle par lui-même.

Ce pourrait être une manière d'atteindre un public cible qui n'a pas été joint.

Ce pourrait être un monologue biographique qui porterait sur un personnage important de l'exposition.

Laissez l'exposition vous indiquer la manière de composer votre pièce.

Today I would like to address the use of theatrical techniques in a Science Museum, and the particular opportunities and challenges that this brings. I wish to discuss here the type of interpretive theatre that is done in the exhibits, using the ideas of the exhibits, where there is no extra charge for admission, and where the performance is held to 15 minutes or so.

Each exhibit poses its own special challenge or unique opportunity for interpretation. It is best if these theatrical animation possibilities are considered during the design of the exhibit so that performance areas, spaces for large groups, etc. can be built in. But they can be included later, quite successfully. The style, the message, the content of the exhibit all dictate the subject and form of the animation. Theatre could be filling a gap, as in the production of *Micro* at the Museum of Science and Technology, which some of you saw yesterday, or enhancing a theme already presented in the exhibit.

I will break the form of the animation down into three ways of "scripting."

Fully scripted work — or a "play" as it is usually called — where you might use one language, or more or none. (A dance or mime piece can be completely set even though there is no language.)

This is usually performed by actors as opposed to demonstrators, who understand the technique of delivering a memorized script, pacing, timing and characterization.

Improvised work — this doesn't mean there is no written flow to the dialogue but it is a more improvised show. The objectives, the sense, the logic are there but a more flexible style allows the demonstration to be tailored to the audience. Historical character interpretation or living history I would see falling into this category. It would also include artisan interpretation in period style.

This type of interpretive work would normally be delivered by content specialists such as historical animators or science explainers.

The third type of work would be a mixture of the two, scripted in some places for a theatrical treatment, but loose in others, having the feel of a demo. Usually, this involves two or more people and the scripted section involves cues and tight rehearsed timing for a special effect. This can be used quite successfully for science shows because given the nature of science demonstrations, some flexibility has to be built in — experiments often take longer than you think, or the equipment fails, or you want audience participation for a certain experiment. We used this technique quite successfully during the 1980s in a science show that toured schools for two years involving a Demonstrator and a Mime/Stage Manager, who ran sound, lights, etc. when she was off stage.

Understanding of these three structures allows flexibility for a wide variety of interpretation of scientific concepts, the use of early technology, historical and biographical content, and the social impact of certain technologies.

Each exhibit presents unique opportunities. Each exhibit has its hidden stories — we just have to find them. Because we are a museum, we have artifacts, and all the special problems those artifacts bring — most notably, Hands off! However, my museum, the National Museum of Science and Technology, did allow me to mount a play that involved climbing all over one artifact. Which one? It was the oldest steam locomotive they had. The theme of the play was the incredible feat of building the Canadian Pacific Railway, told through the eyes of Sir John A. MacDonald's wife.

As another example, we had an exhibit called Canada in Space — Destination Earth that was created with a reading and comprehension level of grade 6 and up. The concepts were sophisticated and the text of the exhibit was quite dense. As a way of reaching our youngest visitors, we commissioned a play that would explain how it felt to live and work on the shuttle in orbit. Two kinds of puppets were involved as a means of reaching the kindergarten set.

I would like to caution you about a few quicksand areas, if you are thinking of using theatrical techniques in a museum setting.

Commitment

The most overwhelming problem with theatre in a museum is the lack of commitment from the audience. When someone goes to a theatre and pays a ticket price they have made a decision to watch a play. At the museum, where they might turn a corner and happen on some presentation, they have no obligation to stay and watch. For this reason, make the theatre piece short — 15 to 20 minutes maximum. Give the audience seating — it's more likely they will stay. Advertise the length of duration of the show so they will be able to plan their time.

Upstaging

In a Science Museum, the big attraction is the hands-on, push-button, try-out stuff. This is engaging and fun. So the demonstration or theatrical is offered as an alternative. Do you present a resting, peaceful, reflective piece or a noisy, audience-involving action piece? The choice is a difficult one. You may only be able to please some of the people, some of the time.

Focus

Another big problem that I have seen in museum demonstrations and presentations is that of lack of visual focus. By this I mean deciding what it is that you want your audience to be looking at or hearing at every particular moment. You must direct the attention of the audience. Too many objects to look at, too many movements, too many themes, can all split the focus and leave the audience wondering what was being said.

Noise

Be very careful *where* you stage your presentation. For the duration of the play, disable sound effects and noisy equipment.

Accessories — set, costumes, props

Most Science Museums have a shop where exhibits are built. I would avoid using these shops for construction of your set, costumes and props, and use someone familiar with theatrical deadlines and requirements.

Why?

- your production is not a priority in their work plan, and deadlines will be shifted
- there is no understanding of the need for rehearsal with the props from almost the beginning of rehearsal period
- theatrical needs do not always coincide with an artisan's desire to make objects exact or durable, e.g., a light, transportable set is a concept unknown

Scripts

Do engage a playwright to write your script. It is a skill, in the same way that exhibit design is a skill. Find a good playwright whose work you have seen or at least read — someone who understands that a script needs conflict, characterization and a climax along with other dramatic values.

Audience participation vs. audience involvement

This sort of interaction within a set play is frequently useful and great fun. Just make sure that it is controllable and that the dynamics of the play are enhanced, not held up by the interaction. There are times when an improvised demonstration or talk serves the purpose better. There is another type of audience participation, which does work extremely well that I will term "audience envelopment." By this I mean that the play takes place all around the audience — the actors are calling and discussing and arguing with each other over the heads of the crowd. This is great fun for both the actor and the audience, and a fine solution.

I will end by reminding you to allow the exhibits themselves in your museum to talk to you about the best method of interpretation. Each one will speak in a different voice.

❖ L'interprétation personnalisée au service d'un thème

Michèle Pérusse
Chargée de projet, Service de l'action culturelle
Musée de la civilisation
Québec (Québec)

At the Musée de la civilisation, the diversified use of the interpretive arts is one of the most popular communication modes for visitors. These arts are integrated with the themes developed at the Museum, using music, theatre, poetry, storytelling and song. Commissioned to enhance an original concept (or, occasionally, a supporting production if it furthers development of a theme), the interpretive disciplines must combine the principles of professionalism, visitor interest in the subject, observance of copyright and dynamic site utilization. Working with such a combination of elements guarantees a rewarding experience.

Alors que dans beaucoup de musées nord-américains les services d'éducation et d'action culturelle sont fusionnés dans ce qu'on appelle les « Public Programs », le Musée de la civilisation a opté pour la création de deux services distincts un peu comme dans les musées européens. Ces deux services font partie d'une même direction. Toutefois, la programmation du Service de l'éducation comporte un secteur important axé sur la clientèle scolaire alors que le Service de l'action culturelle s'adresse davantage à un public adulte ou familial.

Précisons d'abord qu'au Service de l'action culturelle, plusieurs moyens sont utilisés au service des thématiques du Musée : conférences, colloques, débats, ateliers, cinéma, événements spéciaux, créations dans différentes disciplines artistiques, bref, des centaines d'activités sont présentées annuellement.

Cependant, seule l'utilisation des arts d'interprétation sera l'objet de cette communication; d'ailleurs, nous y avons recours abondamment. Soulignons que plus de la moitié du budget annuel du Service de l'action culturelle est consacrée à la présentation d'activités qui font appel à des artistes : comédiens, musiciens, danseurs, conteurs ou chanteurs. C'est dire l'importance que nous accordons aux arts d'interprétation. Ils sont pour nous, plus que de simples accompagnements ou outils pédagogiques. Ils sont plutôt partie intégrante du discours du musée, parce que lieu de parole, celle du texte, celle des gestes, celle du son.

La parole quelle que soit sa langue (sonore ou gestuelle) peut offrir l'avantage d'une plus grande souplesse, d'une plus grande liberté que le discours muséographique de l'exposition et peut contourner l'obstacle du barrage linguistique.

Tout est alors possible, mais rappelons-le, jamais de façon gratuite et toujours au service d'un thème relié soit à une exposition soit à un des grands champs d'exploration privilégié par le Musée.

Voici des exemples de la manière dont nous utilisons les arts d'interprétation au Service de l'action culturelle, en particulier dans les disciplines suivantes : théâtre, musique et danse.

Productions théâtrales

En ce qui concerne les productions théâtrales, le plus souvent, nous retenons un thème relié à une exposition en cours. C'est le cas pour nos programmations estivales. Et là-dessus, j'ouvre une parenthèse pour dire que c'est à l'occasion de nos programmations estivales annuelles que nous faisons surtout appel à l'interprétation personnalisée. Pendant deux mois et demi, du 24 juin au 6 septembre, nous proposons à nos visiteurs un grand nombre d'activités dont nous confions la réalisation à des artistes.

Nous devenons alors les producteurs de capsules théâtrales, de concerts commentés, d'animations de toutes sortes.

La richesse de l'interprétation théâtralisée est infiniment précieuse pour développer un thème et, tous les étés depuis l'ouverture du Musée il y a 6 ans, nous présentons des créations théâtrales originales sous forme de capsules d'une demi-heure au maximum. L'objectif de ces productions est de compléter, d'enrichir ou de développer un aspect du thème de l'exposition retenue. (Il faut ici souligner que, bien entendu, certains sujets d'exposition se prêtent mieux à une interprétation personnalisée que d'autres. Heureusement, au Musée de la civilisation, il y a généralement une dizaine d'expositions en cours, ce qui facilite le choix du thème le plus riche à développer.)

Exemples de productions théâtrales maison

Été 1991 : «Les murs ont des oreilles» (se rattachant à l'exposition «Cités souvenir, Cités d'avenir»	Été 1993 : «Traces et contrastes» (se rattachant à l'exposition «Nomades»)
(diapositives)	(vidéo)
1. Choix du thème	1. Choix du thème
2. Méthode de recrutement : appels d'offre	2. Commande directe à l'artiste

3. Critères de sélection :
 - professionnalisme des candidats
 - respect du thème
 - qualité et originalité du synopsis
 - scénarisation simple
 - intérêt tout public
 - utilisation dynamique des lieux
 - atteinte des objectifs :   - apprendre
                             - divertir
                             - émouvoir
	3. Identiques

Notre rôle comme producteur :

- approbation des étapes et du contenu véhiculé
- suivi budgétaire
- soutien technique
- communications

(Dans un climat de grande liberté et de confiance)

Productions théâtrales accueillies

Il nous arrive aussi occasionnellement d'inviter des troupes à présenter des productions théâtrales qui n'ont pas été créées spécifiquement pour le Musée mais dont le propos convient, s'adapte parfaitement à une de nos thématiques.

Ce sont des pièces produites par des compagnies théâtrales avec beaucoup plus de moyens. Des pièces qui ont été jouées en tournée parfois internationale que nous présentons dans l'auditorium du Musée où nous disposons d'une scène, du personnel et de l'équipement technique nécessaire. En tant que professionnels, cela nous oblige à être vigilants et informés sur les productions disponibles.

Nous avons présenté récemment la pièce «Terre promise -Terra promessa» par Le théâtre des deux mondes qui revenait d'une tournée internationale, une pièce qui convenait remarquablement à un événement organisé sur le thème de l'objet.

Nous invitons aussi régulièrement des troupes de théâtre pour la jeunesse qui ont des productions toutes désignées pour illustrer l'univers du conte, lors d'un événement annuel qui porte sur ce thème.

Des contraintes se rattachent toutefois à la présentation de ce type de créations déjà existantes, disponibles sur le marché du spectacle. Les théâtres de la ville de Québec n'ont pas toujours vu d'un bon œil le fait qu'on présente gratuitement chez nous ce genre de spectacle. À l'occasion, ils nous ont accusé de briser le marché. Nous avons, dès lors, conclu une entente où nous nous engageons à ne pas présenter de pièces qui seraient programmées ultérieurement dans des salles de Québec. Et, évidemment, nous ne jouons en aucun cas le rôle de diffuseurs, ce qui briserait le fragile équilibre du marché du spectacle. Ils sont plus tolérants maintenant puisque dorénavant nous exigeons un prix d'entrée lors de la présentation de ce genre de productions.

Voilà donc quelques exemples de l'utilisation de l'interprétation théâtrale au Musée de la civilisation. Des productions-maison et des productions de l'extérieur, toujours au service d'un thème dans un objectif d'enrichissement du thème mais aussi, bien entendu, pour émouvoir, divertir, travailler en collaboration avec les artistes de chez nous et jouer notre rôle de lieu culturel total.

La musique

Les multiples genres musicaux sont également fortement sollicités à l'intérieur de la programmation de notre Service de l'action culturelle.

Il s'agit pour nous de l'expression idéale pour accéder à d'autres formes de cultures et de participer à un autre grand principe institutionnel qui est celui d'un musée ouvert sur le monde.

Nous mettons à contribution des musiciens d'origine diverses maintenant établis chez nous parce que nous considérons que nous avons des héritages à partager. Il nous arrive parfois d'accueillir des musiciens de passage lors de nombreux festivals qui se déroulent au Québec.

De Sibérie, de Turquie, de Chine et de Bulgarie, entre autres pays, nous avons invité les visiteurs du Musée à découvrir l'ailleurs.

C'est extraordinairement enrichissant pour une programmation estivale alors que nous accueillons des touristes étrangers et locaux et cela contribue à abolir la barrière de la langue.

Lors d'expositions à caractère international comme celles présentées sur la Turquie, la Tunisie, l'Afrique et bientôt sur les trésors d'Autriche, l'expression musicale, celle peut-être qui nous rapproche le plus des peuples, est toujours mise à contribution par une formule de concerts commentés. Les visiteurs accèdent à une autre dimension de la culture des pays que celle traitée dans l'exposition.

Il nous est aussi arrivé parfois d'être producteur à part entière de certains spectacles musicaux. C'est le cas d'un spectacle de chansons d'amour que nous avons monté avec des artistes québécois pour illustrer en chansons une thématique sur l'amour. La conception et la réalisation du spectacle ont été entièrement assumées par le Musée avec la contribution de nos propres services techniques. Cela a donné lieu à un spectacle hautement professionnel, plein d'émotions, un petit bijou qui a provoqué une ovation debout !

Tous les genres musicaux, l'art lyrique, la musique de chambre, le folklore, le rock, le pop, le blues et même la récente organisation d'un rave où les jeunes ont dansé toute la nuit sur de la musique techno-pop, ont eu droit de cité au Musée attirant ainsi des clientèles diversifiées.

Nous poursuivons là aussi un objectif cher au Musée, un Musée ouvert sur le monde et qui reflète le passé, le présent et l'avenir. Un Musée qui fait place aux interprètes de ces réalités.

La danse

Du côté de la danse, nous avons constaté qu'il s'agit peut-être du langage artistique le plus riche pour l'animation de lieux spécifiques.

En ce sens, une expérience originale a été réalisée au Musée pour marquer son ouverture officielle il y a 6 ans. Une jeune compagnie de danse de Québec a été invitée à créer une œuvre originale pour l'inauguration du Musée. Cela nous permettait également d'illustrer la place que le Musée comptait accorder à l'expression artistique.

Nous voulions une création originale, spectaculaire puisqu'il s'agissait de l'inauguration; audacieuse aussi, puisqu'elle devait annoncer la nouvelle approche muséologique d'un jeune musée. De plus, la chorégraphie devait contribuer à la mise en valeur du site, le grand hall du Musée habité par une monumentale sculpture d'Astri Reutch, installée dans un bassin.

Cette chorégraphie, créée par la compagnie Danse Partout, se révèle être une création personnalisée à double titre. D'abord parce qu'elle est le reflet de la personnalité du Musée (audace, parti pris favorable pour l'expression artistique). Et aussi elle personnalise une œuvre, met en valeur un espace et procure une double contemplation : celle d'une œuvre dans une œuvre.

Une belle rencontre de la sculpture, de l'architecture, de la danse, de la musique et... du cinéma puisque l'ONF y a consacré un film.

Donc, la danse permet de personnaliser un site, mais aussi une manière. Cette création annonçait, dès l'ouverture du Musée, la place qu'il comptait donner aux arts d'interprétation et aux ressources artistiques locales.

Les innovations ont été multiples. Que l'on songe à la mise en valeur de la collection de vêtements du Musée dans un spectacle chorégraphié avec musique en direct. On est loin de l'artefact en vitrine! Voilà un autre exemple d'une interprétation personnalisée animant des objets de collection.

La danse contribue, comme la musique, aux rapprochements culturels.

Nous collaborons aussi depuis quelques années à la présentation de spectacles du Festival folklorique des enfants du monde qui se déroule dans notre région. (Diapositives). Ces spectacles sont donnés en façade du musée où nous disposons d'un grand espace ou encore dans le grand hall.

Des troupes de jeunes en provenance d'une dizaine de pays viennent danser pour les visiteurs du Musée.

Il s'agit là d'un animation d'un grande richesse qui attire un public familial et qui nous permet une fois encore de demeurer ouvert sur le monde.

Contes et légendes

Une place importante est aussi accordée à la parole, à la tradition orale. Lors de l'événement annuel la Fête autour du conte, nous accueillons des conteurs de tous les pays qui, en interaction avec le public, nous entraînent dans le monde imaginaire de chacun.

Voilà donc un portrait sommairement brossé de la manière dont on fait appel aux arts d'interprétation dans notre Musée avec, toujours en toile de fond, un thème comme déclencheur de nos choix de programmation.

En conclusion, je dirais que l'utilisation des arts d'interprétation dans un musée personnalise les rapports avec les visiteurs en les interpellant plus directement, plus sensuellement, par la parole, le geste, le son, le contact direct humain, chaleureux avec des artistes.

Les créateurs de leur côté interprètent par leurs visions riches et originales les thématiques du Musée. Ils les rendent vivantes et contribuent à illustrer sa personnalité, sa raison d'être : un Musée qui témoigne de l'aventure humaine et de ses multiples manifestations.

Finalement cette contribution des artistes à la personnalité du Musée en fait une institution ancrée dans sa ville, respectueuse de ses créateurs puisque plusieurs activités sont réalisées en collaboration avec d'autres institutions culturelles : théâtres, festivals, conservatoires de musique, d'art dramatique et bien d'autres encore.

Et si les règles syndicales sont parfois lourdes à gérer, nous nous faisons un point d'honneur de rétribuer correctement les créateurs et de respecter les droits d'auteur.

En terminant, je ne peux passer sous silence la chance que nous avons de travailler dans une ville où abondent des artistes dynamiques, inventifs et compétents. Il s'agit là d'un réservoir riche et stimulant pour ceux et celles qui, comme nous, ont le mandat d'organiser des activités à caractère culturel dans un musée.

❖ L'interprétation personnalisée dans un musée thématique : une richesse, une nécessité au Musée de la civilisation

Pauline Beaudin
Coordonnatrice des guides-animatrices et des guides-animateurs
Service de l'éducation
Musée de la civilisation
Québec (Québec)

The Musée de la civilisation's Education Service has explored the possibilities of theatrical interpretation in a number of ways. From vignettes interpreted at a distance by interpreter-guides to puppeteers and a professional theatre company, we find primary support at the Museum for varied and innovative activities designed to disseminate content knowledge and to reach a range of clienteles. The following is a summary introduction to achievements as of May 1994. At the last workshop, Telltale Togs, young and old were invited to discover an era, a character or a trade by putting on a costume. This was an interactive workshop *par excellence*: stepping into costume, visitors clothed themselves in knowledge, thus becoming visitor-interpreters.

«Interprétation personnalisée», «capsules théâtrales», «animations théâtralisées», quelles autres combinaisons théâtro-linguistiques pourrions-nous inventer pour parler de visites, d'interprétations ou d'animations jouées et présentées en milieu muséal!

De la «capsule théâtrale» à l'animation distanciée d'un guide-animateur en passant par le jeu d'une marionnettiste, nous retrouvons au musée un principal point d'appui - le contenu - et trois pôles de diffusion - l'exposition, les interprètes et les visiteurs - pour arriver à la connaissance.

Schéma

Si nous partons de cette figuration, nous avons le choix de composer et d'innover en explorant les différentes possibilités des trois pôles.

Photo : Pierre Soulard, Musée de la civilisation

Un musée n'est pas un théâtre. Si les gens veulent voir et entendre du Tchékov ou du Tremblay, ils iront «au théâtre». Ainsi, s'ils viennent au musée, c'est non seulement pour apprendre, mais pour se retrouver dans un lieu vivant et dynamique où ils ont un rôle actif à jouer dans leur apprentissage et leur découverte; bref, un milieu où ils connaissent et se reconnaissent.

Notre visiteur choisit parmi les activités qui lui sont offertes. L'interprétation personnalisée, au sens large, est un des moyens à notre disposition pour sensibiliser le visiteur au contenu d'une exposition. De par sa conception, cette forme d'animation a aussi l'avantage de rejoindre des publics variés et plus réceptifs à ce genre de diffusion. L'exposition thématique au Musée de la civilisation s'ouvre aux visiteurs un peu à la manière de ces livres en trois dimensions qui fascinent notre imaginaire depuis notre plus jeune âge. Peu importe le temps du récit de l'exposition qui est présentée, c'est un visiteur au présent et de tout âge qui s'y promène. Le guide-animateur, l'interprète, le conteur ou le marionnettiste devient le narrateur du récit «exposé» ou d'une partie de ce récit.

Dans *Musée de la civilisation, concept et pratiques*, on peut lire : «La personne est placée au centre de tous les choix que fait le Musée de la civilisation» (p. 40). Cette «personne» s'incarne à la fois dans les sujets thématiques présentés, le personnel du Musée, les visiteurs et les différents produits offerts par le traitement pluriel de notre institution.

Photos : Pierre Soulard, Musée de la civilisation

Les guides-animateurs du Service de l'éducation jouent un rôle de premier plan dans la communication auprès des visiteurs. Ils animent les lieux, ils sont le lien entre les visiteurs et les sujets mis en exposition. À l'intérieur de leur travail, ils ont eu à perfectionner différents médiums de communication dont celui de l'animation théâtrale. Au Musée de la civilisation, les guides-animateurs ne sont pas des comédiens ou des spécialistes du jeu; ils sont d'abord et avant tout des communicateurs qui emploient dans le cadre de certains projets, l'approche dite «animation théâtrale». Cette approche a pour principaux avantages de diversifier les activités présentées et de varier le travail des guides-animateurs.

Les tableaux des activités reliées à des expositions qui vous sont présentés plus bas offrent un compte rendu chronologique de l'interprétation personnalisée au Service de l'éducation du Musée de la civilisation et, ce, jusqu'en mai 1994.

En observant ces tableaux, on remarquera que le Service de l'éducation a parfois eu recours au service de professionnels du théâtre mais que la plupart des activités ont été présentées par des guides-animateurs.

Il faut cependant souligner que l'un des derniers ateliers mis sur pied, «Une 2e peau qui parle!» est un atelier de costumes où le visiteur devient le principal interprète. C'est le visiteur qui, en revêtant le costume, découvre le personnage, son époque, ses caractéristiques, etc. et joue un rôle à l'intérieur d'une dynamique de jeu interactif. Le guide-animateur suscite et supporte cette participation et donne les informations. Pour l'atelier «Une 2e peau qui parle!» on s'est inspiré du proverbe «l'habit ne fait pas le moine» et on l'a transposé en «l'habit qui fait le moine qui fait l'habit... ». En fait, c'est comment, par le costume, on peut découvrir une époque (p. ex., le Moyen-Âge en France ou l'époque victorienne) et ses fonctions sociales (p. ex., le chevalier, la paysanne, le tailleur, la femme de l'orfèvre, l'évêque, le fou du roi, la bourgeoise, la servante, etc.), le caractère des personnages de la commedia dell'arte ou du conte (p. ex., Arlequin, Brighella, la princesse, l'ogre, le loup, la petite Alice) ou encore la magie des animaux d'un conte musical (p. ex., le Carnaval des animaux de Saint-Saëns).

Ainsi le visiteur, l'adulte comme l'enfant, revêt* un costume, une deuxième peau, et découvre par le jeu, une époque, des personnages, en plus d'une fonction et d'un rôle spécifique à jouer. C'est le plaisir du déguisement et de la composition spontanée qui est retrouvé.

Petits et grands ont adopté cet atelier de costumes et son succès nous amène à le faire évoluer depuis 1993 en présentant un nouveau thème une fois par année.

*Il est à noter que l'on a conçu un modèle original de costumes pouvant être enfilés par-dessus les vêtements et s'ajustant aux différentes tailles. De plus, on a créé des modèles pour les enfants et pour les adultes.

ACTIVITÉS RELIÉES À DES EXPOSITIONS

LIEU	ACTIVITÉ	INTERPRÈTE	OBJECTIFS	CLIENTÈLES	DURÉE
Auditorium 1	Pièce de théâtre *Parenthèses* (théâtre d'intervention) (1989)	Troupe Bleu Majjiiik (professionnels)	Cadre : exposition **Familles.** Spectacle d'animation sur l'évolution de la vie de la famille.	Groupes scolaires (réservations) Dossier pédagogique remis au professeur.	60 minutes + visite de l'exposition
Hall du Musée	*Monsieur Olivier reçoit* Marionnette, grandeur nature (1990 - 1991)	Marionnettiste (professionnel)	• Faire un accueil magique • Créer un climat de plaisir et de détente • Inviter le public à venir le renconter dans **Objets de civilisation** (exposition)	Familles Grand public	Variable
Expositions : **Objets de civilisation**	*Monsieur Olivier* Marionnette, grandeur nature. Animation d'ateliers pédagogiques	Marionnettiste (professionnel)	Découvrir le sens de l'objet d'une collection dans un musée. Son histoire, son utilisation, sa restauration. Enquête sur l'objet.	Groupes scolaires (réservations)	50-55 minutes
Mémoires	*Monsieur Olivier raconte*		• Redécouvrir le plaisir du conte	Grand public	
La barque	*Monsieur Olivier raconte*		**La barque** : parler des ancêtres, de la vie des commerçants d'autrefois, du transport	Grand public	45 minutes

LIEU	ACTIVITÉ	INTERPRÈTE	OBJECTIFS	CLIENTÈLES	DURÉE
Objets de civilisation (lit de l'Impératrice)	*Le 9e fils du dragon* «Storytelling» (1992 - 1993)	Un guide-animateur du Service de l'éducation (costumes, accessoires)	• Souligner la finesse du travail des artisans chinois, par l'intermédiaire d'un conte. Symbolisme inhérent à leur art. L'observation des détails. • Faire découvrir les collections du Musée.	Grand public	15 minutes (3 ou 4 fois par jour l'été et les fins de semaine)
La Place Royale (site extérieur)	*La charrette* **Atelier mobile d'animation** Un charretier et sa charrette anime ici et là les visiteurs de la Place Royale. (1992 - 1993 - 1994)	Guide-animateur costume + une charrette qui contient différents objets. Matériel: copies d'objets (calumets, pipes, blague à tabac, tabac) et iconographie	Donner de l'information sur les fumeurs du XVIIIe siècle et inciter les gens à aller voir certains objets dans les maisons de la Place Royale où il y a des expositions.	Touristique et estival	Variable selon l'affluence et les questions
Maison Estèbe et Voûtes Pagé-Quercy (site intérieur)	*L'héritage des Estèbe.* **Visite-atelier** Un(e) domestique surgi(e) du passé, et l'archéologue Cafouille, proposent une vision «vivante» de l'histoire de la famille Estèbe et d'un site archéologique (maison Estèbe + Musée de la civilisation (1991-1992)	Guide-animateur • Costumes • Accessoires	Permettre de découvrir et de comprendre le mode de vie de Guillaume Estèbe et de sa famille sous le régime français. (atelier d'archéologie)	Groupes scolaires (réservations) Grand public (fin de semaine)	2 heures Activité complète : 1 heure Capsule du domestique : 20 minutes

LIEU	ACTIVITÉ	INTERPRÈTE	OBJECTIFS	CLIENTÈLES	DURÉE
Ateliers éducatifs au sous-sol du Musée	*Une 2e peau qui parle.* **Atelier évolutif.** Le costume. Le masque et le costume de la commedia dell'arte • Choisir le masque et le costume de la commedia dell'arte • Découvrir les contraintes des «dessous» victoriens • Trouver le costume qui commande un métier. Vie – théâtre – histoire (1993-1994)	**Le visiteur :** qui porte le(s) costume(s) et découvre ainsi le message. Le guide organise le lieu, précise les consignes, donne de l'information et fait une animation où le formel laisse place au ludique.	• Faire vivre et revivre le plaisir du déguisement. • Développer entre les visiteurs une interaction naturelle. • Le vêtement informe toujours sur la personne qui le porte. • Chaque costume ou masque a une histoire à raconter, des informations à révéler.	Groupes scolaires (réservations) Familles et grand public	1 h 30 Variable selon l'intérêt et l'implication des visiteurs

ÉVÉNEMENTS SPÉCIAUX OU FÊTES ANNUELLES

LIEU	ACTIVITÉ	INTERPRÈTE	OBJECTIFS	CLIENTÈLES	DURÉE
Exposition **Mémoires** Zone *Le bon temps!*	• *La Saint-Valentin.* Capsule théâtrale d'animation «Alpide et Philomène». Lecture commentée de leur correspondance. (1992) • *La Saint-Valentin.* Capsule théâtrale «L'homme qu'aimaient les femmes». (1993)	Guide-animatrice Guide-animateur • Costumes • Cartes postales (copies) (documents tirés de nos collections) Guide-animatrice (Mathilde, Éva et Yvonne) Guide-animateur (Roland) • Costumes • Cartes postales (copies) (collection de la Bibliothèque nationale du Québec)	• Origine de la Saint-Valentin • Notion des amours et des fréquentations dans le passé. • Faire connaître l'importance de la carte postale au début du siècle, dans les fréquentations et la relation amoureuse. • Faire découvrir une collection de 266 cartes postales - 1905-1918	Grand public Grand public	15 à 20 minutes 15 à 20 minutes

LIEU	ACTIVITÉ	INTERPRÈTE	OBJECTIFS	CLIENTÈLES	DURÉE
Hall du Musée	*Journée internationale des femmes.* «Le 8 mars et son histoire». Capsule théâtrale mettant en scène Clara Zetkin (1857-1933) et Thérèse Casgrain (1896-1981) (1993)	2 guides-animatrices • Costumes • Accessoires	• Souligner ce jour en rappelant l'origine historique du 8 mars. • Faire connaître ces 2 protagonistes; l'une au plan international, l'autre dans le contexte québécois.	Grand public	20 minutes

❖ Shadow Theatre for Children with Special Needs

Chris Cade
Elmete Wood Special School, Leeds
National Railway Museum
York, U.K.

Présentation sur vidéo de techniques de théâtre d'ombres où des enfants d'une école spécialisée présentant des difficultés d'apprentissage moyennes - de même que des attitudes comportementales et émotionnelles proportionnelles - travaillent avec des enseignants et des artistes. Il en est résulté un impromptu multimédia, «le grand cirque Elmete», dont l'action se passait dans un «chapiteau» amélioré et représenté par des figures en deux dimensions apparaissant sur un écran éclairé par l'arrière. Comme la fanfare commençait à jouer, les clowns, les hommes forts, les acrobates, les jongleurs, les cyclistes, les magiciens et le cheval mimé apparaissaient en même temps en personne et sur l'écran derrière.

Les délégués se sont essayés à faire des «marionnettes» qui avaient un rapport avec leur propre institution et ont improvisé ensemble une histoire. Cette technique a réussi à Mary Burns dans Micro, au Musée national des sciences et de la technologie. Il s'agit peut-être d'une expérience à tenter et de l'apprécier en tant qu'autre forme de langage nous permettant de communiquer, dans des programmes d'interprétation personnalisée.

Alongside my work with Platform 4 Theatre at the National Railway Museum, my full-time job is co-ordinating Creative Arts at Elmete Wood Special School in Leeds. I work with students aged 11-19 who have moderate learning difficulties and associated emotional and behavioural needs.

We have an ongoing close relationship with Artists Whitewood and Fleming with whom we have worked on a number of very varied projects. However, it was the school's Christmas production of 1992 which best highlights artists, teachers and pupils working collaboratively across the arts in a multi-media "happening."

I presented to the delegates a short edited video of *The Great Elmete Circus*, the culmination of a term's cross-curricular work in school.

Shadow theatre "mirroring" the action of *The Great Elmete Circus* at Elmete Wood School.

The Artists had worked with younger pupils making shadow puppets which were to mirror and enhance live performances in "the ring." Two-dimensional backlit figures were in evidence as the Circus came to town both across the screen and "before your very eyes" amongst the audience in the form of real dancing, baton-twirling, pompom-waving majorettes played by older students.

The brass band struck up and clowns, strongmen, acrobats, jugglers, unicyclists, magicians and a pantomime horse appeared in the flesh and on the canvas simultaneously. The "Big Top" extravaganza had been a stimulating experience for all concerned.

The workshop task, following my presentation after an appropriate "finger exercises" warm up, was to make a "shadow puppet" to represent one artefact from the delegate's own museum or heritage institution.

We had a large taut sheet in place across the room with a powerful spotlight strategically in position ready to breathe life into the clever card creations.

Task 2 was to locate colleagues who had made compatible *objets d'art* and to build a short story together and perform it. The inventive and dextrous participants pulled out the stops and within the hour they conjured up some magical kinaesthetics (with accompanying commentary and sound effects)! Language barriers were transcended.

Though I feel strongly that we should never patronise children with Special Needs, a multi-layering of art forms can give more accessibility to the subject matter for all. On Saturday, May 7th, Mary Burns had already shown us the fresh vitality of shadow theatre in her performance of *Micro* at the National Museum of Science and Technology. It is just one of the languages through which we can communicate in live interpretation programmes.

Experiment and Enjoy!

❖ La performance muséologique : Un langage éclaté à la croisée des arts d'interprétation et de la muséologie

Louise-Nathalie Boucher
Responsable des services, Programmes publics
Musée canadien des civilisations
Hull (Québec)

Museological performance art — or performuse — proposes to exhibit artifacts while integrating them in the scenography of a performance primarily designed to present them, using language that is both artistic and scientific. The evocative power of the stage, artists and performance makes it possible to transcend the artifacts by means of emotion. The cognitive language usually predominant in exhibitions is complemented by emotional and responsive language, bringing a new experience to visitors, who become an audience. The very essence of the concept of *performance art* is to go beyond the frontiers of the known, to explore, to innovate. *Museological performance art* involves an ongoing search for new ways of letting artifacts speak by using contemporary stage language (dance, theatre, mime, puppetry, song, etc.) while respecting museum standards. Objects which may seem commonplace at first sight can then be presented spectacularly. Since the primary mandate of museums is to preserve and disseminate collections, these serve as a catalyst for *museum performances.* Nevertheless, it is important to go beyond the artifacts to portray the individuals and societies which created them. The concerned artists and communities will be consulted when initiating the project as their input will surely prove valuable, especially for ethical reasons and since their work may be treated in a non-traditional way. As for narration, if it cannot be heard, it must be readable. Narration content must be based on scientific research, although it is preferable for the form to display originality and creativity.

Obscurité. Lumière sur une courtepointe originale à motifs en étoile de Bethléem exposée sur scène.

Obscurité. Lumière sur une reproduction de la même courtepointe. Une musique de François Dompierre se fait entendre, suivie de la voix d'un narrateur décrivant la courtepointe.

Obscurité. Musique. Lumière sur la courtepointe, et sur six danseurs qui, en une pose théâtrale, tiennent chacun à bout de bras une courtepointe contemporaine, identique à celle exposée, mais taillée et cousue pour les fins du spectacle.

Derrière les danseurs, une diapositive représentant la courtepointe originale est projetée sur un écran géant pour permettre aux spectateurs de voir clairement et de façon impressionnante, l'assemblage des différentes pièces de la courtepointe.

Le narrateur s'exprime à nouveau au sujet de la provenance de la courtepointe, de son contexte social, ses matériaux, etc. Une pièce musicale bigarrée et colorée comme une courtepointe, s'amorce. Les danseurs entament une chorégraphie inspirée des formes, couleurs et motifs de la courtepointe. Ils dansent tout en faisant onduler, en agitant, en jouxtant leurs courtepointes. Pendant la chorégraphie, les diapositives présentent de menus détails agrandis 30 ou 50 fois (points de couture, motifs, assemblages), que le spectateur ne peut voir sur l'original, de son siège éloigné. Les danseurs se fondent régulièrement aux images projetées, en se moulant tantôt aux coutures, tantôt aux motifs en étoile des pièces cousues.

Ce scénario est un exemple de *performance muséologique*[1]. De telles mises en scène permettent de présenter des pièces de collection d'une manière créative et innovatrice en donnant la parole aux objets par l'entremise des danseurs, de la narration et des projections visuelles. Ainsi pour les courtepointes, puisque l'auditoire sait en majorité ce qu'est une courtepointe, à quoi elle sert et comment elle est confectionnée, il est permis de déborder d'imagination, de «s'éclater» afin que le spectateur puisse redécouvrir cet artefact si connu, d'un regard neuf.

La *performance muséologique* propose d'exposer les artefacts en les intégrant à la scénographie d'un spectacle conçu avec l'intention première de les présenter par le recours à un langage à la fois artistique et scientifique. La scène, les danseurs et le spectacle, de par leur puissant pouvoir d'évocation, permettent de transcender les artefacts et de rejoindre le spectateur en empruntant la voie des émotions. Le langage cognitif habituellement prédominant dans les expositions se voit alors complété des langages émotifs et sensitifs apportant une expérience d'un nouvel ordre au visiteur devenu spectateur.

Certains considéreront que le scénario ci-haut évoqué devrait inclure des danses folkloriques de l'époque de la courtepointe originale, des costumes traditionnels et d'autres éléments contextuels pour la rendre significative aux yeux des spectateurs. Bien que cette façon de faire puisse être considérée, l'essence même du concept de *performance* est de dépasser les frontières du connu, d'explorer, d'innover. Par la *performance muséologique*, il s'agit donc de rechercher constamment de nouvelles façons de donner la parole aux artefacts et d'utiliser un langage scénique contemporain pour aborder les cultures. Des objets à prime abord banals pourront se voir présentés de façon spectaculaire.

Prenons un autre exemple. Sur scène côté jardin, trois socles exhibent chacun un vase de verre soufflé. Au centre, apparaîtront sur écran des diapositives ou séquences de film démontrant les différentes étapes de soufflage de verre. Côté cour, une troupe de danse moderne fait son entrée. Nous savons tous ce qu'est un vase de verre, mais il y a par contre moins d'initiés à l'histoire du verre. Une narratrice ouvre donc la *performance* par ces mots :

> « Des archéologues estiment que le verre était connu 4000 ans avant Jésus-Christ. Égyptiens et Phéniciens ont pratiqué l'art de la verrerie; Alexandrie était à cet égard célèbre. Déjà dans l'Antiquité, on travaillait le verre comme aujourd'hui, par soufflage, taille et moulage.»

Pendant que le texte, la musique et la danse alternent, les diapositives, séquences de films ou images numérisées par ordinateur, défilent en illustrant le processus de fabrication : Préparation du mélange vitrifiable, enfournement, fusion, fonte, façonnage, soufflage, coulage, moulage, étirage, cuisson, solidification et finition.

Certaines images seront retenues pour leur esthétisme, telle la flamme rougeoyant le verre brut à l'extrémité du chalumeau. D'autres seront choisies pour maintenir la logique des étapes de fabrication et d'autres pour leur force d'évocation. La chorégraphie intégrera les danseurs aux images en les propulsant au-devant de la flamme, au bout du chalumeau, à l'intérieur du four. Les corps enroberont les vases, se heurteront sur l'enclume et gonfleront avec la pâte de verre. La musique (un air de Kitaro) correspondra à la fois au broyage des minéraux bruts, aux langueurs du verre chaud qui s'étire, à la mollesse du verre encore flasque et aux sonorités cristallines du produit fini.

J'ai réalisé de semblables *performances muséologiques* au cours des années 80 alors que je me demandais comment présenter les artefacts de façon nouvelle à un public rébarbatif aux expositions. Comment étendre la portée des musées et accroître leur achalandage? Est-il vraiment nécessaire de toujours recourir aux expositions pour présenter les artefacts? Ne pourrions-nous pas explorer d'autres médiums pour révéler les pièces de collection au public? Pourquoi ne pas interpréter les objets par un langage plus éclaté, laissant place au risque et à l'audace, afin de rejoindre ceux qui évitent les musées en raison de leur immobilisme et conservatisme?

C'est pour répondre à ces questions que j'ai mis sur pied à titre expérimental, différentes *performances muséologiques*[2] dont la forme d'interprétation peut varier : danse, mime, théâtre, marionnettes, chant, opéra, etc., celle-ci étant choisie pour interpréter l'objet de la meilleure façon possible, sans être une fin en soi. L'essentiel est de communiquer un

Le corps humain devient podium pour *Alli*, un canard de verre soufflé d'Oiva Toikka, designer et maître verrier finlandais dont les oeuvres sont exposées à travers le monde. *Alli* a été conçu en 1980 et fabriqué en série par la suite.

message inhérent aux artefacts par l'entremise d'interprètes en arts de la scène tout en favorisant de nouvelles approches pour laisser parler les objets, dans le respect des normes muséales. Sans être une nécessité absolue, les moyens audiovisuels constituent un important complément au texte et au langage gestuel de l'interprète en créant un univers visuel et sonore éveillant l'intérêt du spectateur.

Le vocable *performance* réfère aux artistes en arts de la scène, comme Marie Chouinard et Michel Lemieux qui utilisaient ce terme alors qu'ils se produisaient dans des galeries d'art, telle Véhicul'Art à Montréal, pour sortir du cadre conventionnel des salles de spectacles. La raison d'être de ces *performances* était de faire éclater les cloisons entre différentes disciplines et d'en repousser les limites. Celle des *performances muséologiques* est de fusionner la muséologie aux arts de la scène et de chercher des façons inédites de présenter les artefacts (et leurs sociétés inhérentes) par un dépassement constant des formes d'interprétation.

Des *performances muséologiques* - ou *performuses* - ont été présentées sur mon initiative au Mexique (par l'entremise d'un stage au Musée régional d'Oaxaca), au Collège de l'Outaouais, au Musée de l'Amérique française, à l'espace de danse Tangente et surtout à l'Université de Montréal alors que j'y enseignais l'ethnomuséologie.

J'ai pu y explorer différentes formules, des plus simples à un seul personnage, aux plus complexes à plusieurs *performeurs* intégrés à des séquences de films, projections de

La projection permet au public de mieux voir les différentes composantes d'*Alli*, soit l'alternance de couches de verre qui se rejoignent en une spirale pour former les ailes. Photo projetée : The Finnish Glass Museum.

diapositives, narration et musiques alternatives. J'y ai privilégié la danse étant personnellement familière avec ce langage, mais comme je l'ai indiqué plus tôt, tous les arts d'interprétation sont à considérer. En s'ouvrant à tous les arts d'interprétation, les *performances muséo-logiques* permettent de joindre un plus vaste auditoire et ainsi de diffuser le patrimoine au plus grand nombre possible.

Comme le mandat premier des musées est de préserver et diffuser les collections, celles-ci constituent le point de départ des *performuses*. Bien sûr il est ensuite important de déborder sur les individus et sociétés qui ont créé et utilisé ces artefacts, ces derniers étant préservés pour témoigner de l'aventure humaine. Mais les *performuses* se distinguent des films, pièces de théâtre ou autres spectacles à caractère anthropologique ou historique en s'identifiant directement à la muséologie et donc aux témoins tangibles des civilisations. Sans pièces de collection ni recherche muséale, point de *performuse*.

Cette façon de mettre en scène des pièces de collection requiert évidemment une prudente application. Les objets doivent être soigneusement sélectionnés, avec la collaboration non seulement des conservateurs mais aussi des représentants des cultures concernées. Le caractère inhabituel des *performances muséologiques* exige également que chorégraphies et

154

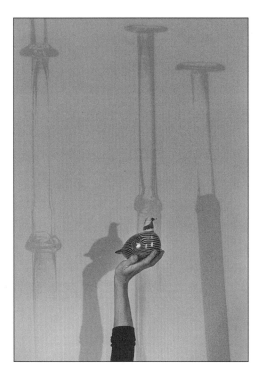

Alli hissé entre *Bambu,* une autre oeuvre de verre soufflé d'Oiva Toikka (1973). Le bras s'allonge tel une tige de bambou pour s'apparier aux formes longilignes des vases. Photo projetée : The Finnish Glass Museum.

scénarios soient soumis, sinon élaborés, avec des représentants des cultures en question. En effet puisque les pièces de collection seront traitées de façon non traditionnelle, il est important d'établir un dialogue avec les communautés culturelles pour éviter que la mise en scène de leur patrimoine tangible ne soit mal interprétée. Ce dialogue présentera l'avantage d'enrichir le spectacle de la perception de ces communautés à l'endroit de leur patrimoine. La nouveauté du processus demande qu'on lui laisse le temps d'être apprivoisé; des rencontres entre artistes, muséologues et représentants des communautés héritières des artefacts retenus sont donc primordiales.

Dans le cas d'œuvres d'art, les droits d'auteur doivent être respectés. Si les artefacts sélectionnés ont été créés par des artistes contemporains, il est important que ceux-ci ou leurs héritiers soient consultés en fonction des droits moraux et de reproduction de leur œuvre.[3]

À la frontière de la muséologie et des arts de la scène la *performance muséologique* entraîne des considérations au niveau de la conservation. Entre autres, les éclairages scéniques et la température ambiante peuvent être nocifs à des pièces de collection que l'on doit protéger pour la postérité. Cet écueil peut être contourné en utilisant des reproductions ou des pièces de collection rassemblées en vue d'être manipulées. Les diapositives et autres illustrations projetées peuvent remplacer les originaux trop fragiles, d'où leur importance première au sein des *performances muséologiques*. Les images projetées ont en fait différentes

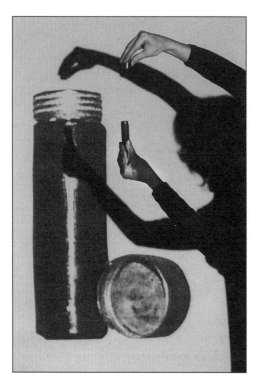

Contenant de verre du XIXe siècle. L'ombre du performeur est ici mise à profit pour compléter l'illustration par une gestuelle qui vient fermer le couvercle. Intégré à la scénographie, un objet à prime abord banal, peut devenir fascinant. Il s'agit d'un article de toilette qui pouvait contenir des sels ou du solvent. Le contenant est de verre rouge et le couvercle de métal.

fonctions : permettre à l'auditoire de voir en grande dimension les objets exposés sur scène, montrer en gros plan de menus détails, situer les artefacts dans leur contexte social, établir des parallèles entre différentes pièces, démontrer les processus de fabrication, recréer des environnements, révéler des vues en coupe, en plan, etc.

Sans être nécessaire, la musique est un autre élément important. Accédant directement aux émotions, elle enrichit considérablement les *performuses*. Ici aussi, jugement et discernement s'imposent avant d'y recourir. Associer des musiques traditionnelles à des objets de tradition différentes peut fausser le message. Et si rien n'empêche d'associer les mêmes musiques aux mêmes cultures, les danses devront alors être elles aussi traditionnelles. Il est donc préférable de choisir des musiques alternatives, plus neutres dont l'appartenance culturelle est plus anonyme.

Quant à la narration, son contenu est vital. À défaut de se faire entendre, elle devra pouvoir être lue. Sans texte, le spectacle est trop subjectif pour bien remplir son rôle muséal. Même le mime porte à différentes interprétations. La muséologie exige précision, authenticité, véracité. Le contenu de la narration doit s'appuyer sur des recherches scientifiques même si la forme doit préférablement faire preuve d'originalité et de créativité. Le texte, tout comme l'ensemble de la *performance* doivent marier les langages scientifique et artistique.

À la narration rationnelle, s'ajoute le langage gestuel, émotif, sensible du *performeur* qui rend accessible le contenu de la narration. Fasciné par ce qui se déroule sur scène, le spectateur est motivé à écouter le contenu de la narration. On a déjà comparé la *performance muséologique* à une conférence *jazzée*; quoique fort réducteur ce commentaire illustre bien cette dualité art et science de la *performuse*, sans compter que si les conférences attirent des auditeurs par dizaines, les concerts de jazz en attirent par milliers!

Les artistes accomplis en arts d'interprétation savent fasciner, émouvoir, passionner, faire rire, enflammer, enrager, bref tout déployer pour capter l'attention de leur auditoire. Rien de plus vivant qu'un être humain pour présenter une pièce de collection et sensibiliser à la culture d'autres êtres humains. Dans le cadre d'une *performance muséologique* le talent des artistes-interprètes vise à transmettre au spectateur le goût d'en savoir plus sur le sujet, quel qu'il soit.

Si plusieurs musées comptent une salle de théâtre dans leur enceinte, d'autres en sont privés. Pour ces derniers, la production de *performances muséologiques* pourra se dérouler dans toute salle où un espace scénique est délimité ou dans des salles de spectacle environnantes. Comme les *performuses* sont exportables, elles deviennent une occasion d'établir des liens avec d'autres organismes culturels et de joindre une nouvelle clientèle. En utilisant un langage contemporain pour ériger un pont entre le passé et le présent, le spectateur habituellement rébarbatif aux «vieilleries» pourra être attiré par une forme d'expression cinétique, répondant à la constante soif de mouvement qui caractérise les publics actuels. Les musées élargiront ainsi l'éventail de leurs ressources pour mieux remplir leur rôle de diffuseur du patrimoine, à l'intérieur tout comme à l'extérieur de leurs murs.

Notes

1. Bien que j'aie présenté une demi-douzaine de performances muséologiques, les extraits de scénarios décrits ici sont présentés à titre d'exemple. Les scénarios réalisés ont fait l'objet d'un compte rendu dans la revue *Musées* (vol. 12, n° 2, 1990).

2. Je tiens à remercier ici les professeurs Müller, Paradis et Bibeau de l'Université de Montréal, qui s'étaient penchés avec moi sur la désignation de *performance muséologique*. De mon côté, j'ai comprimé les deux termes en un diminutif : *performuse*, plus concis et pratique.

3. Les droits d'auteur continuent de prévaloir jusqu'à 50 ans après le décès de l'artiste.

There She Blows! (Elle souffle!) is the title of a new piece written for one of the History Hall environments, a re-created part of a 16th-century Basque whaling station in Red Bay, Labrador. This 15-minute play takes the form of a confrontation between a performance artist, who has come to the CMC to do an environmental piece on saving the whales, and one of the Basque whalers, boiling down whale blubber. The time-slip that brings them together in the visitors' real space and time is, quite deliberately, not fully explained. A "mannequin" of a Basque whaler, frozen in motion as part of the exhibit while visitors are arriving, suddenly comes to life. The artist attributes this vaguely to her powerful "vibrations" — an explanation which accords well with the character created by the playwright and developed by the actor:

Leila: Right now, you're living in my imagination, because of this place . . . and maybe a little because I'm an artist . . . I'm very sensitive to vibrations.

There She Blows! is full of surprises and explores many interesting ideas and issues. One of these is the issue of what exactly an artifact is, and what its relationship might be to the wonderfully re-created, but "non-real" reproductions of original artifacts found in some of the History Hall environments. At one point in the play, Leila notices that a harpoon which forms part of the re-created tryworks environment has carved into its haft the initials of the whalerman with whom she is arguing. She asks the audience to keep a sharp lookout for security guards while she "removes" it from the exhibit to show Txomin, the whaler — clearly again surprising visitors by violating their sense of what is "normal" and "proper" in a museum. In the dialogue and the argument which follow, Txomin tries to form an understanding of how the harpoon he lost in a whale chase can now be here in his hands, as she tries to explain to him how and in what state his harpoon was found, what an "artifact" is, what a museum is, and why the museum has re-created his own, original, decayed and corroded property in this way. As the characters argue, visitors receive much food for thought about their own preconceptions of the museum experience, and what it could and should be.

Source: "Surprising the Visitor: Interpretive Theatre at the Canadian Museum of Civilization," conference proceedings of the Museum Education Association of Australia, September 30 to October 4, 1991.

L'évaluation

PART THREE

Evaluation

❖ Improving Live Interpretation Programs through Evaluation

Harry Needham
Director, Programmes and Operations, Canadian War Museum
Canadian Museum of Civilization Corporation
Ottawa, Ontario

L'interprétation personnalisée subit un examen minutieux. En effet, les gestionnaires de programmes et le personnel essaient d'en améliorer l'efficacité. Ils doivent rendre des comptes et composer avec les coûts qui augmentent et les budgets qui diminuent. Bien qu'il existe plusieurs manières d'évaluer l'interprétation personnalisée, l'évaluation de programme semble être la plus efficace, étant donné que ce type d'interprétation réunit un si grand nombre des divers programmes et activités de l'organisme. L'évaluation de programme examine quatre points fondamentaux : le mandat ou la raison d'être du programme, la réalisation des objectifs, les effets et l'impact de même que les différents moyens de réaliser le programme. Une méthode utile pour faire une évaluation de programme comprend l'étude du dossier, l'observation discrète, des entretiens en profondeur, des groupes de discussion, la revue par les pairs et une recherche-sondage. Au Musée canadien des civilisations, cette approche a été très efficace pour évaluer différents types d'interprétation personnalisée.

Why are people becoming more interested in evaluating live interpretation programs?

Live interpretation poses some major challenges to the evaluator, which likely explains the paucity of studies of museum live interpretation programs. Indeed, in collecting studies from more than 150 institutions in 11 countries, I have only come upon very few examples — and most of these were *very* narrow or superficial or both. I am sure there have been many more but I must still conclude that most museum evaluators prefer to evaluate their exhibits, galleries, school programs, etc.

Yet, in the past few years, there seems to have developed a great deal of new interest in looking at these programs. Why is that?

First, all of us want to improve our programs — to make sure that we are doing the very best job we can, for the sake of the museum, its visitors, or whoever, but this has not made us eager to look at live interpretation in the past, even when we were quite prepared to do all kinds of evaluations of galleries, exhibitions, labels, signage, museum services and just about any other aspect of museum work that you can name.

Is it because we are starting to feel just a little bit uneasy about our live interpretation programs that have chugged along on tracks of their own for what can sometimes have been decades? Are we starting to wonder just what they are achieving, what kinds of real impacts and results they are producing and how well they relate to all our other institutional programs and activities? If so, then we are starting to think about program evaluation and it is long since time we did.

I think the *real* reason is neither of these, but rather the question of money. Live interpretation programs, as we all know, tend to be comparatively expensive, all the more so if lots of intricate costuming, scriptwriting and other bits and pieces are involved. And this is an age when almost all of us are seeing some very nasty trends developing, at least in North America.

First, visitor attendance is dropping, in some cases very quickly. Second, money is getting much, much tighter, especially for those of us funded wholly or in part by government. In this kind of climate, live interpretation is a very visible target in any cost-cutting exercise — and there is no doubt in my mind that, in many areas, *that* is why we are starting, at long last, to evaluate our live interpretation programs.

The Case for Evaluating Live Interpretation as a *Program*

We need to have the program information we need to make *smart* decisions — and we need to make those decisions, not just for a live interpretation program, but for the *totality* of our museum programs.

I suggest to you that using the so-called *standard museological indicators*, which really boil down in most studies to little more than assessing visitor satisfaction and demographics, and, perhaps, some aspects of affective learning, is *grossly* insufficient for the times in which we find ourselves and for our requirements, if our live interpretation programs are not to be first on the block of budget reductions. We need to get deeper into their essence and, at the same time, we need to examine how live interpretation relates to other programs, in carrying out the mandate of the institution. In other words, we need to do *program* evaluation.

Now what is program evaluation and how should we use it to approach the evaluation of live interpretation?

Program evaluation looks at the totality of a program, and its relationship to the carrying out of the mandate and objectives of the whole institution in which it is sited. Rather

It need hardly be said that solid and current research must be the backbone of interpretive theatre.

Much more evaluation work is needed, however, before we can know whether interpretive theatre is an educational method of superior effectiveness.

Source: Stephen Alsford and David Parry, "Interpretive Theatre: A Role in Museums?" *Museum Management and Curatorship*, 10, 1 (March 1991), pp. 21-22.

than evaluating a particular exhibition, for example, a program evaluation would look at the *entire program* of exhibitions and what it does for the institution in which it resides. A program evaluation of live interpretation, by extension, would examine the different kinds of live interpretation, and their relationships with and contributions to the other programs and activities through which the institution exercises its mandate. Only then can management make the right decisions to guide the future development of the institution, especially in times of trouble.

Most institutions that have tried to evaluate their live interpretation programs have done so, in my opinion, far too superficially and with far too narrow a focus. Yes, it's important to know what proportion of your visitors stop to watch. Yes, it's important to know if they like it or not or feel they may have learned something from it. However, unless we measure, in length and in depth the way the interpretation program performs against its mandate and its objectives, and the ways in which it should reinforce and support other institutional programs and activities, we are missing the boat and we will *not* have the information we need to make anything other than superficial programming decisions — and that is simply not good enough, in this day and age.

Classically, program evaluation deals with four issues or groups of issues.

Mandate

The first of these is the mandate of the program. Does it make sense? If it once made sense, does it still do so? Does *your* live interpretation program have a clear and understandable mandate, which it is trying to execute? Is it up to date? *DOES IT **MAKE SENSE**?*

An examination of the program's mandate should be the starting point of any evaluation of a live interpretation or, for that matter, any other kind of program. Let me give you two examples of why this is so. Some years ago, I was responsible for evaluating, for the Ministry of the Solicitor General of Canada, a program that provided funding to centres of criminology in six Canadian universities. The program had been established 10 years earlier, at a time when there were no domestically produced criminologists in Canada — they all had to be imported from the U.K. or the U.S.A. We discovered that, by the time we did the evaluation, we had trained so many Canadian criminologists that few of them could find jobs and they were all leaving in droves for the United States!!! The program was chopped pretty quickly!

I therefore think you should have a serious look at the mandate of your live interpretation program, as a first step to doing anything else. You cannot avoid asking yourself *why* you are doing the various forms of live interpretation that you do and whether or not it *makes sense* to do them.

Objectives Achievement

The second great question that program evaluation asks of a program is whether it is achieving its objectives or, to put it more practically, *Is it doing what we thought it would?*

In 15 years of doing program evaluation, I have found that the most significant problems in a program are usually centred around objectives. They may not exist — the program is like the child Topsy, in Harriet Bleecher Stowe's *Uncle Tom's Cabin*, who said she never had had a mammy or a pappy — she "jest growed."

The program's objectives may be fuzzy and, if this is so, you can bet that the program will not be doing what its originators expected it would. The objectives may not be shared by all the stakeholders. If this is so, the program may be subverted and you can be sure that it will not have much useful articulation with related programs.

It is particularly important, in evaluating live interpretation programs, to examine the objectives, not only of the interpretation programs themselves, but also of all the other institutional programs to which they relate. These include programs of exhibition, education, performing arts and special events, public relations and even commercial programs. It is very important to assess the articulation between the various sets of objectives. If they don't fit, then your live interpretation program, attractive to the visitors though it may be, may not be contributing much to the overall success of the institution.

Impacts and Effects

Program evaluation asks a third question: *What is happening as a result of the program?* In other words, what are its impacts and effects? If we have a clear and unambiguous mandate for the program, and well-defined and measurable objectives, it should be relatively easy to specify just what impacts and effects the program is supposed to produce. (Those can be two very big "if"s!)

This is where we go from the broad perspective to the gory details. Of all the things we had hoped for, what has happened? Equally important, what has happened that was *never* intended, and is it a good or a bad thing? How do we know whether something *is* a good or a bad thing, in the first place?

Just as the institution needs to have a solid philosophy of interpretation to set and assess the program's mandate, it requires a solid understanding of communications and learning processes, as well, of course, as of the methods that may be used, to be able to interpret what is happening. What makes for good evaluation of impacts and effects is the quality of this combination, as applied to the planning of the evaluation.

What questions can we ask?

I think we first need to have some broad understanding of who the audience is. How many people participate in our live interpretation? Do they like it (whatever *that* means!)? How many only watch? How many don't even do that? Who are they? Where are they from? How old are they? Does any of this make a difference? Most of these are questions that simple quantitative methods will answer and will soothe, to some degree, senior management increasingly concerned about the high cost of live interpretation and what kind of "bang for the buck" it may be producing.

But we need to go further. We need to systematically examine, for every impact and effect the program is *supposed* to be producing, what is actually happening out there. If we are trying to produce learning, for example, it is *not* enough to stop at the affective level; there must be some attempt to get at the degree of cognitive learning that is taking place. We must also examine how the impacts and effects of live interpretation interact with those produced by related programs and activities, as this is the only way we can judge whether they are mutually supporting. If they are not, we have a major problem.

Alternatives

The last question the program evaluation asks is, *Are there better ways of producing the desired results*? In evaluating live interpretation programs, this may mean several things. It may involve questioning the *kind or balance* of kinds of interpretation that is going on. For example, it may suggest a move toward more first-person, or more third.

An evaluation may suggest more mundane improvements to your program, involving scheduling, the relative length of performances, better locations, improvements for the comfort of visitors, etc. — things that are related not only to the effectiveness of your live interpretation program, but to its *efficiency*, as well.

The ultimate "alternatives" question, of course, is: *Should the entire program be replaced with something better*?

What Methods Work Best?

File Review

The first method used in most program evaluations is a review of program files. This is the starting point for identifying the program's mandate, objectives and expected impacts and effects. It also helps you understand aspects of the relationship between the live interpretation program and the work of the institution, writ large. Almost every live interpretation program, to get started, required a selling job and the document that did the selling is the place to start. However, there is a major problem with paper — it is often very far from the reality. So file reviews must be verified through the use of other techniques.

Unobtrusive Observation

With file review, unobtrusive observation is the starting point for the evaluation. It very quickly gives you a "feel" for the program, what it offers, how it works and, superficially at least, what kinds of impacts it is producing. What proportion of the visitors stop to watch? How many actively participate? In what ways and to what degree? How happy do they seem? What questions do they ask? How many of them don't even stop but streak right on by? Unobtrusive observation is a technique we all use every day to assess our live interpretation programs, but here, it gives you absolutely critical information to help you plan your study and determine the other methods you will have to use.

Depth Interviews

You are going to have to do a lot of interviewing — and not just of the visitors! You will need to interview program managers and the managers of related programs, to see how everyone understands the mandate, objectives and achievements and feels about how they are being achieved. You must ask the interpreters themselves and, of course, the clients of your institution who participate in live interpretation programs, and — just as important — those who do not, to find out why they don't. I think that, for most live interpretation programs, depth interviews will be at the core of the evaluative process.

Focus Groups

Focus groups can give you much of the same rich information that you get from interviews, but the group dynamic that operates in a well planned and moderated focus group can give you much deeper information, if on a more narrow range of questions. The problems of focus groups are chiefly practical and the biggest problem is getting the right group of people to sit down for a couple of hours to participate in a focus group. This is where the people in the park systems have the advantage over the rest of us;

where they have campsites, it is often possible to collect people together in the evening, after they have participated in live interpretation, for a focus group. The rest of us usually end up paying the visitors to come back and, even then it is a struggle. I tend to use focus groups more for staff and volunteers of interpretation programs, and rely on other means to get at the programs' victims.

Peer Review

Peer review is often used to evaluate live interpretation. It is always useful to have the opinion of an outside professional, *if* he is well-briefed and *if* he's reasonably competent, but it is an unpredictable tool at best and may cause more harm than good. On the other hand, it does give you an independent opinion. Use it with care.

Surveys

I find that, in evaluating live interpretation programs, surveys aren't very useful. While they will give you information on a great many things, the results tend to be shallow, in comparison with what you can get from other means. By all means, use surveys, but use them for the things they do best — to produce the quantitative baseline data that will satisfy your senior management that the program is cost-effective.

Sampling

I'd like to say a word about sampling. I find that live interpretation programs produce quite different effects on different segments of the visitor population, regardless of the institution or type of interpretation. It is very critical that, in planning your evaluation, you determine of whom these segments are comprised and ensure that they are adequately sampled. It is particularly important, for example, to interview not only the visitors who came and stayed for the whole performance, but also those who only stayed for part and those who didn't stay at all. Most evaluations of live interpretation rely only on the visitors who stay for the whole thing. The results are hopelessly biased in favour of the positive as a result, and are therefore useless for any purpose other than program public relations.

What did a program evaluation of our live interpretation program produce for us?

To conclude, I'd like to tell you what we got out of applying this approach to our theatre program in the Canadian Museum of Civilization.

Our evaluation flowed very much from a question of money — our senior management was questioning the cost-effectiveness of our very innovative theatre program and had pretty well decided to chop the program. The managers of the program and I felt the decision was being based on limited and misleading information, and we were able to delay the decision, pending the result of a program evaluation, which we had to carry out in double-quick time.

We looked at the full range of evaluation issues — mandate, objectives achievement, impacts and effects; we also looked at the program in the light of the standard museological indicators and we also compared the program to similar programs in other institutions.

We very quickly discovered that our program was viewed by other institutions as a leader and CMC was seen as an important and active player in the museum theatre community. We found that the program was a success from the visitor point of view, that visitors were stimulated and entertained, that learning was facilitated and that the visitor experience was greatly enhanced by the ways in which the program brought the museum to life. We discovered (not very surprisingly) that the professionalism of the actors was the major key to success. The majority of staff in related program areas felt strongly that live theatre was an essential component of institutional programming. The mandate was right, the objectives were being achieved, the program was producing a significant impact and there was no real alternative to it.

On the other hand, we found that the program did not always articulate well with other programs that it supported or that should have supported it, and that there was the need for better planning and scheduling, improvements to promotion and physical settings, and a need to apply the philosophy of the theatre program to all other areas of interpretation.

We recommended strongly that the program not merely continue, but move into other areas, such as training our uniformed interpreters (our "hosts/hostesses").

The evaluation not only reaffirmed the importance of continuing live theatre, and resulted in a number of changes that have made the program even better, but is having a major impact on the improvement of related programs, drawing them all together to increase the impact of our total museum experience.

We *must* continue not only to improve our live interpretation programs, but also to produce proof of not only their effectiveness, but also their *cost*-effectiveness. This can only be done through evaluation and it appears that the only kind of evaluation that will do it is *program* evaluation.

❖ Evaluating Unscripted Live Interpretation Programs

Chris Parsons
Principal, Word Craft
Monterey, California

Il y a des désavantages à employer des guides ou comédiens de formation non préparés, dans votre musée. Pour me prémunir contre la critique, mais, plus important encore, pour assurer un programme de qualité à nos visiteurs, j'ai mis sur pied un programme d'évaluation des guides-interprètes à l'aquarium de Monterey Bay lorsque j'y ai pris en charge la formation des bénévoles en 1985. Cet article soulève la question des défis que comporte l'instauration d'une évaluation dans un programme d'interprétation déjà en place, du développement des instruments d'évaluation, de l'organisation matérielle pour effectuer l'évaluation et des leçons tirées de l'expérience.

Introduction

A curator drops into your office to tell you that he just overheard one of your interpreters use the word "testicles" instead of "tentacles" to describe part of an octopus's anatomy. He suggests that you increase the number of lectures on invertebrates for the next interpreter training course and immediately offer an enrichment session for your current interpreters.

Your supervisor drops into your office and tells you that she has just witnessed one of your guides at an artifact cart. The guide didn't seem very interested in talking to visitors. She spent more time rearranging the items on the cart than engaging visitors in conversation or answering questions. Your supervisor suggests you spend more time in the galleries supervising your guides.

How many of you have had similar situations involving docents, interpreters or guides at your museum? These and similar situations often put the supervisor or trainer of interpreters in an awkward position and sometimes in a panic mode. The situations show the major drawbacks of having trained, but unscripted interpreters or docents at your museum.

To counter the criticisms, but more importantly to ensure we had a quality program for our visitors, I instituted a docent evaluation program at the Monterey Bay Aquarium when I took over volunteer training in 1985.

At that time, docents (called guides at the aquarium) completed a 16-week training course, the equivalent of a semester course at the local community college, before they interacted with visitors at the exhibits. The main stations for guides were the Touch Pool, Kelp Lab and Sandy Shores aviary. Guides also worked at other exhibits throughout the aquarium, narrated feeding demonstrations at the largest exhibits, and led tours.

Objectives

For this paper, I plan to cover:

- the challenges of introducing evaluation to an already established interpretive program
- the development of an evaluation instrument
- the logistics for conducting the evaluation
- the lessons learned.

Overview

I wanted evaluation to become a natural part of a volunteer's job and the senior education staff's responsibility. However, as I mentioned, the interpretive program had been in operation for a year when I began the evaluations. I knew that if it was not handled delicately and with attention to the needs and experiences of the guides, the evaluation program would fail.

Because the guides' interpretation was unscripted and generally without clear goals and objectives, I decided it would be easiest and safest to start with evaluations by the education staff who had trained the guides. I felt the guides would be more comfortable with feedback from us than from the public. I was also interested in improving the training program and wanted some information on the skills that needed upgrading or reinforcement.

If I were developing this evaluation program today, I would include visitor feedback as part of the evaluation of the guides.

The goals for the evaluation program were:

- to evaluate every guide (approximately 400) once a year to improve the quality of the interpretation provided to visitors
- to correct inaccurate or misinterpreted information
- to set up an ongoing, one-on-one communication and feedback loop between volunteers and education staff
- to identify strengths and weaknesses of our training program
- to identify strengths and weaknesses of the volunteer program
- to get to know the volunteers better.

The procedures for the evaluation were as follows:

Each week we would poll the senior education staff to see which day (if any) each member was available to evaluate a guide. Then, we randomly selected the names of guides who worked during the shifts when staff were available. (We randomly selected names to ensure fairness in the selection and to avoid stigmas such as problem or poor interpreters.)

We informed the guides in person that during their shift the following week they would be evaluated. We gave them a copy of the evaluation instrument (see attached) with a cover memo that explained the procedures in writing.

When the guide checked in for his/her shift the following week, the evaluator and guide met briefly. The evaluator was available to answer any questions the guide had. The evaluator received the guide's schedule for that shift (guides rotate during a three-hour shift to three stations in the aquarium). The evaluator unobtrusively observed the guide for at least 15 minutes during the shift. The evaluator and guide then met after the shift to discuss the evaluation.

Once we had worked out the logistics, I started with a memo to all guides explaining the program in detail and held several meetings to discuss the issue. I also spent more time than usual on the floor visiting guides while they were working in the aquarium to answer any questions they might have or address concerns.

I had a few guides who were very concerned (and met with them individually), a few who didn't care, a few who said they would leave if subjected to an evaluation, and most who understood the need for the evaluation and saw it as an opportunity to talk with education staff about the volunteer program.

Evaluation Instrument Development

Using the *Good Guide* (Grinder 1985), along with the aquarium's Guide Training Manual and Policies & Procedures Handbook, we developed a list of skills we thought were most indicative of a "good guide" engaged in quality interpretation.

Then, we developed a rating scale. The original scale used scores of 0 to 5, with 0 indicating the skill was not done (but could have been), 1 indicating poor performance, to 5 indicating great performance. Not applicable (n/a) was also an option for skills not performed and not applicable to the particular situation.

In hindsight, I found the rating scale too subjective, and so for this paper, have changed it to a rubric. Where a rating is a judgment made about the relative position of ability or performance, a rubric scores key traits of performance. I feel the rubric is less subjective.

When we originally developed the instrument we didn't involve the guides. If I were doing this program today, I'd have the guides work with education staff to determine the list of skills. *(Note: This is not the definitive list of skills. I believe each institution should develop its own list based on current research on interpretive techniques and the philosophies of the particular institution.)*

We tested the evaluation instrument on several guides and on education staff to determine the ease of use and instrument validity. We also tested instrument and observer reliability several times by having two education staff members evaluate the same interpreter, then compare results.

We made a few adjustments — adding, deleting and modifying the skills list — to refine the instrument.

Evaluation Instrument

Date/time of day	Crowd:	light	medium	heavy
Guide's Name	Evaluator's Name			
Station	Amount of time observed			

n/a = not applicable in this situation
0 = could have, but didn't do
1 = did, but needs improvement
2 = did okay
3 = did well

Skills Rating	n/a	0	1	2	3	Comments
Was appropriately dressed	n/a	0	1	2	3	
Looked receptive, ready to talk	n/a	0	1	2	3	
Was friendly and positive	n/a	0	1	2	3	
Faced audience while talking	n/a	0	1	2	3	
Stood so audience could see exhibit(s)	n/a	0	1	2	3	
Had a theme or focus	n/a	0	1	2	3	
Spoke loud enough	n/a	0	1	2	3	
Spoke clearly	n/a	0	1	2	3	
Used hands to direct attention	n/a	0	1	2	3	
Modeled appropriate behavior	n/a	0	1	2	3	

Used props appropriately	n/a	0	1	2	3
Gave accurate information	n/a	0	1	2	3
Used suitable vocabulary	n/a	0	1	2	3
Used appropriate anecdotes	n/a	0	1	2	3
Related information to visitors' lives	n/a	0	1	2	3
Encouraged participation with open-ended questions	n/a	0	1	2	3
Listened to questions and remarks	n/a	0	1	2	3
Credited questions	n/a	0	1	2	3
Encouraged the use of 2 or more senses	n/a	0	1	2	3
Solved problems gently & effectively	n/a	0	1	2	3
Closed talk by directing audience to exhibit(s) of interest	n/a	0	1	2	3

Guide's Strengths

_____

_____

Guide's Weaknesses

_____

_____

Suggestions for improvement made by the evaluator

_____

_____

Suggestions for improving the program made by the guide

_____

_____

Overall Rating of the Guide's Performance

Excellent   Very Good   Good   Fair   Poor

Recommendations

        _____ Re-evaluate in _____ month(s)

        _____ Retraining (specify) _____

        _____ Other (specify) _____

Guide's Signature _____ Date _____

Evaluator's Signature _____ Date _____

Lessons Learned

We found it sometimes difficult to schedule an education staff member with enough content knowledge and interpretive skills, who was also available to conduct an evaluation. To meet our goal of evaluating all the guides on an annual basis, the evaluation duty often fell to me. However, it was very valuable to have senior education staff conducting evaluations. They gained a better understanding of the problems and issues the volunteers and I faced.

Some guides were intimidated by some education staff members, particularly the director of the department, mainly because of his position and high regard.

Once we started the evaluation, the Volunteer Coordinator began requesting evaluations of "problem" guides, and we often had to dispense with choosing guides randomly. I was concerned this would change the guides' perception of the evaluations from "for everyone" to "for problem guides."

We found we had some good guides and some not-so-good guides. For those who needed improvement, we offered suggestions and scheduled a follow-up evaluation within a few months. Some guides improved and some didn't. The few who didn't were referred to the Volunteer Coordinator, who had procedures for reassigning them to a volunteer job that didn't include public contact or for dismissing them.

In addition to individual differences among guides, we also found certain skills were consistently weak, such as "related information to visitors' lives" or "had a theme or focus." We used results from the evaluation to develop enrichment classes and make changes in the training course.

Suggestions for improvement made by the guides were insightful and useful. Although we couldn't always make changes, it was beneficial to discuss the issues with guides.

The evaluation focused on observable skills, not on visitors' responses to the interaction with guides. If I were doing this today, I would include interviews with visitors to see if the skills we identified actually contributed to quality interpretation.

Summary

Overall, I think the program was well received, after some initial trepidation. I learned a great deal from the guides and, as a result of evaluations I conducted, I developed some very close friendships that I maintain today.

And although it was sometimes a logistics headache, I found the evaluation program very useful in developing, maintaining and improving the guide training program, as well as improving the quality of interpretive presentations. I would recommend a similar evaluation program to anyone responsible for unscripted interpretive programs.

References

Butler, P. H., III and R. J. Loomis (1992). "Evaluation for an Historic House Museum: The Moody Mansion as a case study." *Visitor Studies: Theory, Research, and Practice, Volume 5. Collected Papers from the 1992 Visitor Studies Conference, St. Louis, MO.* Jacksonville, AL: Visitor Studies Association.

Canadian Museum of Civilization (1992). "Evaluation of the Live Interpretation Program at the Canadian Museum of Civilization" reprinted in *Perspectives on Museum Theatre*. Washington, D.C.: American Association of Museums, Technical Information Service's Forum.

Evans, C. W. (1984). "Coaching: A system of evaluating interpretive presentations." *the Interpreter* (Fall): 18-22.

Graft, C. (1989). "Incorporating Evaluation into the Interpretive Planning Process at Colonial Williamsburg." *Visitor Studies: Theory, Research, and Practice, Volume 2. Proceedings of the 1989 Visitor Studies Conference, Dearborn, MI.* Jacksonville, AL: Center for Social Design.

Grinder, A. L. and E. S. McCoy (1985). *The Good Guide*. Scottsdale, AZ: Ironwood Publishing.

Huberty, B., A. Sigford, et al. (1984). "Networking: On the road to excellence." *the Interpreter* (Fall): 15-17.

Mager, R. F. (1988). *Analyzing Performance Problems*. Belmont, CA: Lake Publishing.

Parsons, C. (1986). "Using Computers to Evaluate." *AAZPA Regional Conference Proceedings*. Washington, D.C.: AAZPA.

Rossett, A. (1987). *Training Needs Assessment*. Englewood Cliffs, NJ: Educational Technology Publications.

❖ Conclusion

Au-delà du théâtre...
L'interprétation personnalisée au musée

Jean-Marc Blais
Planificateur principal en interprétation
Musée canadien des civilisations
Hull (Québec)

Phénomène qui gagne en popularité dans le domaine muséal, l'interprétation personnalisée est reconnue pour la multiplicité de ses approches et la diversité de ses langages. Le symposium présenté en 1994 démontrait le côté novateur, voire provocateur de ce moyen de communication.

Comme l'ont souligné plusieurs auteurs, l'interprétation personnalisée est un des moyens qui permet de transmettre un savoir, de partager un engouement, mais surtout de faire vivre des émotions. C'est là que réside la particularité de l'interprétation personnalisée : permettre aux visiteurs de vivre «l'expérience muséale» dans son intégralité. Au cours des dernières années, les musées se sont taillés une place fort respectable parmi les industries de la culture. Toutes les statistiques de fréquentation indiquent un accroissement réel, significatif et constant du public. Si le musée est devenu plus familier, ses utilisateurs exigent que la visite soit valable aux points de vue économique (on en veut pour son argent), éducatif (le désir d'apprendre est manifeste) et social (le musée est un lieu d'interaction). Dans ce contexte, l'interprétation personnalisée constitue le moyen par excellence de répondre à ces exigences.

Les musées sont passés maître dans l'art de faire appel à l'intellect des visiteurs. Point besoin de faire l'inventaire des techniques traditionnelles de mise en exposition où le savoir encyclopédique sur l'objet présenté constitue la raison première de toute action muséale. Malgré le discours dominant qui prône l'approche «publique», il n'en demeure pas moins que les besoins de ce public sont considérés comme un mal nécessaire. Dans plusieurs institutions, les professionnels versés dans l'interprétation personnalisée sont confrontés à cette réalité toujours bien présente. Ils sont souvent appelés à combler, en catastrophe, les lacunes d'une exposition et doivent rapidement concevoir des approches d'animation qui touchent au visiteur.

«Toucher au visiteur», voilà l'objectif difficile de la muséologie actuelle. Afin d'atteindre cet objectif, nos approches doivent être davantage holistiques; toutes les fonctions du musée doivent concorder à faire de ce dernier un lieu pertinent, valorisant et vivant pour ses utilisateurs, voire pour ses partisans. Pour ce faire, nous devons tout mettre en place afin que nos présentations (expositions, programmes, collections, etc.) soient plurielles tant dans leur approche que dans leur contenu. En plus de faire connaître, de faire découvrir, il nous faut émouvoir.

Faire appel à l'émotivité des visiteurs n'est pas chose facile, mais je crois que les professionnels de l'interprétation personnalisée réussissent cette tâche à merveille. À la lecture des textes présentés dans cet ouvrage collectif, il est fascinant de constater la richesse des techniques de l'interprétation personnalisée toutes centrées sur les visiteurs. L'hétérogénéité de ceux-ci et la diversité des lieux à interpréter expliquent en bonne partie la variété de ces techniques : personnages interactifs, capsules théâtrales, interprétation à la troisième personne, animation avec des objets à manipuler, visites guidées non conventionnelles, chansons, contes, pièces de théâtre, performances, etc. Chaque technique a son propre langage et prend diverses formes selon l'auditoire visé.

Pour que l'interprétation personnalisée et ses langages soient employés judicieusement et efficacement, il est impératif que les concepteurs d'expositions l'intègrent au tout début d'un projet. En discutant avec plusieurs participants au symposium, il m'est apparu manifeste que les spécialistes de l'interprétation éprouvaient des problèmes d'intégration similaires au sein même de leurs institutions. Je crois que l'interprétation personnalisée et ses langages auront l'impact souhaité par ses créateurs lorsque ceux-ci participeront pleinement au processus de décision entourant les projets d'exposition. L'interprétation personnalisée est en fait un moyen de communication ou de présentation supplémentaire à la disposition des muséologues. Cependant, son énorme potentiel d'évocation ne devrait être ignoré par personne. Que faudrait-il pour convaincre nos collègues de la pertinence de nos approches et du rôle bénéfique que nous pourrions apporter lors de l'élaboration des objectifs d'un projet d'exposition?

L'interprétation personnalisée doit perdre son côté accessoire. C'est un moyen muséographique non négligeable qui permettra sûrement de transformer la mise en exposition à la condition d'être pleinement intégré. Déjà, certains musées *théâtralisent* davantage leurs expositions. Il est donc possible de s'inspirer des langages de l'interprétation personnalisée dans l'organisation du discours même d'une exposition. Sans être une panacée, les techniques de communication de l'interprétation personnalisée sont complémentaires aux autres et peuvent nous aider à rendre nos musées plus pertinents aux yeux de nos visiteurs actuels et potentiels.

Plusieurs questions et interrogations furent soulevées lors du symposium et par les collaborateurs de cet ouvrage. Elles laissent la place à un approfondissement de notre réflexion commune sur le rôle de l'interprétation personnalisée et de ses langages comme moyen de communication. En voici une compilation succincte.

Bonne réflexion!

À qui s'adresse l'interprétation personnalisée?

Quelles sont les limites de l'interprétation personnalisée?

Qui a l'apanage de l'interprétation personnalisée? Le comédien, l'éducateur, l'animateur? Avec quelle formation?

L'interprétation personnalisée est-elle complémentaire à l'exposition ou fait-elle partie de la muséographie?

Quel est le rôle exact du théâtre comme moyen d'apprentissage?

Les langages utilisés permettent-ils vraiment d'établir des connexions avec le vécu des visiteurs?

Sommes-nous devenus spécialistes de l'*edutainment*?

En terminant, je tiens à remercier tous ceux qui ont contribué à cet ouvrage et au symposium de 1994.

❖ Conclusion

Beyond Theatre . . .
Live Interpretation at the Museum

Jean-Marc Blais
Senior Interpretive Planner
Canadian Museum of Civilization
Hull, Quebec

Live interpretation, a phenomenon that is growing more and more popular in the museum world, is recognized for its multiplicity of approaches and diversity of languages. The 1994 symposium demonstrated the innovative — sometimes provocative — aspects of this means of communication.

As many authors have pointed out, live interpretation is a means of transmitting knowledge, of sharing enthusiasm, but more importantly of giving life to emotions. The particular strength of live interpretation is that it enables visitors to undergo the "museum experience" in its entirety. During the last few years, museums have established a respectable place for themselves within the cultural sector; statistics show a very real, significant and steady increase in museum attendance. While museums are becoming more familiar, visitors are coming to expect more: the visit must be worthwhile economically (value for money is important), educational (a desire to learn is obvious) and social (a museum is a place for interaction). Live interpretation is the perfect means through which such expectations can be met.

Museums are connoisseurs at appealing to the intellect of their visitors — no need to list the traditional techniques in exhibiting artifacts where the goal of imparting encyclopedic knowledge motivated all museological activity. Despite the dominant view that advocates a "public" approach, it is clear that the needs of this public are seen as a necessary evil. In many institutions, the professionals who are well versed in live interpretation frequently face this reality. It is these people who are often called upon in panic to fill the gaps in an exhibition and readily come up with interpretive approaches to engage the visitors.

"Engaging the visitor" is the challenge in today's museological thinking. To achieve this goal, our approaches must be more holistic, the museum en masse must work towards making itself a relevant, worthwhile destination that is alive for its visitors — that is, its supporters. To this end, we must do all that we can to make sure that our presentations (exhibitions, programmes, collections, etc.) are multifaceted, both in approach and in content. We have much more to offer than a "presentation": if we want visitors to explore what is behind a presentation then we must make it come alive.

It is not easy to touch the emotions of visitors, but I believe that the professionals involved in live interpretation do a marvelous job. Reading through this volume gave me insight into the great variety of live interpretation techniques aimed at visitors. The range of visitors and the variety of sites to be interpreted explain in large part the diversity of techniques employed: interactive characters, theatrical vignettes, third-person interpretation, hands-on animation, unconventional guided tours, songs, stories, plays, performances, etc. Each technique has its own language and takes a different form according to its intended audience.

To ensure that live interpretation and its languages are used judiciously and effectively, it is essential to have the support of exhibition designers from the outset of an exhibition. Talking to other symposium participants made it clear that specialist interpreters face similar integration problems in their own institutions. I believe that live interpretation and its languages can have the impact intended by their creators if they are able to participate fully in the decision-making process in planning an exhibition. After all, live interpretation is a supplementary means of communication or presentation available to museologists. Its enormous evocative potential, however, should not be ignored. How can we convince our colleagues of the effectiveness of our approaches and the value of our role in exhibition planning?

Live interpretation must rid itself of its subordinate side. When fully integrated, live interpretation can be a valuable museographic means of transforming the presentation of an exhibition. Some museums have already made their exhibitions more theatrical, allowing the languages of live interpretation to inspire organization of the very message of an exhibition. The communication techniques of live interpretation are not a panacea: they should complement other techniques and can help us make our museums more relevant in the eyes of our current and potential visitors.

The symposium and the contributors to this volume raised numerous questions that encourage us to reflect more thoughtfully on the role of live interpretation and its languages as a means of communication. Questions that came up included:

For whom is live interpretation intended?

What are the limits of live interpretation?

Whose prerogative is live interpretation: that of the actor, the educator, the moderator? And with what training?

Does live interpretation complement exhibitions or is it more a part of museography?

What exactly is the role of theatre as a means of learning?

Do the languages employed really help visitors to relate to their own life experiences?

Have we become specialists in *edutainment*?

In closing, I would like to thank all those who have contributed to this volume and to the 1994 symposium.

David Parry
1942-1995

❖ Annexe / Annex

Measure sur mesure

Henry Price, un administrateur anglais et futur gendre de Mme Marguerite Bacon tente de faire comprendre à cette dernière que le lit qu'elle lui offre en cadeau de mariage n'a pas les dimensions qu'elle croit. Cette situation illustre bien les difficultés qu'engendra en Nouvelle-France, l'adoption du système anglais de poids et mesures. (Situation qui n'est pas sans rappeler notre adoption du système métrique, il n'y a pas si longtemps.) Devant cette confusion, ils n'ont que deux choix : compromettre l'alliance des deux familles ou trouver le compromis entre la raison et la passion.

In *Measure*, then, we have tried to go the whole way. The piece is thoroughly bilingual. But the playwright has subtly turned the tables on the audience, and created a very clever structure where both characters have agreed to speak the other's language in their discourses, where they criticize each other when one fails to live up to the agreement, and where they also constantly correct the other's mistakes. To overcome prejudice in the audience, both characters look to the audience constantly as if for sympathy and perhaps support in their obvious difficulties in dealing with the other character. This presentational mode also allows the audience to construct a bridge between their own experiences and the historical realities and emotions described in the play.

Source: David Parry, "A Question of Identity," p. 20-21.

Mr. Henry Price, an English administrator, and Madame Marguerite Bacon try to reach an amicable agreement regarding the size of a bed for the proposed marriage of Mr. Price to Madame Bacon's daughter. Confusions over the new English system of weights and measures, and whether the bed will fit into Mr. Price's house almost wreck the alliance (a situation which may well have arisen in a household or two in our own area, when the metric system was first introduced!). But reason and passion reach a compromise, and love triumphs in the end.

Lieu : Place publique de la Nouvelle-France, Salle du Canada
Location: New France Public Square, Canada Hall
Texte bilingue / Bilingual text
Auteur / Author : Jean Herbiet

MEASURE FOR MESURE

par / by Jean Herbiet

© Musée canadien des civilisations / Canadian Museum of Civilization

Madame Bacon sort de l'auberge. Monsieur Price, qui semblait l'attendre, la rejoint.

Mr. Price   Madame Bacon, madame Bacon...

Madame Bacon ne lui répond pas et presse le pas

Mr. Price   Madame Bacon, please answer me.

Il se place sur son chemin

Mr. Price   Madame Bacon, please, please, listen to me...

Elle le repousse et presse le pas

Mr. Price   Madame Bacon, this is not fair...

Elle se retourne

Mme Bacon   Not fair? Not fair? And you, jeune homme, you think that you are fair?

Mr. Price   Yes, I am.

Mme Bacon   No, mister Price! First, you forget your own "convention". To understand each other better, you told us! We have agree that you and my "dauteur" Marguerite and the rest of my family we will exchange our language when we talk together: you will speak french and we shall speak inglish... Like this, you say, we can improve our mutual misunderstanding.

Mr. Price   Understanding, madame! Je m'excouse pour l'anglaise, j'étais très *excité...*

Mme Bacon   Excité?

Mr. Price   How do you say "upset"?

Mme Bacon   Ennuyé, agacé...

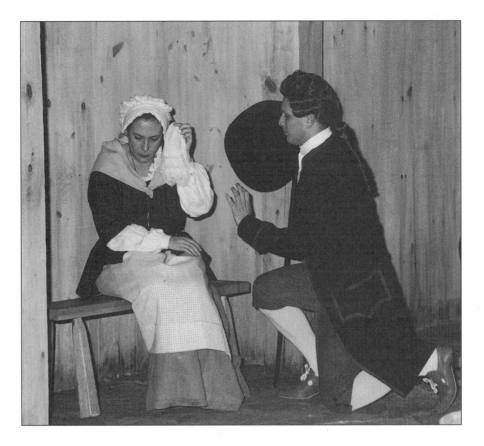

Mr. Price   Voilà : agacé.

Mme Bacon   May I know why?

Mr. Price   À cause d'hier-*nouit*.

Mme Bacon   We say: "hier soir". And why you was upset, please?

Mr. Price   Parce que votre fille m'a dit que je *souis* une tête de cochon.

Mme Bacon   That is *trou*.

Mr. Price   Madame Bacon, je ne suis pas a *pork*, n'est-il pas?

Mme Bacon   Jésus-Marie-Joseph! I hope not for the *vertu* of my *dauteur*!

Mr. Price   Madame Bacon!

Mme Bacon	Mister Price, "Tête de cochon" mean in french "entêté". It is an expression.
Mr. Price	But...
Mme Bacon	Monsieur Price, en français!
Mr. Price	*Mais, j'étais raison.*

Mme Bacon	"J'avais raison". And she was not right?
Mr. Price	Of course... She was wrong.
Mme Bacon	Monsieur Price!
Mr. Price	Pardonnez-moi...
Mme Bacon	Tell me: on what thing you had that *agreement*?
Mr. Price	«Argument», madame Bacon, not agreement. Elle ne l'a pas dit à vous?
Mme Bacon	No. My *dauteur* is crying in her room since yesterday night when you bring her home. She don't want to see everybody, she don't want to eat everything, she don't want to work, she don't want everything.
Mr. Price	O, my God!
Mme Bacon	And what is... pis, euh...
Mr. Price	Worse?
Mme Bacon	Worst!... she don't want to see you never, never.
Mr. Price	O, my God! By the way, say "does not", madame Bacon, please.
Mme Bacon	Why?
Mr. Price	You are hurting my ears.
Mme Bacon	Je vous casse les oreilles?
Mr. Price	Pas casser, euh..., abîmer.
Mme Bacon	Je lui abîme les oreilles à cet *inglish*! To finish, and because you insist, "she does not want" to marry you for ever. Adieu, mister Price.

Elle s'éloigne

Mr. Price	O, my God! Wait! Madame Bacon, please!

Elle revient

Mme Bacon	And I have say the good news to madame Aubry and I will said it to everybody in the Québec City and in the Château-Richer.
Mr. Price	Vous avez dit à madame l'aubergiste...
Mme Bacon	That is "fini"! F-i: fi, n-i: ni, fi-ni! No *mariage* with Marguerite.

Elle s'éloigne

Mr. Price	O, my God!

Elle revient

Mme Bacon	And you know? I am very glad of it!
Mr. Price	Pourquoi?
Mme Bacon	You are a jolly fellow, Mister Price, with good manners et tout ça... you are not totally *eugli* for an *inglish*...
Mr. Price	Thank you...
Mme Bacon	You have good work with the new *inglish gouvernement*, you have a good *hèlte*, you does not go out with bad girls...
Mr. Price	Here, we say "don't".
Mme Bacon	You don't see *prostituées*!
Mr. Price	Madame Bacon!
Mme Bacon	At our knowledge anyway...
Mr. Price	Madame Bacon, please...
Mme Bacon	And you look very *affectious* and *lovely* with Marie-Marguerite.
Mr. Price	Pas *look*, madame! Je suis très en amour.
Mme Bacon	And she were in the love with you *aussi*.
Mr. Price	We say: she was...
Mme Bacon	I said it: she was, en effet.
Mr. Price	Madame Bacon, si je suis tout ça, n'est-ce pas, pourquoi êtes-vous si joyeuse que mon relation avec Marie-Marguerite... is over?

Mme Bacon Because this *mariage* will be very *difficoult*, young man, and you know why.

Mr. Price Madame Bacon, vous l'avez accepté, n'avez-vous pas?

Mme Bacon My husband more than me. Contrary to me, he is not very attached to the *catholic* religion. Ô mon Dieu! For much years, I have dream a *magnifique* ceremony for my girl! Poor darling, she will have only a vague *bénédiction* from one of your anglican preacher... And what about my family and my friends? You don't not know what they say, you know...

Mr. Price Quoi?

Mme Bacon That we have make peace with the devil. Imagine: marry my sweet Marguerite with a protestant...

Mr. Price Madame Bacon, des *marriages* comme cela à Québec déjà il y a eu entre Britanniques et Canadiennes.

Mme Bacon My people don't like this...

Mr. Price J'ai juré à votre mari, à vous et à Marguerite que je respecte ses croyances vraiment, ...

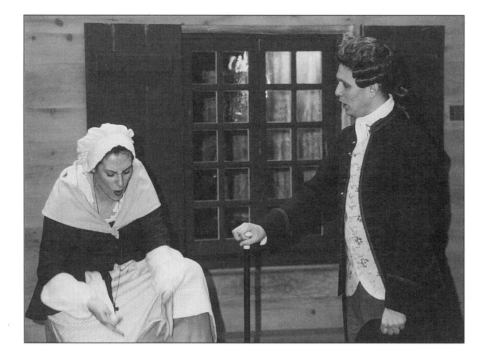

Mme Bacon   Respecterais…

Mr. Price   Que je respecterais ses croyances vraiment, même si hérétiques.

Mme Bacon   Comment ça, hérétiques?

Mr. Price   Nous avons reçu l'*advice* de ne pas *ridiculiser* les erreurs de cette fausse religion que les Canadiens fréquentent.

Mme Bacon   «Pratiquent», monsieur Price! Vous «fréquentez» ma fille adorée, mais vous «pratiquez» une religion diabolique.

Mr. Price   What do you mean by *diabolique*?

Mme Bacon   Laissez faire! Je comprends qu'elle vous tienne rigueur d'un pareil entêtement; vous ne la convertirez jamais! La tête de cochon vous va comme un gant! Adieu, monsieur.

Elle s'éloigne

Mr. Price   Madame Bacon, listen to me, please!

Elle revient

190

Mme Bacon	Tenez-le vous pour dit, young man: catholiques nous sommes, catholiques, le resterons. Votre Roi a plus de parole que vous : lui, nous l'a garanti !

Elle s'éloigne

Mr. Price	What? Wait!

Elle revient

Mr. Price	Nous n'avons *dispouté* rien sur la religion, hier.
Mme Bacon	On what subject, then, to put my poor girl in that state?
Mr. Price	Nous avons *dispouté* sur les pieds.
Mme Bacon	The feet?
Mr. Price	Yes, les pieds anglaises et les pieds françaises.
Mme Bacon	We does not have the same feet?
Mr. Price	You know perfectly well we don't. Les pieds anglaises sont *plous* petites que les pieds françaises.
Mme Bacon	Since *which*?
Mr. Price	*Depouis* toujours.
Mme Bacon	Ma fille a renoncé à son mariage pour une histoire de pieds?
Mr. Price	Yes!
Mme Bacon	This is ridiculous!
Mr. Price	I know.
Mme Bacon	Are you serious?
Mr. Price	Damned it, yes! I tell you!
Mme Bacon	Explain this to me.
Mr. Price	Hier, j'ai aidé Maggy à…
Mme Bacon	Qui c'est celle-là?

Mr. Price	C'est Marguerite. En secret, mon cœur ainsi l'appelle : Maggy.
Mme Bacon	And your feet, how they call her?
Mr. Price	My feet?
Mme Bacon	What is the dispute about your *inglish* feet smaller than the french feet of my *dauteur*? You *does* not like her feet? That is what she has the best!
Mr. Price	Wait, please! Yesterday, we measured the small bedroom in my modest residence to see how we could fit the big bed you have so kindly given to Maggy.
Mme Bacon	En français, s.v.p.!
Mr. Price	Hier, nous avons *mésouré* le chambre de mon petite maison pour savoir comment coucher le lit que vous avez donné à Maggy. J'ai *mésouré* en verges et...
Mme Bacon	En quoi?
Mr. Price	En verges! In yards.
Mme Bacon	Ah! This *ridiculus inglish* measure...
Mr. Price	I beg your pardon, madame Bacon! Le verge est une *ounité* de *measurement* très pratique. Les Français n'avaient pas le verge; ce n'était pas pratique pour les Anglais. Maintenant tous les Canadiens ont le verge anglaise.
Mme Bacon	We are *conting* in *aunes* since *centouries*... It is the same thing!
Mr. Price	No, madame Bacon and you know it. The yard... euh!... le verge a trois pieds...
Mme Bacon	L'aune aussi!
Mr. Price	No. La aune a trois pieds et *houit* pouces. It is not the same thing, it is longer.
Mme Bacon	So what? When you *conte*, just take off *étes* tumbs each time...
Mr. Price	We say inches, madame, not *tumbs*... euh, thumbs!

Mme Bacon	Anyway, take off *étes* pouces each time and it will be like us.
Mr. Price	No!
Mme Bacon	Why?
Mr. Price	Parce que le pied française est *plous* grande que le pied anglaise.
Mme Bacon	Comment ça? There is douze pouces dans notre pied-de-roi et *twelf* inches in votre feet anglais. It is the same thing. Everybody can understand that!
Mr. Price	This is precisely my quarrel with your daughter: vos pieds sont un peu *plous* grandes.
Mme Bacon	How many *plous* grandes?
Mr. Price	One inch, more or less, per foot.
Mme Bacon	So what?
Mr. Price	So what! Si je achète une terre de dix arpents de longueur, j'ai combien de pieds?
Mme Bacon	You have ten times one hundred and *éty* foot because one arpent is one hundred and *éty* foot.
Mr. Price	We say feet.
Mme Bacon	When?
Mr. Price	Quand c'est *plous* que un.
Mme Bacon	So what is the problem?
Mr. Price	Le problème est *celoui*-ci, madame Bacon : si nos pieds sont *plous* petites, nos arpents sont *plous* petites. Si je achète une terre à monsieur Bacon en arpent française, je vais avoir une terre *plous* grande qu'en arpents anglaises.
Mme Bacon	Tant mieux pour vous! Et ma fille là-dedans?
Mr. Price	J'été *mésouré* le chambre...
Mme Bacon	«J'avais»!

Mr. Price J'avais *mésouré* le chambre avec mon *yard*. Le lit pouvait être là. Tout *jouste* mais pouvait être là. Hier, Maggy a *mésouré* avec sa pied-de-roi française et le lit ne pouvait *plous* être là. Elle dit : Henry, il manque huit pouces pour mettre le grand lit de grand-père et elle a pleuré. She cried. I hate that!

Mme Bacon And what?

Mr. Price The same damned room, pour moi il a *houit* pieds par *houit* pieds et pour Maggy il a seven feet four inches by seven feet four inches.
Elle dit : Le lit ne va pas entrer! Il est trop grand.
Je dis : Yes! Il va entrer! Il est assez petite!
Elle dit : Non! Il est trop grand!
Je dis : Maggy, yes!
Elle dit : Vous ne savez pas compter!
Je dis : Yes!
Elle dit : Non et non!
Je dis : Mon verge est perfectly good and legal, Maggy, but your pied-de-roi is no good anymore. Then, she cried again.
Elle dit : Henry, vous êtes fou et vous avez une tête de cochon!
Je dis : Certainly not!
Elle dit : Je rentre à la maison! Et voilà!

Mme Bacon C'est tout?

Mr. Price Madame Bacon, I am right, you know.

Mme Bacon Why?

Mr. Price Because dans la Province de Québec, c'est maintenant la yard anglaise qui est *legal*. Elle a trois pieds ou thirty-six inches, mais c'est *plous* petite, une pouce *plous* petite pour chaque pied.

Mme Bacon Depuis quand?

Mr. Price Since 1762. You know it! Every Canadien knows it. But, as usual, you don't want to...

Mme Bacon What about the bed?

Mr. Price Madame Bacon, Maggy wants that bed in the room. And she said it is not possible! But it is! She said : le chambre est trop petite pour la lit... But I know it's not...

Mme Bacon	You know why she want the bed so dearly?
Mr. Price	I don't care! Anyway, that bed is old and clumsy.
Mme Bacon	Monsieur Price, behave yourself! That bed is one of the first bed made in Nouvelle-France... by my great-grandfather. Des générations de Rancourt sont nés, ont dormi, ont aimé, ont accouché, ont été malades et sont morts dans ce lit. You understand that?
Mr. Price	Yes, madame Bacon.
Mme Bacon	Monsieur Price, do you love Marguerite?
Mr. Price	Yes, madame.
Mme Bacon	She loves you too.
Mr. Price	Not anymore...
Mme Bacon	Ben oui, ben oui...
Mr. Price	Oh! Madame Bacon, je suis si malheureuse!
Mme Bacon	Monsieur Price, you have to learn about us. We have suffered lot, you know, since many years. Now, we are fraid...
Mr. Price	Afraid...
Mme Bacon	I say the rest in french! Nous avons peur de perdre ce que nous sommes. Vous êtes les maîtres, c'est entendu... Vous voulez changer les choses selon votre bon plaisir? Change them! Mais laissez-nous vivre comme avant, même si vous nous trouvez difficiles, capricieux, ignorants et pleins de préjugés.
Mr. Price	Madame Bacon, pas moi, pas moi!
Mme Bacon	Écoutez-moi, jeune homme! On va s'habituer à vos mesures à l'anglaise et à vos manières... Only, be patient... Si vous voulez vous faire aimer de Marguerite, respectez son passé.
Mr. Price	Madame Bacon, je...

Mme Bacon	Taisez-vous un instant, doux Jésus! Je ne vous demande pas de comprendre, mais de respecter. Let us be as we are. Monsieur Price, n'abîmer pas nos souvenirs, nous pourrions troubler votre avenir.
Mr. Price	I understand, madame Bacon. That was the reason why I wanted to learn French.
Mme Bacon	It is not *éneuf*, young man, not *éneuf*. I know: you will do more, vous allez marier ma fille.
Mr. Price	I will?
Mme Bacon	Sure. At one condition...
Mr. Price	Which?
Mme Bacon	Don't ever call her Maggy.
Mr. Price	Je promets d'appeler toujours Maggy, Margaret...
Mme Bacon	Monsieur Price! Allez! Allez faire la paix avec votre promise...
Mr. Price	À la ferme?
Mme Bacon	Non. Elle vous attend chez madame Aubry.
Mr. Price	À l'auberge?
Mme Bacon	À l'auberge.
Mr. Price	Elle est là?
Mme Bacon	Elle vous attend, je vous dis! Allez lui demander pardon.
Mr. Price	Pardon? But, madame Bacon, I was right!
Mme Bacon	Elle a pleuré. She cried, does she not?
Mr. Price	So what?
Mme Bacon	Ici, quand une femme pleure, c'est qu'elle a raison!
Mr. Price	J'ai peur...
Mme Bacon	Marguerite is a bit *difficoulte*, but she loves you, comprenez-vous, elle vous aime...

Mr. Price	Venez avec moi.
Mme Bacon	Quel enfant vous faites!
Mr. Price	Vous avez dit qu'elle a mauvaise caractère.
Mme Bacon	Monsieur Price, why do you think I give her to you.
Mr. Price	Parce que elle m'aime et je l'aime.
Mme Bacon	No, monsieur Price, to get rid of her.

Mr. Price   Madame Bacon! De moi, vous riez!

Mme Bacon   Bon courage, jeune homme! Attendez un peu pour parler à ma fille de verges, de yards, et de mesures anglaises; ça l'énerve ces jours-ci...

Mr. Price   Madame Bacon, what about the bed?

Mme Bacon   Take your wall down.

Mr. Price   Even if I know it can fit in the room?

Mme Bacon   Yes! I trust my *dauteur*!

Mr. Price   Impossible! Impossible!

Mme Bacon   You took many walls down already in the Québec; for one more, who cares?

Mr. Price   But, this is my house!

Mme Bacon   Then do it like us, with your hands and not with your guns. Au revoir, monsieur Price. You bring back Marguerite to the Château-Richer; my husband who like you very much, want to talk at you.

Mr. Price   De quoi?

Mme Bacon   You know... *diary*...

Mr. Price   You mean "dowry"!

Mme Bacon   Yes, yes, contrat, notaire... all that.

Mr. Price   Madame Bacon, pourquoi est Marguerite à l'auberge?

Mme Bacon   To get drunk!

Mr. Price   O, my God!

Mme Bacon   Parce qu'elle vous aime, bêta! Is this a good answer for an *inglish*?

Mr. Price   The best, madame Bacon, the best.

Il s'éloigne, puis se ravise et revient

Mr. Price   Madame Bacon, je veux essayer le lit dans le chambre. Mes *mésoures* sont *joustes*, j'en *souis sour*!

Mme Bacon	Very good *taut*, mon gendre! Take it à the Château-Richer.
Mr. Price	May I?
Mme Bacon	Certainly. You will take my mother with it. She is lying in that bed.
Mr. Price	O, my God! Is she dead?
Mme Bacon	Not yet. Paralysée, monsieur Price! But she will live very long and she has the same *temperment* as Marguerite...
Mr. Price	O, my God!
Mme Bacon	Bon courage, futur gendre. If you want to misunderstand Marguerite, remember this: Our mind is in our *hart*, not in our brain.
Mr. Price	Then, je peux demander ce que vous avez dans le cervelle?
Mme Bacon	French feet, my dear Henri, french feet...
Mr. Price	O, my God!

Ils s'éloignent, lui, soucieux, vers l'auberge, elle, pâmée de rire, vers la sortie.

FIN / THE END

The rhetorical goal is thus stated at the end of the play after some of the initial prejudices of the audience have, perhaps, been overcome. What is not stated outright is the hope that the audience will examine themselves, and the climate of uncertainty they are living in, and think about its relationship to what they have just seen in New France in the period of the play.

Our experience has certainly been that some audience members are provoked and disturbed by the play. Interestingly, although this piece has actually considerably more French than English, francophones have sometimes complained of having trouble fully understanding the play "because most of it is in English."

Source: David Parry and Sara Snow, "A Question of Identity: Interpretive Theatre and the Politics of Language at the Canadian Museum of Civilization," paper presented at the annual conference of the Speech Communication Association, Chicago, 1992, p. 18.
